Banana

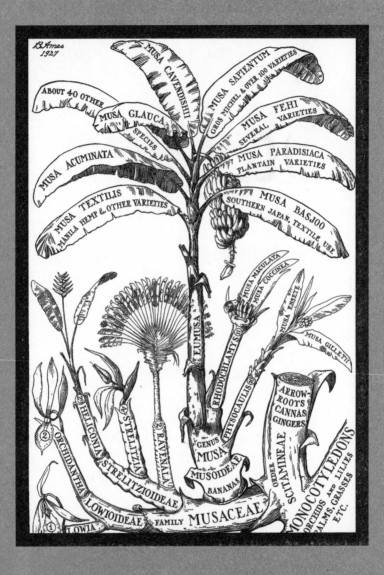

Banana

The Fate of the Fruit That
Changed the World

Dan Koeppel

HUDSON
STREET
PRESS

HUDSON STREET PRESS
Published by the Penguin Group
Penguin Group (USA) Inc., 375 Hudson Street, New York, New York 10014, U.S.A. • Penguin
Group (Canada), 90 Eglinton Avenue East, Suite 700, Toronto, Ontario, Canada M4P 2Y3
(a division of Pearson Penguin Canada Inc.) • Penguin Books Ltd., 80 Strand, London
WC2R 0RL, England • Penguin Ireland, 25 St. Stephen's Green, Dublin 2, Ireland (a division
of Penguin Books Ltd.) • Penguin Group (Australia), 250 Camberwell Road, Camberwell,
Victoria 3124, Australia (a division of Pearson Australia Group Pty. Ltd.) • Penguin Books
India Pvt. Ltd., 11 Community Centre, Panchsheel Park, New Delhi – 110 017, India • Penguin
Group (NZ), 67 Apollo Drive, Rosedale, North Shore 0632, New Zealand (a division of Pearson
New Zealand Ltd.) • Penguin Books (South Africa) (Pty.) Ltd., 24 Sturdee Avenue, Rosebank,
Johannesburg 2196, South Africa

Penguin Books Ltd., Registered Offices: 80 Strand, London WC2R 0RL, England

First published by Hudson Street Press, a member of Penguin Group (USA) Inc.

First Printing, January 2008
10 9 8 7 6 5 4 3 2 1

REGISTERED TRADEMARK—MARCA REGISTRADA

LIBRARY OF CONGRESS CATALOGING-IN-PUBLICATION DATA
Koeppel, Dan.
    Banana : the fate of the fruit that changed the world / Dan Koeppel.
        p.   cm.
    Includes bibliographical references and index.
    ISBN 978-1-59463-038-5 (hardcover : alk. paper)
    1. Bananas.   I. Title.
    SB379.B2K66 2008
    634'.772—dc22   2007038398

Page ii: Originally published in *The Banana: Its History, Cultivation, and Place Among Staple Foods* by
Philip K. Reynolds. Page 5: Courtauld Institute Galleries, London; published under Wikimedia
Creative Commons license. Page 11: Photo by Alan Lakritz. Licensed under Creative Commons.
Original image at www.Flickr.com/photos/35188692@N00/133805120/. Page 54: Courtesy Ann
Lovell. Page 61: Author's collection. Page 61: Author's collection. Page 118: Courtesy Ann Lovell.
Page 163: Jeffrey Weiss. Page 163: Jeffrey Weiss. Page 165: Jeffrey Weiss. Page 203: Library of
Congress. Page 209: Dan Koeppel. Page 242: Jeffrey Weiss.

Printed in the United States of America
Set in Van Dijck with Walbaum MT and Bureau Eagle Book • Designed by Sabrina Bowers

To Kalee, with love

CONTENTS

PART III: Corn Flakes and Coup d'Etats

PART IV: Never Enough

PART V: Good-bye, Michel

PART VI: A New Banana

The World's Most Humble Fruit

IF YOU ARE AN AVERAGE AMERICAN, about forty years old, you're probably approaching banana ten thousand, just as I am. You've probably never given the fruit much thought, and until recently neither had I. Bananas had always just *been here*, waiting to be purchased, waiting to be enjoyed. Bananas were likely the first fruit you ate as an infant, and they may be the last fruit you eat in old age. To most of us, a banana is just a banana: yellow and sweet, universally sized, always seedless.

I first began thinking about bananas in 2003, after reading a small story in a magazine called *New Scientist*. I was fascinated by what the article revealed: that bananas are more loved, consumed, and needed than any other fruit on earth; that Americans eat more bananas per year than apples and oranges combined; and that in many other parts of the world, bananas—more than rice, more than potatoes—are what keep hundreds of millions of people alive. The story also talked about a disease spreading throughout the world's banana crop—a blight with no known cure.

Surprised by how little mainstream publicity the disease was getting, I pitched a story on the banana to *Popular Science* magazine, to which I frequently contribute. I wanted to write something that picked up where that original article left off: showing that the banana blight was on the verge of becoming a major agricultural crisis and explaining how it happened.

While researching the article, I traveled to Honduras and spent a week on a banana plantation. What I discovered there, however, was abundance. Where were the shrunken banana plants, their diseased remains? Where were the dark and deserted farms? There seemed to be nothing wrong with the rows and rows of bananas down there, or anywhere in Central and South America, which is where nearly all of the bananas eaten in the United States come from.

It was this seeming paradox that compelled me to learn more about the banana. The more I researched, the more it became clear that there's nothing we eat—that the world eats—*more* paradoxical than the banana. The humble treat we pack into our lunchboxes is among the most complex crops cultivated by humans. In ancient times, the fruit helped the earliest farmers put down roots and establish communities. In the modern era, the banana—literally—has destroyed nations and ruined lives.

The plantation I visited in Honduras is the product of all that history and contradiction. But it—and the bananas grown in similar places across the globe—is threatened. The disease I couldn't see in Honduras *is* spreading. There *is* an epidemic underway, one far more ominous than I'd realized. In a matter of decades, it could essentially wipe out the fruit that so many of us love and rely on.

ALMOST EVERYTHING I LEARNED ABOUT THE BANANA was surprising. For all its ubiquity, the banana is truly one of the most intriguing organisms on earth. A banana tree isn't a tree at all; it's the world's largest herb. The fruit itself is actually a giant berry. Most of us eat just a single kind of banana, a variety called the Cavendish, but over one thousand types of banana are found worldwide, including dozens of wild varieties, many no bigger than your pinky and filled with tooth-shattering seeds. The banana's original migration from Asia to Africa and finally to our breakfast tables is a tangle of the known and unknown, as is the fruit's evolution, over millennia, from a handful of jungle species to a complex farmed plant with a unique reproductive system. (The bananas we eat today never reproduce on their own. They *must* have human assistance.) Bananas were one of the earliest plants to be cultivated by humans—they were first farmed more than seven thousand years ago—and they remain one of the most important: They are the world's largest fruit crop and the fourth-largest product grown overall, after wheat, rice, and corn.

The banana's past is also rich with historical significance. At the end of the nineteenth century, a few rugged and ruthless entrepreneurs built a market for a product most Americans had never heard of. The fruit proved to be a commercial miracle. Within twenty years, bananas had surpassed apples to become America's best seller, despite the fact that the banana is a tropical product that rots easily and needs to be shipped up to thousands of miles, while apples grow within a few hours of most U.S. cities. The companies that are the direct ancestors of today's Chiquita and Dole—founded by those early banana barons—had to invent ways to bring bananas out of dense jungle and to control and delay ripening throughout the fruit's long distribution chain, all the way to local markets. The companies cleared rain forests, laid railroad track, and built entire cities. They invented not just radio networks but entire technologies—some still in use today—to allow communication between plantations and cargo vessels approaching port. Banana fleets were the first vessels with built-in refrigeration and banana companies the first to use controlled atmospheres and piped-in chemicals to delay ripening. None of these innovations, now in wide use, existed before bananas; there was no such thing as a "fruit industry." Apples and oranges and cherries and grapes were supplied by small farms and regional distributors.

Everywhere bananas have appeared, they've changed the cultures that embraced them. In the most ancient translations of the Bible, the "apple" consumed by Eve in the Garden of Eden is the more suggestive banana. In the African nations surrounding Lake Victoria, the word for food, translated from Swahili, is also the word for banana. In Central America, bananas built and toppled nations: a struggle to control the banana crop led to the overthrow of Guatemala's first democratically elected government in the 1950s, which in turn gave birth to the Mayan genocide of the 1980s. In the 1960s, banana companies—trying to regain plantations nationalized by Fidel Castro—allowed the CIA to use their freighters as part of the failed Bay of Pigs invasion of Cuba. Over and over again, the banana is linked with triumph and tragedy: Banana workers in Honduras wrote epic novels, poems, and songs about the difficult conditions they worked under. Eli Black, the chairman of Chiquita, threw himself out the window of a Manhattan skyscraper in 1974 after his company's political machinations were exposed. The term *banana republic* reflects the excess of influence banana producers wielded throughout the twentieth century.

THE BANANA THAT IS DYING, the Cavendish, is the most popular single variety of fruit in the world. It is the one that you and nearly everyone you know eats today. But, as I first learned through my research for *Popular Science*, it's *not* the fruit your grandparents enjoyed. That banana was called the Gros Michel, which translates as "Big Mike." By all accounts, Big Mike was a more spectacular banana than our Cavendish. It was larger, with a thicker skin, a creamier texture, and a more intense, fruity taste. It was the original banana that arrived at American tables, and from the late nineteenth century until after World War II, it was the only banana Americans bought, ate, or thought of.

But the Gros Michel disappeared. A disease began to ravage banana crops not long after the first banana trees were planted in Central America. The malady was discovered in Panama and named after that country. Panama disease—actually a fungus—is particularly virulent. It is transmitted through soil and water. Once it hits a plantation, it quickly destroys, and then moves on.

The reason Panama disease is so devastating isn't just because the malady is strong. It is also because bananas, at their core, are weak. That's another contradiction, because everything we see or can intuitively conclude about the banana implies the opposite. Our banana's thick skin makes the fruit tough enough to survive not only being stacked in boxes on the way to the grocery but also being tossed over the back of a mule in Ecuador or strapped in bunches to a motor scooter bumping through a humid, dense plantation in the Philippines. Unlike peaches or plums, bananas all ripen at nearly the same rate, arriving at the store green and cycling from yellow to flecked with brown in almost exactly seven days. There is no fruit more consistent or reliable, which is one of the reasons we eat so many of them. A banana's taste and visual appearance are as predictable as a Big Mac's.

There's a simple explanation for this, and you can find it—or, more accurately, can't find it—when you peel a banana: no seeds. You will never, ever find a seed in a supermarket banana. That is because the fruit is grown, basically, by cloning. One banana begets another in a process similar to taking a cutting from a rosebush—and multiplying it by a billion. Every banana we eat is a genetic twin of every other, whether that banana is grown in Ecuador, where most of our fruit comes from; in the Canary Islands, which supply Europe; or in Australia, Taiwan, or Malaysia. The banana sliced into Swiss muesli is the same one we cut into Rice Krispies. The banana Hong Kong action star Stephen Chow slipped on in *Shaolin Soccer* (2001) is as identical to its cohorts as the Gros Michel that caused a pratfall in *The Pilgrim* (1923), starring Charlie Chaplin, was to its brethren.

Yet because every banana is the same, every banana is equally susceptible: Billions of identical twins means that what makes one banana sick makes every banana sick.

That's what happened to the Gros Michel. Panama disease spread from the country in which it was first discovered to neighboring nations, moving north through Costa Rica all the way to Guatemala and south into Colombia and Ecuador. The process took decades. By 1960, fifty years after the malady was first discovered, the Gros Michel was effectively extinct. The banana industry was in crisis, itself threatened with disappearance. It was only at the last minute that a new banana was adopted.

The Cavendish was immune to Panama disease, and in a few years the devastated plantations resumed business as usual. The change happened so quickly and smoothly that consumers barely noticed. The Gros Michel era ended not just with a new banana but with an assumption: The old banana, now gone, was uniquely frail. Cavendish, convenient and delicious, was strong.

But it wasn't strength that kept the Cavendish healthy. It was simply a matter of being in the right place at the right time. Many of the world's non-Cavendish varieties of bananas—eaten and grown in Asia and Africa, in India, through the islands of the South Pacific, all the way to Australia and New Zealand—are also susceptible to Panama disease. When the malady hits, it is always devastating. The difference is that these are *local* bananas. They may provide sustenance for an entire Pakistani state or a single village in Uganda, but because their growing area is limited, many outbreaks simply reach a dead end.

This was even true with the Gros Michel, though the biological cul-de-sac was a big one: an entire hemisphere. Panama disease never moved across the Atlantic or Pacific because the commercial banana crop didn't mingle with the fruit people grew and ate closer to their homes. But the Cavendish was introduced into a different, faster-moving world. At first, it was grown in the same places as its predecessor. But by the end of the 1970s, the world's appetite for bananas began to change. Populations across the globe were moving to cities, and if they wanted the fruit, they needed one that could be transported great distances intact, ready to ripen, and with consistent enough taste to be a reliable performer on greengrocers' shelves.

One such place was Malaysia. Cavendish plantations were new to the country in the 1980s, but they quickly became big business. Thousands of acres of rain forest and former palm oil plantations were being shifted to banana production, the first time the fruit was grown on a commercial scale in that part of Asia. But within a few years of breaking ground, the newly planted fruit began to die. An unknown pathogen was working its way into the roots of the plant, discoloring leaves, and choking off water supplies.

It took several years for scientists to identify the malady, and it came as a shock: Panama disease, hitting the banana variety that was supposed to be invulnerable. It took longer, still, to discover why. It turned out that the Cavendish had never actually been immune to the blight—only to the particular strain of the sickness that destroyed the Gros Michel. That version of Panama disease was only found in the Western Hemisphere. But the sickness lurking in Malaysian soil was different: It was not only deadly to the Cavendish, it killed and moved faster and inspired more panic than its earlier counterpart. I saw this firsthand during the last banana trip I made before this book was published. In early 2007, a Chinese scientist named Houbin Chen led me through a patchwork of plantations in the southern province of Guangdong. There, I witnessed row after row of stunted, rotted fruit. (Whatever disease and destruction I had originally expected to see in Honduras, I, sadly, was seeing now.) The blight became big news in China during the middle of the year, when a newspaper article described the malady as "banana cancer." Within days, scores of consumers and farmers were avoiding the fruit, fearing that it would make *them* sick. Within a month, banana sales across China had plummeted. The rumor had transformed: The fruit was now said to cause AIDS—and government officials were frantically issuing pronouncements that bananas were safe to eat. True enough: people can't catch any disease from bananas.

That doesn't mean the Chinese crop is safe, however. A dejected Chen told me that the epidemic could only spread. "We're going to try to stop it," he said. "But I don't see how."

TODAY, THE BLIGHT IS TEARING THROUGH banana crops worldwide. It has spread to Pakistan, the Philippines, and Indonesia. It is on the rise in Africa. While it has yet to arrive in our hemisphere, in the dozens of interviews I have conducted since 2004, I couldn't find a single person studying the fruit who seriously believes it won't.

For the past five years, banana scientists have been trying—in a race against time—to modify the fruit to make it resistant to Panama disease (as well as more than a dozen other serious banana afflictions, ranging from fungal, bacterial, and viral infections to burrowing worms and beetles). Researchers are combing remote jungles for new, wild bananas; they're melding one banana with another and even adding genetic material from altogether different fruits and vegetables. By the time you read this, they'll likely have cracked the banana genome.

The best hope for a more hardy banana is genetic engineering—work in the lab that adds DNA from one organism to another. But even if that succeeds, there's an excellent chance people won't want to eat and won't be allowed to eat (such products are currently banned in much of the world) bananas that gain newfound strength from the insertion of genes originally found in everything from radishes to (and this is real) fish.

A parallel and competing effort is underway to somehow cross the threatened bananas with a variety that has resistance to the new blight. But that's tough, too: The resulting fruit needs to taste good, ripen in the correct amount of time, and be easy to grow in great quantities. Right now, nobody knows if the banana can—or will—be saved.

The fate of bananas is the fate of millions. After the *Popular Science* article that first got me hooked on the banana hit newsstands in 2005, more people knew about the threat to their favorite fruit. But that knowledge is only the tip of the iceberg. My goal in writing this book is to show just how important bananas are—and how fascinating they can be.

In these pages, we'll travel from past to present, from jungle to supermarket, from village to continent, and to kitchen tables around the world. This book begins with banana myth, then moves into the ancient world, when people first brought the fruit—and themselves—out from jungles and forests and into the fields. In many parts of the world, we'll see, the banana is what made that possible. We'll follow the fruit as it journeys, over a period of thousands of years, across oceans, deep into continents, accompanying and sustaining people nearly every place they settled. We'll follow the banana of the crusaders and conquistadores into the modern era. From that point, the journey becomes intertwined with politics, culture, greed, and ultimately our own lives. As the banana arrives in the present, it is endangered, and hundreds of people are working to save the fruit that millions love. We'll see that there may be ways to preserve the banana—if we're bold enough to embrace them.

Ultimately, that's what this book is about: saving the banana. It is a book about what, exactly, *needs* to be saved. It is science, but it is also biography and adventure story—though the details of the plot and the characters are still playing out. It searches for the ultimate solution to a crime in progress—the mortal wounding of a beloved companion—one hidden in history and science, in the immutable past, and in a future that is yet to be determined. My hope is that it does not also turn out to be forensics.

PART I

FAMILY TREES

CHAPTER 1

And God Created the Banana

IF THERE IS AN ANSWER TO PANAMA DISEASE, it begins further back than even the earliest recorded history. It starts in myth. It starts when people—and bananas—were born.

It is humanity's oldest story. There's probably not a single person you know who isn't familiar with it. The odds, however, are also good that nobody—not you, me, or perhaps even your local pastor—has gotten it quite right.

In the beginning, God spent a week creating heaven and earth. Fruit appeared on day two. Man arrived after the sixth dawn. After resting, God created a companion for his progeny, and Adam and Eve became a couple. Their Eden was a classic utopia. Everything was there in abundance, for the taking, with a significant exception: "You may freely eat of every tree in the garden," God said, "but of the tree of knowledge of good and evil you shall not eat, for in the day that you eat it, you shall die."

When she encounters the snake, Eve, being Eve, is easily convinced that the prohibited fruit is not poison, but a source of power selfishly guarded by God. A taste confirms it: "The tree was good for food," the Bible says, "and a delight for the eyes." The first woman shares with her mate, and Adam, also, doesn't perish. Instead, the couple realizes that they're naked, and they fashion clothes from leaves. God discovers the transgression . . . you know the rest. Common wisdom holds that Eve's temptation was an apple, a piece of which lodged itself in Adam's throat, giving that particularly male anatomic feature its name.

The apple is so prominent in the Western world's collective imagining of Eden that it came as quite a surprise when I learned, while researching this book, that many of the most ancient biblical texts, written in Hebrew and Greek, never identified the fruit as such. That now-common representation emerged around AD 400, when Saint Jerome, patron saint of archaeologists, librarians, and students, created the Vulgate Bible, a version of the book that united the older texts into a cohesive Latin form. Jerome's work—conducted in Rome at the behest of Pope Damasus I—was one of the first to make scripture available to a wider audience. Over the next six centuries, other translations of the Bible began to appear. Then, in 1455, Johannes Gutenberg invented movable type and published the first mass-produced edition of the Bible. Gutenberg's Bible was a close transcription of Jerome's millennium-old volume, in the original Latin.

Like English, Latin is a language that contains many homonyms—words that sound alike, but have different meanings. When Jerome translated the Hebrew description of Eden's "good and evil" fruit, he chose the Latin word *malum*, which, according to biblical archaeologist Schneir Levin, was intended to mean something similar to "malicious." *Malum* also can be translated as "apple," however, derived from a Greek word for the fruit, *melon*. When Renaissance artists referred to their Gutenberg bibles, they took the term to be a reference to the fruit—and began painting apples into their Gardens of Eden.

NOT EVERYONE INTERPRETED the term that way, though. Over the centuries, scholars outside of Renaissance Europe asserted that the identification should have been the banana.

Lucas Cranach the Elder's Adam and Eve, *1526.*
It should have been a banana.

Among these scholars was Swedish scientist Carolus Linnaeus, father of modern taxonomy. Early in the eighteenth century, Linnaeus made two entries for the fruit in his *Systema Naturae*, a seminal catalogue of over four thousand species of fauna and seven thousand kinds of plant life. A deeply religious man, Linnaeus saw his work as no less than creating a complete inventory of God's creation. He both believed in Eden and that the banana belonged there. The scientific name he gave to the sweet, yellow banana was *Musa sapentium*, from a Latin term meaning "wise" (as in the tree of knowledge). The green banana—our plantain—was called *Musa paradisiaca*, "the banana of paradise."

Linnaeus's family designation for banana, *Musa*, derives from *mauz*, the Arabic word for the fruit. This makes sense, since the Koran also situates the banana in the sacred garden. There, Eden's forbidden tree is called the *talh*, an archaic Arabic word that scholars usually translate as "tree of paradise" (or sometimes even more directly as "banana tree"). The Islamic sacred text describes the tree as one whose "fruits piled one above another, in long extended shade . . . whose season is not limited, and [whose] supply will not be cut off." Sure enough, that description matches the concentric rings of banana bunches and the plant's multigenerational life span.

But let's swing back to the Judeo-Christian Bible, for a moment. In the Western story of Eden, Adam and Eve are said to react to their nakedness by covering themselves with "fig leaves." Fig greenery might cover the essentials, barely. Banana leaves are actually used to make clothing (as well as rope, bedding, and umbrellas) in many parts of the world, even today. In this case, the word for the Edenic fruit isn't mistranslated, just misunderstood: Bananas have been called figs throughout history. Alexander the Great, after sampling the fruit in India, described it as such, as did Spanish explorers in the New World. The clincher comes from ancient Hebrew. In that language, the language of the Torah (the first five books of the

Old Testament, including Genesis), notes Levin, a word for the forbidden fruit translates directly: It is called the "fig of Eve."

AS THEY IMAGINED EDEN, the authors of the Bible would have,
most likely, drawn from the landscape around them. And what was
around them? Over the centuries, there have been dozens of attempts
to scientifically locate the "genuine" Eden. Some have been exercises
in theological speculation (like the Mormon notion that Eden sat
somewhere near St. Louis). Others try to match landmarks in the
text with real geological features. In Genesis, for example, four
rivers—the Tigris, Euphrates, Pison, and Gihon—are said to have
bounded the paradise. The first two still exist today, flowing through
Iraq and Iran. The other pair are mysteries. In the early 1980s, however, archaeologist Juris Zarins used satellite imagery to locate
vestiges of two long-vanished waterways. By calculating variations
in climate and terrain, Zarins concluded that the four rivers did
intersect in what was once lush valley, now submerged offshore in
the Persian Gulf.

A Middle Eastern Eden could have been hospitable to bananas,
and the people living there almost certainly would have been familiar with the fruit. Even today, the region is a growth center for the
fruit, which is farmed in Jordan, Egypt, Oman, and Israel. Those
same areas are not terribly friendly to the apple, which grows there
today in limited quantities, and with the assistance of modern
agriculture.

Finally, it's interesting to note that mankind's true condemna-
tion to a life of struggle doesn't begin when Adam and Eve are cast
out of biblical Eden but afterward, in the story of Cain and Abel.
The brothers work diligently and, from the abundance around them,
make offerings to God: Abel makes an animal sacrifice and Cain
fruit. Cain's tribute displeases God, and, angered, Cain kills his
younger brother. As punishment, God condemns Cain to "till the

ground," which will "no longer yield to you its strength." Just like farmers today, in the Holy Land and across the world, Cain was forced to struggle with weather, drought, pests, and blight. In that struggle, the first human communities sought out crops that were easiest to grow: roots (like taro, yam, and cassava) and fruit—like bananas.

Which brings us to our next chapter, about the banana plant itself and how it lends itself to cultivation.

CHAPTER 2

A Banana in Your Pocket?

IF YOU'VE EVER SEEN A BANANA TREE—one that is fully fruiting—you've likely thought to yourself, "This is the strangest plant I've ever seen."

Not just strange: almost obscene. If the banana itself has always been a crude phallic symbol, the part of the plant called the inflorescence mirrors nothing less than a Georgia O'Keeffe painting.

Inflorescence is a fancy word for a plant's flowers and the way they arrange themselves while they're growing. A banana inflorescence, though, is not simply the agricultural equivalent of a florist's bouquet—it's the part of the plant that includes the fruit (flowers, as they mature, give way to the edible part of the banana).

The first time I saw a fully formed banana inflorescence was on a plantation in Ecuador, which grows more of the commercial version of the fruit than any other country. (Until then, I had only seen plants that had already been harvested.) It was hot out, humid. Sweat stained my shirt. I'd expected something like an apple tree:

neat, in fine symmetry, with orderly fruit arranged amidst spreading leaves and branches. Instead, I saw a pendulous extremity, nearly as big as a football, extending from a thick stalk that emerged from the very top of what looks like the banana's trunk (since the banana isn't technically a tree, it *actually* has no trunk; the proper term for the plant's central support is a *pseudostem*).

The base of the inflorescence, which eventually grows into the bunches of fruit that are harvested and brought to market, holds the banana plant's female organs. (Yes, despite the phallic symbolism of the banana, the part we eat is feminine.) The bunches are composed of "hands"—those are the sections we buy in the supermarket—which are broken into the individual "fingers" that we eat. Spirals of gender-neutral flowers pour forth from beneath the plant's base, as well. Then comes the most bizarre-looking part of the banana plant: a heavy, teardrop-shaped bud that droops toward the forest floor, weighing down the upper part of the inflorescence the way a caught trout pulls on a bamboo fishing rod. This is the tree's male component. Like the female equivalent above it, the male is sterile. The bud doesn't produce pollen, as male plants usually do. The most extraordinary thing of all, to a banana innocent, is the color of the bud. A banana plantation is mostly a swath of green. But the giant buds are a deep, dark purple.

The transformation from flower to fruit takes about six months. As the first fruit appears—tiny, green, and not much longer than a half-used pencil—it curves upward, toward the top of the tree. The fruits arrange themselves in spirals, perfectly positioned for maximum sun exposure. The arching bunches also look strange, and not just because they seem to bend the law of gravity. When we see bananas in the field, our tendency is to think that they are somehow upside down. The opposite is true. The "top" of the bananas we eat, the "pull tab" where we start to peel away the fruit's convenient packaging, is actually the bottom. And the tiny nubbin at the banana's opposite end is all that's left of the flower.

SO, IF BANANAS ARE SEEDLESS AND SEXLESS, you may now be desperate to know, where do baby bananas come from?

Like poinsettias, lavender, and strawberries, bananas are a perennial, meaning they grow and flower multiple times over a period of

A Polynesian fe'i *banana in full bloom.*

years. A banana plant's life cycle divides into two distinct stages. The "vegetative" phase comes first, a preparatory growth period prior to the inflorescence, the appearance of which marks the second, or "reproductive," phase. The heart of the banana, and the fruit's true stem—as opposed to the trunklike pseudostem (bear with me here)—is the corm, a bulblike part of the plant that lies under the ground. In short: the pseudostem grows out of the corm, and the leaves and inflorescence grow from the pseudostem. Bananas, like most plants, also have roots. This underground vascular system extends up to twenty feet around the plant, though not very deep, and brings it water and nutrients. The roots can also bring attackers—like Panama disease.

It all comes down to this: One corm begets another—and a handful of corms can become a plantation. The reproductive process is accomplished via a branchlike appendage that also grows from the corm, called a "sucker." The sucker is the essential element of banana husbandry: about a dozen emerge from a typical corm, shooting horizontally through the surrounding soil. Eventually, the new corms push aboveground, sometimes at a distance of up to five feet from the original corm, sometimes growing almost directly from it. Small plants begin to appear beneath fully grown plants. They're genetically and visually identical, and the two are often referred to as mother and daughter. Eventually, the daughter outgrows the mother, and the cycle begins again.

A SINGLE BANANA PLANT can produce as many as three or four harvests during its lifetime. A typical flowering Cavendish produces about a dozen hands, each with as many as twenty individual fingers (fruits). Though many plantations have modern packing and irrigation facilities, actual harvesting is still done manually. Workers chop the bunches down and haul them to central processing areas, sometimes on their backs, sometimes via mechanical pulley systems.

The fingers remain green as long as they're on the tree. But as soon as they're cut down, they begin to ripen. Picking the fruit is a trigger for the release of ethylene gas—a simple hydrocarbon. The presence of ethylene throws a switch for a series of events that prepare the banana for your lunchbox: Acid flavors begin to mellow. Pectin (an enzyme used in jam making) content decreases, making the fruit softer. Chlorophyll breaks down. The fruit turns from green to yellow. Most importantly, starch—which makes up most of the green fruit's physical mass—begins to transform into sugar. An uncut banana contains about 1 percent fructose. By the time it has been harvested, shipped, purchased, and is turning brown on your kitchen counter, that amount has risen to nearly 80 percent. (After that, rot and fermentation begin, at which point banana wine or beer—both popular in Africa—can be distilled. Both beverages are an acquired taste, and the taste is difficult to acquire.)

The plantation is maintained by constantly replanting, a process as simple as digging up a sucker, complete with corm, and burying it elsewhere. In commercial agriculture, this is done at carefully measured intervals. Village bananas are usually transplanted more randomly. In either case, each sucker forms a new plant. After about three or four years, the mother plant stops producing suckers. At the end of its life, the banana corms rise from beneath the soil, forming what growers call "high mat," where dried roots and leaves are arrayed thickly on the ground. (As I was leaving the Honduran banana field I visited back in 2004, one of the workers I'd spent the afternoon with pointed to a section of the farm where the plants were in high mat. These were the biggest banana trees I'd yet seen—not as high as thirty feet, which is pretty much the plant's maximum, but close to triple my own height. "You don't want to walk around in there," he told me. The reason, he explained, was that bananas in high mat are no longer well anchored to the ground; they're ready to topple, literally hanging on by a thread. "People get killed or crushed," the banana grower told me, "if they're not careful.")

By the end of a banana plant's life, it may have produced dozens of daughter plants that are still thriving. Those offspring have also reproduced. For a celibate organism, this is a rather impressive form of immortality. It can go on nearly forever. Or at least, that's what's supposed to happen.

CHAPTER 3

The First Farm

IF YOU WERE TO DRAW A MAP showing the earliest human efforts to remove bananas from the wild and grow them in the gardens and plowed terraces of prehistory, it would, appropriately, resemble the shape of a banana. The elongated oval would enclose the equator. India would be at the fruit's stem. From there, a bulging line would trace northeast, just encompassing Taiwan and coastal southern China before turning south. It would brush Sri Lanka and trace the Sunda Arc, a fiery ring of volcanic islands and coastline where the India and Burma continental plates grind into each other. It would include all of Southeast Asia, the Malay Peninsula, and the Philippines. Borneo would be near the oval's center. The curve would terminate at northern Australia and the edges of the Coral Sea, just west of the Great Barrier Reef. Most of this area is ocean. But somewhere along the strips of land that dot this perimeter the first banana farms emerged. Kuk Swamp, an obscure swath of wetland no bigger than your average shopping mall, is one of those likely spots.

Today, the marshy patch is tucked between mountain ridges, deep in a green valley. The surrounding peaks are not high, but they form an imposing rampart, running along the spine of Papua New Guinea. Wind and moisture rush in from the ocean, bringing rain—sometimes almost constant rain—to the bottomlands. Even now, this area is a riot of biodiversity, with hundreds of unique species of birds, flowers, and insects. Seven thousand years ago, this land was as rich and fertile as anywhere else on earth, at anytime in history.

The swamp is not hard to find. It is just a few miles from the modern town of Mount Hagen, which is famous for an annual festival where dozens of members of different highland aboriginal groups gather to dance and celebrate (it began in the 1950s as a way to encourage rival tribal groups to work out their differences without violence). Attendees display a stunning array of traditional costume—body piercings, tattoos, and varying kinds of headgear and jewelry, each representing a different aboriginal division. The native occupants of the area—the festival's home team, if you will—are the Melpa, a social group that numbers about sixty thousand. The first encounter between the Melpa and outsiders—even others from New Guinea—happened only seventy years ago.

Against the backdrop of both recorded and geographical history, Kuk Swamp is a relatively new feature. Before humans arrived, it was mostly grassland. But as global temperatures rose following the end of the last ice age, melting glaciers released huge amounts of water. The moist, rich land gave rise to deep forests, all across the planet.

In the warmest parts of the world—the fertile crescent along the Mediterranean and the tropical coastlands along the great banana-shaped map—people found that it was easier to grow what they ate than to go search for it, and that meant they needed to stay close to the crops they were tending. They needed to settle down. They needed to create, for the first time, villages. Kuk Swamp is one place where this happened: Before almost anywhere else in the world, people there emerged from the wild and found ways to live with each other in an agricultural community.

THE EARLIEST SCIENTISTS TO ARRIVE in Kuk Swamp didn't expect to find an ancient farm. Their mission was to investigate whether the area could be used for modern agriculture. Yet, starting in the 1970s, as they dug through the terrain, they realized they wouldn't be the first to take advantage of this fertile landscape. There were no pottery shards, burial sites, or human remains hidden beneath the soil. Instead, twenty feet down, investigators found the remnants of a collective garden: over two hundred primitive drainage ditches, traces of ancient plowing, and holes that once held posts made from felled trees. The discoveries turned the site from what scientists described as a "Neolithic backwater" into an anthropological breakthrough: Until Kuk Swamp, the conventional wisdom was that farming societies likely originated in mainland Asia. But the farm at Kuk Swamp was more than three thousand years older than the earliest supposed time of contact between the two regions. "Only a few regions [in the world] were suited to become the homelands of full agricultural systems," wrote German archaeobotanist Katharina Neumann. "New Guinea seems to have been one of them."

Those discoveries quickly yielded an understanding of what the earliest people to live there *did*. But it seemed impossible to know exactly *what* they were growing in the tilled soil scientists were unearthing. Bananas don't leave fossils (toss one onto your front lawn on a hot summer day, and you'll see why). Vegetable roots usually rot away, leaving no indication of their presence. But if you're very determined, and willing to take the time to look, traces can be found: miniscule, ghostly shadows, which can last for thousands of years.

The word *phytolith* literally means "plant stone." A phytolith is a miniscule sandlike body that forms in a stem as it rises from the ground. The tiny grains mold themselves to the plant's cells, creating an impression as accurate as a plaster casting (and beautiful under the microscope; geologists often compare them to opals). Phytoliths are fingerprintlike evidence of a particular plant's presence, left in place, right where the plant grew, once the actual organism has died and rotted away. The challenge with phytoliths is their size. A frozen-in-time tyrannosaur isn't hard to identify. Determining whether an antediluvian grain of sand came from a banana is more difficult.

In 2002, in what sounds like one of the most tedious and painstaking jobs in the history of science, Australian researchers sifted through tons of soil dug from Kuk Swamp's ancient trenches, gathering and sorting thousands of phytoliths. They then compared them to a control group of samples from bananas found in contemporary New Guinea. The visual examination corroborated the identity of the tiny stones. Their presence confirmed that this small, ancient village—one of the first on earth—grew bananas.

THE NEXT QUESTION IS HOW AND WHY those early farmers managed to do that. Wild bananas are so inedible that biting into one can send you screaming to the dentist, so it seems odd that people would attempt to cultivate the fruit at all. One possible answer, according to Edmond De Langhe—a Belgian botanist who has spent the past fifty years combing the jungles and forests of the world's equatorial regions for undiscovered wild bananas—lies with the subterranean part of the fruit: the corm. Though it tastes something like a wooden turnip, the corm can be cooked and used as a starchy vegetable. You'd have to be very hungry to do so, but that condition was as common in prehistory as it is today. In Africa, people still turn to the corm during times of famine.

The hunters and gatherers of ancient New Guinea might have started by eating this part—then the only edible portion—of the banana. A changeover to cultivation could have begun when a few of the plants yielded mutated fruit, most likely with fewer rock-hard seeds. These variations could quickly have been selected and grown. Forest was likely cleared and fields tilled. Eventually, as bananas became sweeter and bigger, corms would have become mostly what they are today: the base material for something much more delicious. At Kuk Swamp, as well as in Malaysia, China, and possibly India—all along the fruit-shaped arc—the banana was eventually transformed from a wild foodstuff into a staple.

CHAPTER 4

All in the Family

I T MAY SEEM ODD to jump from a concept so ancient—farming—to one so supremely modern: genetics. And yet, before we continue with our story, exploring just how the banana went from being a primordial crop to a ubiquitous cereal accessory, it's helpful to know something about the fruit's genes, its family tree.

It was a desire to learn more about the banana's genetic heritage that, in 2004, took me from the plantations in Honduras to the world's preeminent banana research facility—far from Central America and Papua New Guinea and even the United States—in the bustling town of Leuven, Belgium.

THE BANANAS I SOUGHT OUT IN BELGIUM are both artifacts of the past and hope for the future. After my flight from Los Angeles landed in Brussels, I boarded a commuter train, and—after fifteen minutes of staring from a rain-streaked window onto a chilly, industrial landscape—I arrived in the town of Leuven. I exited the main station, walked across the town square, and checked into my hotel. A few minutes later, I was on the city's Number Two bus. The destination, CAMPUS, was posted on the windshield, and the vehicle was standing-room only, full of students. We made our way through the town's market plaza, passing the ornate city hall, built in 1438, with over two hundred sculpted gothic statues on its stone facade. They depict artists and scientists, a tribute to the city's academic heritage: Leuven has been a college town for over five centuries. Cartographer Gerardus Mercator, whose flattened, orange-peel map of the world is still in use today, studied at Leuven. In 1517, over a millennium after Saint Jerome conducted his own linguistic enterprise for the Holy See, the university launched Europe's first post-Enlightenment foreign languages curriculum, where students learned to translate between Greek, Hebrew, and Latin.

Today, Leuven is the world capital of banana research. The university's Laboratory of Tropical Crop Improvement is run by Rony Swennen—he's tall, thin, and looks a bit rugged, like the banana explorer he once was (he was made an honorary tribal chief in Nigeria for helping a local village grow the fruit). His lab holds the world's largest collection of the fruit's genetic material, gathered from both wild and cultivated specimens.

About thirty students and technicians work there. They come from around the world, but especially from banana-growing nations. The countries provide education sponsorship. When the young scientists return, they'll go to work improving and protecting local crops.

The Leuven holdings—genetic material in dishes and hundreds of tiny plantlets held in test tubes—are housed in a series of cryogenic vats and refrigerated rooms in the basement of Swennen's facility (the only full-grown bananas in Leuven are in the small, attached greenhouse). But you can get a good idea of what the collection contains without putting on a parka by examining what's essentially the banana version of a museum catalog. The "Musalogue" (*Musa* being Linnaeus's genus designation for banana) is over two hundred pages long. It begins with a brief summary of how the fruit is named and classified. There's also a handy glossary and a pictorial reference to the parts of the banana. But the heart of the "Musalogue" is its gazetteer of the world's 172 known banana accessions—the primary banana types held as samples for breeding and study. The Cavendish, our banana, is found on page 67; the particular variety of Cavendish we eat, called Williams (that's one of the ones with the Chiquita label), is described as having a "milky sap" and flowers that are cream, rust, yellow, and white. The apex of the Williams Cavendish is "lengthily pointed," and the fruit is "curved upward." The reference sample in the book was originally grown in South Johnstone, Australia. Three other Cavendish varieties are noted: the Petite and Grande Naine (translated: small and large dwarf) from the Caribbean, and the Dwarf Parfitt, part of the Belgium assortment. The Cavendish types vary slightly in appearance and taste, but genetically they're identical twins. A few identifiable differences are evident, but they have the same DNA and thus the same traits, strengths, and weaknesses.

I SPENT FIVE DAYS AT THE LAB, commuting back and forth in the rain, eating at the school cafeteria, and—every day for almost the whole day—using the copying machine to make duplicates of hundreds of pages of banana research papers, some dating back more than a century. They were records of long-ago banana collecting forays in Asia and Africa; they detailed the very first efforts by scientists to create "improved" (the word used to describe human efforts to find new breeds) versions of the fruit; and the modern ones illuminated the discovery of the fruit's most obscure genetic secrets. I met with the banana students and struggled through explanations of banana heredity. At night I sat in a local tavern, drinking Belgian beer and studying the oversized directory.

The "Musalogue" also maps out the banana family tree, which looks less like something from an orchard and more like a pyramid, with wild bananas and related species at the bottom and the fruit that we consume at the narrowed top. The banana is part of a larger plant order known as the Zingiberales, which, as the name slightly implies, includes ginger as well as turmeric and the banana-like traveler's palm. (Ginger is another ancient plant whose destiny is irrevocably tied to humans. Though it probably first appeared in India about five thousand years ago, the world today is completely devoid of any truly wild version of the root-based spice.)

A level up, the family Musacae divides into Linnaeus's *Musa*, and a lesser-known cousin called the "false banana," or *Ensete*. False bananas are grown mostly in East Africa, not for fruit, but for their corm, which is slightly better tasting than a true banana's corm, especially when fermented, baked, and served as *kocho*—a flat bread similar to the kind you'll find at an Ethiopian restaurant.

Another step up the pyramid moves us closer to our bananas. There are four types of *Musa*, but the ones we eat come from just two of them: Australimusa and Eumusa. Australimusa are rare and delicious. You may have tried one if you've been to Fiji or Tahiti, where they're known as *fe'i*. On the tree, they ooze a magenta sap, a hue no other banana comes close to generating (no matter what the color, banana sap is among the most sticky and stubborn substances on earth. You will never get it off your clothes). They have a rich texture and strong, even complex taste; multiple tones of flavor come through in each bite; many have orange flesh and are nearly as fat as they are long, giving them a mangolike shape. Except for these island fruits, the banana everyone else eats is of the Eumusa type. There are eleven species of Eumusa, but our banana cultivars (the term is a combination of *cultivated* and *variety*) occupy an even more narrow level restricted to two species: *Musa acuminata* and *Musa balbisiana*, abbreviated as A and B.

From there, basic genetics take over. Different banana cultivars contain different combinations of A and B genes. Wild bananas, and a few edible ones, are AA, containing two sets of like chromosomes. AB and other combination bananas are usually the result of human hybridization. Our Cavendish is an AAA banana (hybrid plants can have more than two sets of chromosomes). So was the Gros Michel that preceded it. Nearly all sweet bananas, as well as those grown for beer making in Africa, are also AAA. Most plantains are AAB.★

Any combination other than an AA banana is not found in nature's original stock of the fruit. It was either consciously bred or grew from a wild mutant and was then brought to plantations. There are now very few parts of the world where AA bananas make up any portion of the daily diet. Of the twelve listed in the "Musalogue," nine are from New Guinea, one is from the Philippines, and another is of unknown origin. The twelfth, called Pisang Mas, is a staple in Malaysia. The reason the Leuven banana collection and the "Musalogue" exist is not just to show what a broad foundation our few bananas are built on. The Leuven samples are kept for a more important reason: hope—that one of them, somehow, will help reduce the fruit's vulnerability, that it can be bred to create a new banana that tastes good, grows well, and resists disease. But progress has been slow, and the search for undiscovered bananas continues. In the meantime, though the number of bananas people consume rises every year, into uncountable billions, genetically they're all still crowded into one very small, very frail, basket.

★ Officially, bananas that are sweet, like our Cavendish, are called "dessert bananas," while bananas eaten green are called "cooking bananas." In this book, we'll consider them more or less interchangeable, since the genetic differences between them are limited.

PART II

EXPANSION

CHAPTER 5

Asia

WHEN I RETURNED FROM BELGIUM, I began sorting through the documents I'd collected—so many that I had to buy an extra suitcase—along with a virtual mountain of reports, papers, and stories I'd downloaded from library databases and the Web sites of more than a dozen universities, agricultural research organizations, and individual archives. I spent weeks dividing them into three-inch binders organized by topic. There are over sixty such binders on my office shelves now, the result of a considerable investment of time, as well as toner and paper.

The first thing I wanted to do was to devise a map charting the banana's original journey—from its origins in Africa, around the globe. (Hard as it now is to imagine, there was a time, not so long ago, when the fruit did not even exist in the Western Hemisphere.) It was not an easy path to reconstruct. Bananas did not move in a straight line. Instead, the fruit moved in waves and spurts, traveling east, west, north, and south. Sometimes the tracks crossed over one another; other times they doubled back. Each trajectory took

varying amounts of time, ranging from dozens to hundreds to thousands of years. Making the task even more difficult, many of the
routes the banana might have taken are in dispute, the subject of
constant and shifting scientific debate. Kuk Swamp was one of
the places that jolted conventional wisdom; until traces of ancient
bananas were uncovered there, it was thought that human cultivation of the banana originated in a single place—probably modern-
day Malaysia—and spread uniformly. But the New Guinea studies
indicate that people may have started to grow the fruit in multiple
places, and that it likely traveled multiple routes.

The result today is both variety and confusion. Across the globe,
people grow different kinds of bananas (though they fight the same
kinds of banana diseases). The more modern a banana is, the easier
it is to determine where it came from (the origin of every banana
grown in our hemisphere is well-known, since they are recent arriv-
als and there are few varieties); the older it is, the more difficult.

In sorting through the stacks of reports, maps, and stories I'd
acquired about the fruit, I was able to get a broad sense of the banana's
course of expansion throughout the world—a journey that ultimately
carried it (and me), across continents and millennia, from the banana's
ancient past to its entrance into American history books.

BEFORE THE EARLIEST FARMERS began cultivating bananas, the
fruit grew wildly in the lonely masses of forest that stretch from
South China into Southeast Asia and on to India. Even today, there
are more indigenous banana species in that region than anywhere
else. Some of the fruit grow in the Himalayas, as high as six thousand
feet. Others are found in deep jungle.

Because there were so many early varieties of the fruit in Asia,
the number of cultivated bananas that have evolved from them
reaches into the hundreds. All are closely related. Some are meant to
be cooked; others are eaten raw. At a single marketplace, you might
find yellow and green bananas alongside orange, brown, and magenta

ones. If banana consumers were as enthusiastic and inquisitive as wine lovers, a tour of Asia's groceries and plantations would be the equivalent to a visit to Bordeaux or the Napa Valley. But most of these fruit you and I will never taste, because—like their feral counterparts—they often have a very limited range.

A few years ago, I vacationed in North Vietnam. I ended up on Cat Ba Island, a national park that sits in Ha Long Bay, at the edge of the South China Sea. There are a few towns on the Manhattan-sized island, but the interior is mostly rain forest growing around a series of undulating karst mountains that jut above the trees. A path winds across the center of the island, through forests of thick vines and spiny rattan palms. After a long day of hiking, my group and I finally emerged at the village of Kim Ngan. At sea level, the island is humid and oppressively hot. As we entered town, several residents greeted us, pointing to tables in front of their modest homes, where they were selling cold drinks.

There were four of us, and we eagerly purchased the offered refreshments. The boat waiting to take us back to the island's main town was docked about two miles away, and we were in a bit of a hurry, since it would soon be dark. But I lagged behind. There were people, mostly women and children, working in the collective rice paddies that surrounded the village. But front-yard farming was mostly a family enterprise, and mostly bananas. I couldn't tell what kind they were, but as I stared, two children came out of one of the houses. They stared for a minute or two, ran inside, and returned with their mother. She came back with a plate of ripe bananas. Normal practice, I suppose, is to politely refuse such offerings for a while, then gratefully accept them. Being both famished and thrilled at the prospect of trying this strange new breed of banana, my excitement got the better of me, and I took one right away. The fruit was bright yellow, a little stubby, with a very thin skin. I was surprised that it was unbruised. It had a tart taste with firm flesh. I was quickly coming to the conclusion that every other banana on earth is more flavorful than our Cavendish, which makes sense if you think about it: the most common commodities generally favor the least common denominator.

I was late. The rest of the group was out of sight. I thanked the family, pointing to my watch. The mother nodded and went inside again, motioning me to wait. A minute later, a teenage boy emerged from the back of the house, pushing a moped and holding a bag of bananas. He started it up and motioned for me to get on. With a wobble, a puff of black exhaust, and the bananas in my hand, we sped toward the boat.

I COULD SPEND the next two hundred pages talking about the bananas of Asia (and I'd love to do that, but space is limited, and I suspect you might tire of reading descriptions of hundreds of Asian bananas). Instead, I'll focus on the one place that isn't just most representative of that continent's fruit but defines and encompasses much of what we know about bananas today.

That place is India, and there is no country on earth that loves bananas more. There are more varieties of the fruit found there than anywhere else. If you visit, I recommend you search for the lovely Thella Chakkarakeli, a candy-sweet fruit that is moist enough to almost be considered juicy, grown in residential gardens in the southern state of Tamil Nadu, or the Kerala region's Nendran variety, with its heavy skin and starchy texture. India's passion for bananas has a long history. Hindus call the fruit *kalpatharu*. In Sanskrit, that means "virtuous plant." The country's bananas are the ones Alexander the Great sampled in 327 BC. Indian mystics are said to have chosen banana plants to provide shade as they meditated; the fruit was believed to be an incarnation of Lakshmi, goddess of wealth, beauty, and wisdom. Throughout history, husbands presented bananas to their new brides as a symbol of fertility.

In India, even those you assume would maintain a technical comportment when it comes to bananas sometimes verge on the mystic when describing the fruit. During a 1998 conference on bananas and food security (the umbrella term for efforts to guarantee adequate nutrition for global populations), Palaniyandi Sundararaju, director of the country's National Research Center for the Banana, gushed that the fruit is, "Mother Nature's most wonderful gift."

The banana is also one of India's most plentiful offerings. The country grows 20 percent of the world's bananas—about 17 million tons—each year. That's three times more fruit than the world's number two banana-producing nation, Ecuador—but unlike its South American rival, hardly any of the fruit produced in India is sent abroad. (In Ecuador, nearly every banana exits the country. Domestic consumption represents less than 2 percent of total output.)

A typical Indian market sells dozens of banana types, including the country's favorite, Mysore, best described as a sweet-and-sour banana, with a skin no thicker than a few sheets of the paper this book is printed on. Peeling and eating the fruit is just the beginning of Indian banana cuisine. Bananas are used in curries and stews; banana leaves are used as plates in many parts of the country. The fruit is formed into cutlets, as a meat substitute. Banana chips— over a hundred brands—are the nation's most popular snacks. Even banana peel is eaten, usually grated, fried, and mixed with black-eyed peas. Most horrifying of all to Americans, the Indian banana is used as a substitute for tomatoes in ketchup.

INDIA'S BANANA MANIA isn't just an indicator of affection, or even necessity. It is also a sign of diversity. More than 670 types of bananas, cultivated and wild, grow in the country. Thirty-two forest bananas are so rare that only a single plant or two has been discovered. There are likely many others that no person has ever encountered. But what India, and many of the banana-loving nations of Asia, wants to do these days is not only eat the fruit but sell it. India grows a considerable amount of Cavendish for domestic

consumption. Exporting the fruit could provide a boon to strug-
gling rural economies, which have largely been left out of the prosperity brought by India's urban technology revolution.

But there's a downside to globalizing Indian bananas. The
Cavendish—the only fruit suitable for such an enterprise, as described earlier—is pushing out many local varieties. Already at least
one of the country's garden species has been lost: *Musa acuminata*
subspecies *burmannicoides*, also known as Calcutta 4, is now found
only in botanical gardens.

New plantations don't just mean fewer choices for family tables.
Wild bananas thrive in many of the places that might be cleared for
commercial agriculture. These isolated fruit are not just curiosities or
an excuse for a jungle trek. Many of them are resistant to existing
banana diseases. Others, though inedible, might be thick skinned.
They might grow on smaller trees, which would make them more
resistant to being blown down in hurricanes—a big problem in Latin
America. And any one of these traits might be transferable, through
genetic engineering, to a new banana: one that might be stronger and
that might be the answer to saving the fruit that millions rely on.

How much of India's wild banana stock is already gone? Nobody
knows. But NeBambi Lutaladio, a banana expert with the United
Nations Food and Agriculture Organization, warned in a 2006 report
that it is almost certain that "many valuable gene sources have now
been lost."

There's risk at the opposite end of the commercial equation as
well. When diversity evaporates, with multiple varieties replaced
by just one, the chances of that single banana coming down with
some kind of illness are increased. The likelihood that the malady
will spread, once it arrives, is guaranteed.

I SAID EARLIER that you probably haven't tried any Asian bananas—
that almost all of our banana supply comes from Central America.
Technically, that's true. But some migrant bananas that began in Asia

are now present in our hemisphere. You, or a member of your family, are almost certain to have tried at least one of these transplanted fruits, even if you've never left your hometown.

These bananas made intermediate stops as they found their way to the Americas, arriving mostly via Darwin-era explorers, who carried them to greenhouses around the world.

One is from Southeast Asia, where it was just one of many local varieties that people enjoyed. At the beginning of the nineteenth century, a French naturalist named Nicolas Baudin encountered the fruit when he visited the region. He liked it enough to pack a few corms and carry them with him on his travels. Baudin finally deposited the plant at a botanical garden on the Caribbean island of Martinique. Growers there loved the banana so much that they named it after the explorer, calling it the Figue Baudin, or "Baudin's Fig."

The fruit grew as well in our hemisphere as it did in Asia. In 1835 another Frenchman, botanist Jean François Pouyat, carried Baudin's fruit from Martinique to Jamaica. Again, the fruit was renamed for the person who'd borne it, becoming the Poyo banana. Pouyat was also awarded a prize of a single gold doubloon, worth about $400 today. Four decades later, the Far East import had spread across the region. By that time—it may have disappointed Baudin and Pouyat to know—the name of the fruit had changed again: It was now called Gros Michel. (The origins of the name are unknown, but the fruit *is* rather large, and perhaps masculine.)

A century later, that banana could no longer survive in the region. But there was another fruit, in another local garden, that could. That one came from China, where it had also been grown for centuries. It was called the Cavendish.

CHAPTER 6

Pacific

AS BANANAS TRAVELED FROM ASIA out into the rest of the world, they were both improved and diminished. Fruits that succumbed more easily to maladies were culled from the agricultural gene pool, reducing the number of total varieties as they dispersed. Through miles of ocean, from island to island, The banana made its first great journey, across the Pacific, settling on island after island, key cargo on a voyage east conducted over three thousand years by human history's most daring navigators.

Determining the exact course of that epic traverse is even more difficult than looking for phytoliths in the remains of an ancient farm. But there's a similarly useful clue: language. The word people used for "banana" progressed as methodically as evolution, traveling at the same slow pace as human settlement did along a rough circumference of ocean and landmasses beginning near the earliest cultivations in Southeast Asia and Papua New Guinea, moving counterclockwise around Australia, New Zealand, and Polynesia, and finally ending at Hawaii.

There are three similar-sounding terms for bananas in this vast area. One is believed to have originated near Samoa and sounds like that island's current term for the fruit, *mei'a*. Linguists have uncovered similar words in the Maori language of New Zealand (*maika*); in Hawaiian (*mai'a*); and, on the very fringes of this great banana circle, on Easter Island (also *maika*). In Indonesia, the fruit is known as *pisang*. The same word appears in the Philippines, Malaysia, and New Guinea. Two other Papuan terms for the fruit—over eight hundred languages are spoken on the world's second-largest island—are *pudi* and *fud*. These words are echoed, over a thousand miles of ocean, in the Solomon Islands, where the fruit is called *huti*. In Fiji, it is *vud*. In Tonga (mutating a bit from the original root word), it's *feta'u*, and, finally, in Tahiti (mutating some more), the fruit is called *fe'i* (which also sounds a bit like Hawaii's *mai'a*). Tracing those words along a map turns an exercise in linguistics into a physical logbook of the banana's movements.

ABOUT A YEAR AGO, I was visiting my local Whole Foods Market in LA; I'd gotten in the habit of cruising the fruit section first, not to look at bananas—they're pretty much all the same—but at banana stickers and boxes, which usually indicate where they were grown. (I confess that I've become a bit of a banana obsessive these past few years.) But on that afternoon, something caught my eye (actually, it sent me into a state of glee). It was a chunky, short banana—twice the diameter of the ones we usually eat and about two-thirds as long. There were only a few bunches, and they cost three times as much as the yellow bananas that far outnumbered them on the shelves, but I had to try it.

The banana was a Lacatan. It may be the only exotic banana most American consumers will ever get the chance to try. They occasionally appear in U.S. stores, but I'd never seen one. Though any Lacatan you or I might buy in a local market is Caribbean-grown, the fruit was transplanted there from the Philippines, where

LACATAN

it is considered to be the best-tasting banana anywhere. The fruit's flesh is the color of crème brûlée. The taste is lush and full bodied, with an intense flavor that recalls homemade banana ice cream. "True nobility among bananas," gushes the Web site run by Jon Verdick, owner of a San Diego nursery that sells more than two dozen types of banana plants for home growing (don't expect much fruit, if any: our climate makes bananas a rather lovely decorative plant but little more).

The only problem with eating this regal banana is that afterward you may feel—as I now do—condemned to living in a world turned drab when you bite into an ordinary Cavendish. That's not a problem in the Philippines, however, the world's fifth-largest banana producer, where Lacatan are piled high at nearly every street market and fruit stand. The Philippines also grow several close banana relatives. Manila hemp, woven from the fibers of the Abaca plant—a cousin—is the raw material for the strong, thick rope used to secure boats and ships to docks. Our most familiar application of the fiber also derives from the substance's strength: it is the key ingredient in our Manila envelopes.

Lacatan isn't an endangered species in the Philippines, but bad omens are appearing. The Abaca plant is susceptible to many of the diseases that affect its edible counterpart, and these maladies are running rampant. In 2005, the governor of Southern Leyte province, part of the Visayan Islands at the center of the Philippine archipelago, asked that the region—where Abaca disease had spread from just 400 acres in 2001 to over 18,000 acres—be declared a disaster area.

Banana sickness is spreading as well. Large-scale commercial growing of the fruit began in the late 1970s, using bananas imported from Latin America. Those bananas brought disease with them. A scramble began to fight the maladies, even as new plantations were being established. "It went from one farm to the next," says Gus Molina, Philippine coordinator of an Asia-wide effort to save the fruit. (The campaign is funded by a coalition of banana researchers and scientists from around the world and is called Bioversity International, formerly known as the International Network for the Improvement of Banana and Plantain, or INIBAP. Bioversity International is also a sponsor of Rony Swennen's Belgian banana-preservation project.)

Panama disease was not one of the originally imported maladies. The ones that did arrive—some bacterial, some fungal, and some pests—were controllable, sometimes with crop rotation, more often with expensive chemicals.

I first spoke to Molina in 2005. At the time, when I asked him if any Panama disease had been found in his nation, he said there wasn't enough data. A regional survey was underway, but with seven thousand islands, checking every farm in the Philippines was nearly impossible. "We don't know if it can be found in any one place, or anywhere in the country," he told me. Even if the Philippines were to get a clean bill of health, places nearby were in a similar state of uncertainty. No comprehensive information on Panama disease was available from mainland countries like Thailand, Vietnam, Myanmar, or Cambodia, though the disease had been seen in Indonesia, where it had spread from the Asian mainland to the islands of Sumatra and Borneo.

Within the past few years, Philippine uncertainty has vanished. In 2006 pockets of Panama disease were found in Davao, a province on the island of Mindanao. The island is the second largest in the nation, and the soil is some of the world's richest. Bananas, coconuts, rice, and pineapples grow adjacent to forests of teak, ebony, and cypress. The appearance of the incurable banana malady there is more than cause for scientific alarm. For decades, Mindanao has been the center of a guerilla war pitting government forces against Muslim rebels. The conflict has claimed an estimated 120,000 lives. The fighting is as much about poverty as religion; two years ago, a banana plantation opened with the express purpose of providing jobs for the rebels. More than two thousand of them chose work instead of combat, according to news accounts. (It wasn't a totally smooth process. At first, the new employees insisted on carrying their weapons in the field. A compromise was eventually reached: Wives would hold the firearms while their husbands were on the job.) Within a year, however, the largest banana growers in the Philippines were bracing for an epidemic. A task force of agricultural technicians, specially trained to recognize signs of the disease, fanned out across the countryside, hoping to teach farmers quarantine measures that slow the malady down. The biggest obstacle, a spokesperson for one of the growers said, came from small-scale, family operations. "If their fields are infected," she said, "it will likely spread to our farms."

It is difficult for an individual grower to fight Panama disease. But even a large plantation can only buy time. For families working the banana fields—especially ones who have known only fighting, and are just beginning to experience even the most threadbare prosperity—there may not be enough time.

BEYOND THE PHILIPPINES, farther into the Pacific, are bananas even more alien to us—and the rest of the world—than Lacatan. Even the tiniest islands can host a dozen or more banana types. On Pohnpei, the largest island of the Federated States of Micronesia (the landmass is about one-quarter the size of Paris), over twenty odd-looking bananas are grown. Most are short and fat, with skin sometimes as dark as crimson or purple. Their flesh can be nearly pure white (like the Utin varieties) or deep orange (like the Karat). Most Pacific bananas are related to one another, but they're also different from the rest of the world's, having emerged in isolation as people paddled from island to island—sometimes in canoes made from banana stalks—over a period of several millennia.

There's a chance that a hybrid grown from Pacific fruit may one day come to a store near you. This isn't just because it would taste good. Bananas from this part of the world are healthier for you than any other. One of the global hallmarks of malnutrition is a lack of beta-carotene, a precursor of vitamin A. The World Health Organization estimates that about 150 million children worldwide have vitamin A deficiencies, which can lead to blindness as well as an increase in the risk of death from malaria, measles, and diarrhea. American children, especially those living in poverty or with substandard health care, are also at risk.

As the term implies, the best-known source of beta-carotene is carrots. Cavendish bananas have barely any. But Pohnpei's fruit is rich in the substance. A single Utin Lap banana contains 6,000 micrograms (mcg) of beta-carotene, about the same as a carrot (and is a lot easier to grow). Even the most humble Pacific banana can contain as much as 1,000 mcg of the substance, more than the daily requirement for a child. That's not as much as the world's best-known orange vegetable—but which would your kid rather eat?

The bananas that spread across the Pacific traveled north, south, and east from the Asian mainland. The word chains followed. For years, it was thought that the term for banana hadn't gone west. Yet the *huti*, *vud*, and *pudi* that likely originated in New Guinea did make it one step in that direction, to East Timor—at the junction of the two oceans—where one of the local words for banana is *hudi*.

Banana scientists and anthropologists still search for undiscovered words for banana. In 2001, they uncovered *huti*—a clear relative of the word used in the Pacific—in Tanzania, on the east coast of Africa, across six thousand miles of open ocean.

CHAPTER 7

Africa

ACCORDING TO AFRICAN LORE, Kintu—not Adam—was the first human being. He lived alone, on the shores of Lake Victoria, watched over by Gulu, the creator of the universe. Gulu allowed his daughter, Nambi, to marry the lonely herder. But as she set out for her new, mortal life, her angry and protective brother also found his way to earth. It is his malicious presence, as the story goes, that turned the world from a paradise into a place of conflict, pain, and sickness. But there was a remedy. Kintu and Nambi would carry a banana root on their travels, and though the fruit couldn't end all of humanity's suffering, it did well enough.

The Eden of Kintu and Nambi is easy to locate. It was called, both in legend and through much of modern history, Buganda. Today, it is Uganda, the nation that relies more immediately on bananas than anywhere else. The Ugandan fruit—known as the East African Highland banana and also eaten in the circle of nations surrounding Lake Victoria—is more than just something to eat. Songs are written about it, but they are not commercial jingles;

they're more like historic documents, chronicling birth, death, and renewal. Bananas are sometimes used as money. A farmer might take out a small loan and pay it back with bananas; the harvested crop might then work its way through a network of middlemen—usually transported from village to village by bicycle—the same way a dollar bill goes from your pocket to the till at your grocery store and on to another shopper as change. There's a special breed of banana that's consumed when twins are born. Another type marks the passing of a relative. Families are guaranteed prosperity if a mother buries her afterbirth under a banana tree. There's a banana that, when eaten, helps return a straying spouse. A breed called the Mpologoma banana represents the lion and is said to improve male potency.

At the center of it all is *matoke*, the word that is used interchangeably, in many parts of this region, for both "food" and "banana." For Ugandans, nothing says "welcome home" more than this comfort food, served on a banana-leaf saucer. It is the macaroni and cheese of the highlands. The dish is made by mashing green plantains, wrapping them in their leaves, and roasting them over a smoky, open fire. A proper *matoke* will be accompanied by *tonto*, a banana beer, and if it is a special occasion—the arrival of a guest from far away will do—the meal might conclude with toasts made over glasses of *waragi*, a kind of gin distilled from the fruit.

A trip across Africa's middle—from Ghana and Cameroon on the Atlantic, east to Uganda, Rwanda, and Burundi in the mountainous regions surrounding Lake Victoria, Lake Tanganyika, and Lake Kivu—is a trip across what most consider the world's most important bananalands. Uganda grows 11 million tons of the fruit each year. That counts out to more than 500 pounds per person annually—twenty times more than we peel and eat in the United States. In remote villages, where there are few other crops, banana consumption stretches toward the impossible: as much as 970 pounds each year for each person. Ugandan bananas—with names like Monga Love, Mbouroukou, and Ngomba Liko—are grown green and are never exported much farther than regional markets. All are about double the size of our Cavendish and even cooked taste less sweet than starchy, somewhat like a potato. Surveying Ugandan bananas is a nightmare. There can be up to a hundred names for a single variety, making identification more like doing a crossword puzzle than science. In some communities, a banana tree can be found in front of every household, grown for generations, feeding infants and grand-parents: a century of nutrition in just a few square feet.

This banana bounty makes Ugandans slightly better off than their neighbors. The country is having some success in fighting the HIV epidemic that plagues much of Africa. Uganda is a democracy. It isn't a paradise—refugees from Rwanda and Burundi are crowded into camps on the country's borders; an estimated 1.5 million orphans live in them. Uganda's cities are impoverished, and basic services are lacking. But one problem the nation has rarely faced is hunger.

"Uganda doesn't endure famine, and to a great extent that is because of bananas," said Joseph Mukiibi, the former director of the Ugandan National Agricultural Research Organization, at the 2003 opening of a banana-research lab in that country. If famine and war are cyclical counterparts—as a 1991 International Red Cross report determined—then the Highland banana is more than just a nutri-tious or ritual object. On a scale thousands of times greater than in the Philippines, the African banana is a peacekeeper.

Though other African nations dependent on bananas aren't doing as well as Uganda, the crop is cautiously considered a success story across a continent that desperately needs good news. And while we don't eat African bananas in the United States, and most of us are barely aware they exist, we'd surely come to know the consequences of their loss.

MOST AFRICAN BANANAS are rarely sold more than fifty miles from where they're grown; the majority of the fruit is consumed just a few feet from the place it is picked. Ugandan bananas are not bagged or boxed; they are not treated with chemicals, held in atmosphere-controlled ripening rooms, or affixed with cute stickers. But as local as they are, it could also be said that they are among the best-traveled fruit on earth. Bananas reached Africa from the Pacific over a journey of thousands of years. They arrived in four waves, according to current (though sometimes disputed) scientific thinking. The bananas of Uganda and the surrounding countries grow at altitudes of about three thousand feet, and are restricted to a relatively small area: ultraconcentrated biodiversity. The continent's second most important banana is the African plantain. It is a different-looking, different-tasting—but just as important—kind of fruit. If you were to look at a map of Africa, plantain territory would appear like a river flowing westward along the equator, with an island at the center, where Highland bananas grow; one kind exists isolated and surrounded by another.

The theorized reason for this is that the banana settled twice on East African shores. Both times, it came across the Indian Ocean (the best example of one of those long-distance bananas is the Tanzanian *huti*, the fruit that shares a name with the South Pacific varieties). The plantain came first, probably about three thousand years ago, carried from the coasts and into the rain forests by tribes transitioning from hunting and gathering to more permanent settlements. The Highland fruit came a millennium later. Scientists speculate that as the climate changed and Africa got dryer, the two types of bananas eventually became crops distinct to their particular regions. The rain forest plantains spread through the wetter locales across the continent's width, while the later-appearing fruit became a mainstay in the geographically isolated, less-humid areas. Plantains kept moving. The bananas of Uganda and its neighboring countries stayed put.

THE JOURNEY OF THE BANANA from Asia to Africa began with hundreds of varieties of the fruit. Over thousands of years of agricultural trial and error, that number narrowed to no more than a dozen or two. By the time bananas reached Africa, the fruit's genetic pool was in the single digits. For two millennia, the African plantain and the East African Highland banana were the only varieties of the fruit on the continent. If things had stayed that way, there's a good chance our cereal bowls would have remained forever unadorned. But at some point during the time Europe was experiencing the Dark Ages, a third kind of banana appeared in Africa. While the continent's first two varieties had grown on their own long enough to have gained genetic distinction from fruit found elsewhere, the new bananas were similar to ones found along the Indian Ocean's coastline, from the Middle East to Malaysia.* Some of this type might have been brought by sea, while others likely took a land route, carried by traders. Many fruit arrived as a byproduct of the slave trade between Arab nations and North Africa, which lasted from about the seventh century AD until just before World War I. In some places, the banana even became a luxury good. An Iraqi poet named Ali al-Masudi—writing during the tenth century—included the fruit in his recipe for *kataif*, a confection made from almonds, honey, and bananas. (The sweet is still served today, though the formula doesn't commonly include bananas.)

This third type of banana is the one that was ultimately noticed, and actively consumed, by Europeans, who would eventually bring them to the African colonies they were establishing—Guinea and Senegal, on the Atlantic Coast, and the Canary Islands—and ultimately (along with 20 million African slaves) across the Atlantic. The technical term for fruit from that third wave is IOC, or "Indian Ocean Complex" bananas. We have a different name for them, one that the traders from the Middle East brought with them as the fruit moved from continent to continent. Linneaus borrowed an Arabic word, *mauz*, and adapted it as *Musa*, the taxonomic genus for the fruit. But to the average person, another Arabic word is more familiar and has become the better-used term for our favorite fruit. That word translates in English as "finger." The word is *banan*.

---

* A fourth African banana type is modern, brought to the continent within the last century or so.

CHAPTER 8

Americas

B Y THE TIME THEY REACHED THEIR FINAL STOP, our hemisphere, the number of bananas making the round-the-world journey had narrowed. Prior to the arrival of Europeans in the fifteenth century, and depending on which theory you subscribe to, the number of bananas that grew in all of what would become the Americas was none—or one.

The chain of islands that stretches east from the tip of the Malay Peninsula ends 2,300 miles from the coast of South America. The banana of Rapa Nui—we call it Easter Island—is the *maika*. Samoans and Hawaiians use similar words for the fruit. If that banana arrived on our continent, then it would contradict one of the most hardened bits of conventional thinking about the fruit: that it was first brought here by Europeans. It would mean our bananas, rather than coming from one place, arrived—like the winner of a long race in which every other runner has dropped out—in the same kinds of waves that carried the fruit around the rest of the world.

There's no physical or fossil proof that the banana grew on the Pacific shores of either South or Central America before the years following the first voyage of Christopher Columbus. Without such evidence the case becomes circumstantial. But it is still strong. The argument, first posited by historian Robert Langdon, begins with what we know: Almost everywhere Polynesian sailors went, they brought bananas. So it is a reasonable assumption that if they came to this hemisphere, they brought the fruit along with them. Next would be to show that people from the Pacific arrived on American shores. In the 1970s, archaeologists found a cache of artifacts near Ecuador's Bahía de Caráquez, which is today a popular beach resort a hundred miles north of Puerto Bolívar, the country's busiest banana-shipping center. The objects, estimated to be more than one thousand years old, included pottery, figurines, and personal-care items. Not only were these unlike anything else found in South America, they were nearly identical to articles used in Asia at the same time.

Also interesting to note: If native tribes in that part of South America did grow bananas, there's no trace of it in current language. But those tribes do grow, even today, another crop that Polynesians are known to have carried. In the eastern Pacific, the word for sweet potatoes is *kumara*. Ecuador's Quechua Indians call the root crop *cumar*.

The word used today for the region's cooking bananas, *plátano* or plantain (the term has been adopted worldwide), is almost universally assumed to have originated in the Western hemisphere. Yet, while *plátano* is a Spanish word, it originally had nothing to do with fruit. It was used to describe the sycamore tree. Langdon argues that the Spanish may have encountered a similar-sounding native word for bananas already growing in parts of South America. At least one pre-Columbian term that may indicate so has already been deciphered: Scientists reconstructing a Mayan dialect in the 1940s concluded that a *plátano* sound-alike was, in fact, present during the pre-European period of that culture.

The case in favor of the banana's early presence in North America was further bolstered in 2007. Early in that year, archaeologists working in Chile found fifty prehistoric chicken bones during a dig near the Arauco Peninsula. The site is as close to Easter Island as any point in the Americas and a feasible jump for the exceptionally skilled marine adventurers who settled the Pacific. When DNA was compared to genetic material from prehistoric chicken remains collected in Tonga and Samoa, scientists got a direct match. The time line for travel from Rapa Nui to South America fits perfectly with the patterns of settlement that brought people to the farthest reaches of the South Pacific: Easter Island was settled sometime between eight hundred and one thousand years ago. The Arauco bones date just a little bit later; they're between six hundred and seven hundred years old. But there's little trace of migrating *people*—no human bones, no artifacts other than the Ecuadorian ones that appear to be from Asia—in South America. If Polynesians or Asians came all the way here, where did they go? It turns out that throughout history Pacific wanderers have rarely settled where people already lived. Native tribes have inhabited coastal South America for thousands of years. But the early navigators could have made briefer stays—stays that were never meant to be permanent (the Vikings did the same thing, around the same time, in North America). Whether they planned to take up residence or not, the renewable food resources we're pretty sure they brought, sweet potatoes and egg-laying chickens, would almost certainly have been accompanied by the most reliable long-distance traveler of all.

THEN AGAIN, IF THAT BANANA *didn't* arrive in the Americas, if Polynesians were *not* roasting chickens along the western edge of South America, then the progression of bananas from many in Asia to a good number in the Pacific to a few in Africa only continued to the Americas with the advent of the modern world.

Either way, in 2016 the banana associated with European husbandry will celebrate its five hundredth birthday in our hemisphere. If the from-the-Pacific theory is discounted, those bananas, the ancestors of our plantains, were brought to the Americas by just a single person. Once they arrived, the fruit moved with a velocity that would become a hallmark of the expansion of the New World. It took just decades for the starchy staple to extend across a continent.

"One hears on all sides that this special kind [of fruit] was brought from the Island of the Gran Canaria in the year 1516 by the Reverend Father Friar Tomás de Berlanga of the Order of Predicadores, to this city of Santo Domingo, whence they spread to the other settlements of this Island and to all the islands peopled by Christians. And they have been carried to the mainland, and in every port they flourished," wrote Gonzalo Fernández de Oviedo, royal historian to the Spanish court of King Ferdinand and Queen Isabella, in his 1526 *Sumario de la natural historia de las Indias* (Santo Domingo is today the Dominican Republic). The fruit didn't become an African-like staple in Latin America, but it came fairly close and remains so today: A serving of cooked green banana is an essential part of any meal in most of the Spanish-speaking Caribbean.

Nurtured by farmers, and carried by sailors, merchants, conquerors, and pioneers, the banana took seven thousand years to complete its circle around the globe. By the time the United States was founded, nearly the whole world was eating the fruit. Except us.

PART III

CORN FLAKES AND COUP D'ETATS

CHAPTER 9

Bringing Bananas Home

THE WORLD'S BANANA MAP was fairly fixed until modern times. Starting around 150 years ago, however, the places the banana went, and the way it traveled, would become more tangled—and, for the first time, laced with tragedy. America's part in that story, and it is the main part, began on its hundredth birthday.

America's centennial was not a time to look toward the past. The Civil War had ended just eleven years earlier, and the nation was transforming from one that expanded slowly toward a western frontier, to one that moved faster and faster, with pioneers and farmers being replaced by immigrants and industrialists. This new, forward gaze reached its peak at the Philadelphia Centennial Exhibition, held in the summer of 1876. Over 10 million visitors, one-fifth of the U.S. population, marveled at fantastic new inventions from around the world, including automated butter churns, steam engines, and mechanical pencils. They ate sausages slathered with a new condiment called Heinz Ketchup (made, as it should be, from tomatoes). And they listened, stunned, as voices—real, human voices—came through a wire: The exhibition marked the first time Americans saw Alexander Graham Bell's telephone.

Against such a backdrop, a display of exotic fruit might have seemed unremarkable. But to one seven-year-old, wandering amidst the astonishments, the banana was a thrill. "To my young and impressionable mind, this was the most romantic of all the innumerable things I had seen at any of the [exhibition's] vast buildings. It was the tangible, living, and expressive symbol of the far-distant and mysterious tropics," wrote Frederick Upham Adams in his 1914 book, *Conquest of the Tropics*. (Adams was also an inventor—he built the first streamlined locomotive, predecessor of today's bullet trains.)

Bananas were available in the United States immediately following the Civil War. But they were a luxury item, like caviar, consumed more for status than taste (plantains, for cooking, however, had been a staple in the southern parts of the hemisphere since Spanish times). The bananas North Americans ate were sold at a dime apiece—about two dollars today—and came peeled, sliced, and wrapped in foil, mostly to prevent the fruit's suggestive shape from offending Victorian sensibilities, according to Virginia Scott Jenkins, author of *Bananas: An American History*. Shorn and overripe, these bananas offered hardly a clue that they'd one day become so widespread.

The closest place to the United States where bananas could be grown was, at the time, Jamaica. The trip from that Caribbean island to the ports of the American Northeast could take as long as three weeks aboard the sail-driven schooners of the day, far beyond the average fruit's shelf life. But if the winds were right, a shipment of bananas could fetch a fine price. Six years before they appeared in Philadelphia, a Cape Cod sea captain named Lorenzo Dow Baker brought 160 bunches, hoping to keep them fresh on the voyage north, from Jamaica to the docks at Jersey City, New Jersey.

In almost every respect, Baker was the picture of a nineteenth-century New England seafarer. He was weathered, broad-chested, with a rough beard framed by sometimes-wild sideburns. He didn't speak so much as shout, and he possessed the classic circumspection that characterizes both his home and profession. "He rarely scowled," noted his biographer, Charles Morrow Wilson, "and rarely laughed."

Baker's banana career happened almost by chance, as a byproduct of one of the era's most daring maritime escapades. In 1870, after setting out from Cape Cod, he sailed his ship, the *Telegraph*, across the Caribbean, to the mouth of Venezuela's Orinoco river. His passengers were ten gold miners, all anxious to search for riches in the excavations near Ciudad Bolívar, three hundred miles upstream. The Joseph Conrad–like journey upriver took three months; Baker deposited the prospectors at their destination, collected his pay—$8,500 in gold, or about $125,000 today—and turned toward home.

The *Telegraph* was leaking badly, and Baker put in for repairs at Jamaica. As he prepared to head north, he spotted the bananas and decided to take on the cargo. Baker reckoned he could make the mainland in two weeks. If wind and weather were favorable—he'd keep the bananas on deck, in order to expose them to cool air—he could recoup some of the money he'd spent refurbishing his vessel. The timing was perfect. Baker made the passage in eleven days, arriving with bananas fresh enough to wholesale at $2 a bunch, netting him the current equivalent of $6,400.

Within a year, Baker was the biggest banana exporter in the Caribbean. He became so enthusiastic about the undertaking that he bought land at Port Antonio, Jamaica, where he planted acres of fruit and built a sprawling estate. The world's first banana export hub was a classic boomtown, similar to the gold rush communities of the American West. At the height of banana mania, flush-with-cash plantation workers would literally rampage through downtown, drinking, gambling, cavorting in bordellos, and—as the legend goes—lighting their cigars with five-dollar bills.

The fruit grown on the Jamaican plantations was the Gros Michel, descended from the samples Jean François Pouyat carried from Martinique forty years earlier. No one would have predicted that the island's banana surge would eventually wither; Jamaica was among the first spots to be hit by a disease—at that time unnamed—that, as we now know, would ultimately destroy the hemisphere's entire banana crop.

But the bust was years away. While bananas were earning huge profits, the fruit hadn't yet become something everyone could eat and enjoy. They remained costly, and transporting them even a moderate distance from the ports that received them was impossible. Still, America's biggest cities of the time—New York, Boston, and Philadelphia—were falling in love with the tropical import.

ONE OF THE BENEFICIARIES OF BAKER'S INITIATIVE was Andrew Preston, a twenty-five-year-old New England produce buyer who couldn't keep enough of the tropical fruit in stock. For over a decade, Preston had risen at a conservative pace at a Boston grocery

*Elegant Victorian women could eat bananas
without a trace of impropriety.*

wholesaler, advancing from janitor to bookkeeper to in-the-field representative. His job was to meet ships at the docks and bargain for whatever fruits and vegetables they were unloading. When he encountered the Jamaican bananas, he was instantly taken: "I saw 'em, I bought 'em, and I sold 'em," he later said.

Baker and Preston became partners in 1885. The two men couldn't have been more different. If Baker was a traditional Yankee salt, Preston saw himself as positively Brahmin (in spite of his modest origins), covering his ambition with a veneer of haughty detachment. Eight other investors contributed $2,000 apiece to form the world's first commercial banana company. Boston Fruit was the first of four names the endeavor would adopt. Today, it is known as Chiquita.

Preston didn't just want every American to pick up a few bananas now and then. He wanted the fruit, he told his partners, to be "more popular than apples." But apples could be delivered to grocers within a day or two of harvest. Even after the fledgling banana industry abandoned sailing ships for steam-powered vessels—cutting the Caribbean passage to less than five days—the trip north remained a chancy one. Entire loads sometimes arrived overripe and rotting.

Preston decided to try something never before attempted on any large scale: refrigerated shipping. Chilled air keeps bananas green, allowing them to travel farther distances. The banana entrepreneur set up a series of cold-storage warehouses throughout the United States, connected to a network of shipping facilities and railroad hubs. The Fruit Dispatch Company became the first of more than a dozen interlocking subsidiaries under the company's control. (The structural labyrinth would lead to repeated antitrust battles over the next century, along with a nickname that is still used in Latin America: El Pulpo, or The Octopus.)

Late nineteenth-century refrigeration wasn't the system of condensers and compressed gases we're familiar with today. Instead, Boston Fruit's storerooms, boxcars, and cargo vessels operated exactly like the old-fashioned cooling units our grandparents or great-grandparents used. They required blocks of ice—thousands of them. Ice became so essential to banana profitability that at least one banana merchant—an importer named Joseph Vaccaro, based in New Orleans—bought up every ice factory along the Gulf Coast. His reduced, no-middleman cooling costs made his company the second big success story in the banana industry. Vaccaro called his company Standard Fruit, and it remains Chiquita's primary competitor, now operating under the Dole brand name.

What Preston and Baker accomplished with their bananas should have been impossible. They brought consumers a highly perishable tropical product, intact and ready to eat, thousands of miles from the place where it grew, at a price everyone could afford. They did it by developing a formula the banana conglomerates still employ today: Work on a large scale, control transportation and distribution, and aggressively dominate land and labor. The result? The banana cost half as much as apples, and Americans couldn't get enough of the new fruit. But Caribbean property was growing scarcer, and coordinating shipping between multiple islands was too costly. The enterprise—and the banana—needed to move west.

CHAPTER 10

Taming the Wild

CENTRAL AMERICA'S CLIMATE was perfect for bananas. There were just two problems: There was no place to grow them and no way to move the fruit in the quantities required to make it as ubiquitous as Preston and his colleagues desired. Except for a few coastal areas, the entire isthmus, from Guatemala to Panama, was thick forest, filled with everything from malaria-carrying mosquitoes to jaguars and poisonous snakes. Apart from a few capital cities, what few villages there were in Central America's interior were tiny; most of their residents lived an unadorned existence, sometimes amidst the ruins of fabulous Mayan cities.

Early attempts to tame the land had ended in disaster. Since the sixteenth century, Europeans had dreamed of a continental bypass, a canal that would stretch fifty miles along the region's narrow point, from the Caribbean Sea, over the mountains, to the Gulf of Panama. But the first serious effort to build a water route to the Pacific, undertaken by the French—they'd already built the Suez Canal, a project that cut through flat, dry terrain—had ended tragically. More than

25,000 Panamanian and French workers died during the attempt, which was abandoned in 1893, thirteen years after it was begun. If the French had paid attention to a project undertaken a bit farther north a few years earlier, they might have understood the risks involved. Banana men were also attempting to cut their way inland. Their effort proved just as deadly—but it would succeed.

HENRY MEIGGS, an East Coast businessman, arrived in San Francisco during the 1849 gold rush. Soon after landing in the booming city, Meiggs began to solicit backers for an ambitious undertaking—building a huge dock and cannery complex at the northwest edge of the city. Meiggs finished the job but failed to repay his investors. "He was a scheming, nefarious, unscrupulous businessman who got run out of town with a vengeful posse nipping at his heels," wrote historian Bernard Averbach. The project, originally called Meiggs Wharf, was eventually renamed Fisherman's Wharf.

No longer welcome in the United States, Meiggs headed to Chile, where he built that country's first railroad, running 75 miles of track between the Pacific port of Valparaiso and Santiago. He then moved on to Peru, where, over the course of a decade, he laid over 1,200 miles of track. The former con man became wealthy and powerful, and, as Don Enrique, he was considered the nation's de facto monarch.

Nearly every other country in Latin America began clamoring for railroads, and for Meiggs to build them. His nephew, Minor C. Keith, was also a self-reinvented man; he'd grown up in Brooklyn, New York, but lately had become a rugged Texas cattle rancher. In 1871 Meiggs lured Keith to Costa Rica, where he was to oversee construction of a rail line between San José, the country's capital, and the eastern port of Limón. The distance between the two was twice that of the still-uncompleted Panama Canal and counted as one of the most formidable expanses human enterprise had ever attempted to conquer. Deep swamp and dense forest spread amidst towering peaks.

Every day was searing and humid. Late afternoon showers dumped inches of rain in minutes, turning everything to mire. To avoid these obstacles, to the extent that they could be avoided, Keith and his two brothers, who'd also joined him on the project, mapped out a path that first ran north through the jungle then swung south around the ten thousand-foot Irazú volcano. Conditions weren't much better at higher altitudes. The volcano had erupted ten times since 1735, and it rarely stopped spewing smoke and ash on the land below.

Keith hired hundreds of Costa Rican workers. Nearly all of them died, some of yellow fever or malaria, others of dysentery and dehydration. Those remaining eventually refused to work for Keith, who returned to the United States and contracted two thousand mostly Italian immigrants, tempting them with promises of steady work and high pay. After arriving and learning how deadly the job was, many of the recruits chose to escape into the wildlands rather than continue with the railroad. Few who attempted to walk out of the Costa Rican forests were ever seen again. Desperate for help, Keith then enlisted prisoners from the jails in New Orleans. Only those with no hope of otherwise being released agreed to take on the assignment. Of the seven hundred who volunteered to work on the Costa Rican railroad (in return for a pardon after the project was finished), only twenty-five survived.

Keith had other problems. In 1877 Meiggs died, leaving his nephew with full control of the Costa Rican venture but with little of the capital that had backed him up. In 1882, with the project still thirty miles from San José, Keith went broke. So did Costa Rica's government. But Keith was determined to complete the project. He traveled to England and borrowed £1.2 million—about $175 million today—and made an irresistible offer to Costa Rican president Próspero Fernández Oreamuno: Keith would build the railroad at no cost, in return for a ninety-nine-year concession to run the route, full control of the port at Limón, and 800,000 acres of land—tax free—adjacent to the tracks.

The first thing Keith did along his newly acquired railroad route was to plant bananas. The fruit was initially meant only to feed his workers. But Keith soon realized that he could also carry the bananas back to Limón, and from there ship a modest amount to the United States, even before the railroad was finished. Keith's plantations grew as the railroad inched toward completion. In 1890 the final spur into San José was laid. The effort had cost over five thousand lives, including those of Keith's brothers. (The Limón railroad ran until 1991, when rockslides destroyed portions of the track, and the government decided not to rebuild.) With the train lines complete, Keith turned his attention to the banana plantations along the tracks. Soon, the fruit he grew was worth more than the railroad. As the turn of the century approached, Keith was Costa Rica's richest man, establishing himself further in San José by marrying the daughter of a former president. One newspaper account described him as "the best-liked American south of the Rio Grande." One way Keith maintained that affection was by tossing gold coins to children at dockside whenever he was departing for a sea voyage.

While Preston and Baker were dominating the banana trade in the Caribbean, Keith had become the undisputed monarch of the Central American end of the banana world. Most of the former rancher's fruit was sold in the American Southeast. The Boston-based enterprise controlled most of the Northeast. The two were poised to do battle for the U.S. market when one of Keith's creditors suddenly declared bankruptcy, calling in the railroad builder's British loans. Keith couldn't pay them back. Once again, he was broke—and Preston stepped in. The men had complementary skills. Keith understood how to get bananas growing. Preston's genius was in getting the fruit to market and convincing people to buy it once it arrived. Keith would continue building railroads—and continue financing them with lopsided land-for-track deals—throughout Central and South America, and opening plantations in Panama, Guatemala, Honduras, Nicaragua, Colombia, and Ecuador.

United Fruit's Great White Fleet docked at New Orleans
(c. 1910).

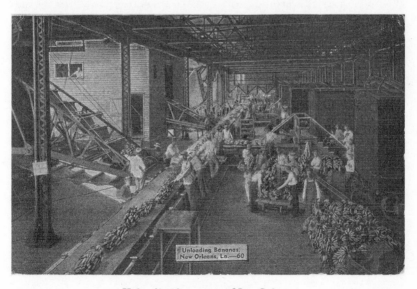

Unloading bananas at New Orleans
(c. 1910).

For their part, Preston and Baker (mostly Preston—as bananas became more of an industry, his partner, who was primarily a sailor, found his active role decreasing) continued to look for ways to make bananas more popular and profitable. Preston began early efforts to advertise the fruit and even found a way to squeeze extra income from his fleet of refrigerated banana boats. The elegantly painted Great White Fleet—the hue was chosen to reflect sunlight, thereby saving on cooling costs—started offering cruises on return trips to the tropics, guaranteeing that boats would be full on both ends of the journey. The fleet's ships could be converted from cargo vessels to luxury liners in a matter of days. Special vents, leading directly from the refrigerated holds, were installed in each passenger cabin. A guest could "turn on the cold," as one historian put it, simply by sliding open a panel.

The merged company, renamed United Fruit, was born on March 30, 1899, with Preston as president and Keith as second-in-command. Within a decade, it would grow bananas on acreage equal to the size of Connecticut. Fresh bananas were now within reach of 65 million Americans. One estimate stated that if all of the bananas United Fruit sold in the United States in a single year were to be loaded into box-cars, the resulting chain would stretch from Philadelphia to Portland, Maine.

CHAPTER 11

Why Banana Peels Are Funny

THERE WAS A CLEAR SENSE of manifest destiny in the building of the banana empire. It was both part of and, sometimes, the cause of an increasing assertion of control over Latin America by the United States. The Spanish-American War began one year before United Fruit was chartered. The fighting continued through the summer of 1898, climaxing with the charge by Theodore Roosevelt and his Rough Riders up San Juan Hill, near Santiago de Cuba. On August 12, Spain surrendered, and the United States gained control of the island, opening a naval base at Guantánamo Bay. Over the next thirty-five years, the U.S. military intervened in Latin America twenty-eight times: in Mexico; in Haiti, the Dominican Republic, and Cuba in the Caribbean; and in Panama, Honduras, Nicaragua, Guatemala, Costa Rica, and El Salvador in Central America.

The biggest consequence of those incursions was to make the region safe for bananas. One of the first U.S. businesses to enter Cuba was United Fruit. The banana and sugar plantations it established would eventually encompass 300,000 acres. An 1899 article in the *Los Angeles Times* described Latin America as "Uncle Sam's New Fruit Garden," offering readers insight into "How bananas, pineapples, and cocoanuts can be turned into fortunes." A later story in that newspaper was more direct. The story's headline read: "Banana Growing . . . Returns of Wealth from Lazy Occupation Are Immense." The headline's use of "lazy" makes the story seem like it was reported from a hammock. This assertion was made despite the fact that, while growing the fruit *was* easy compared to other crops, there was not even a hint of smooth sailing when it came to opening plantations or working in them, as thousands of native workers would have testified, had they been allowed to do so.

The workers had no such voice. Though the banana moguls exhibited some altruism, building hospitals and schools for their workers, the notion that the fruit companies were an unqualified benefit to the countries they controlled—as was frequently claimed— was surely disputable. The public knew little about events like the 1912 U.S. invasion of Honduras, which granted United Fruit broad rights to build railroads and grow bananas in the country. They weren't aware that in 1918 alone, U.S. military forces put down banana workers' strikes in Panama, Colombia, and Guatemala. For every direct intervention, there were two or three softer ones, accomplished by proxy through local armies and police forces controlled by friendly governments. One of the few observers to take note of the situation was Count Vay de Vaya of Hungary, who traveled the world as a representative of Pope Benedict XV during the late eighteenth and early nineteenth centuries. Upon returning from a visit to Latin America, he described the banana as "a weapon of conquest."

THE NEED FOR NEW PLACES to grow bananas continued to be stoked by consumer desire. The banana was one of the first convenience foods. It fit nicely into the brown bags and lunchpails of a rapidly urbanizing America. The fruit was agreeable to just about everyone, from infants to old folks. It was also becoming the object of culinary innovation (or at least the creation of memorable treats).

In 1904 David Strickler, an apprentice pharmacist and soda fountain operator at a drugstore in Latrobe, Pennsylvania, began serving a concoction made of three scoops of ice cream nestled between halves of a banana. He charged ten cents for the creation and even had special boat-shaped dishes manufactured for serving the extra-large sundae. (His recipe for the dessert was one banana, cut lengthwise; scoops of vanilla, chocolate, and strawberry ice cream; a drenching of chocolate, pineapple, and then strawberry sauce; and a final sprinkling of nuts and a trio of whipped cream dollops topped with cherries.)

Three years later, a version of the delicacy appeared at a restaurant owned by E. R. Hazard, 275 miles away, in Wilmington, Ohio. Hazard called his creation a "banana split." Both towns now claim to have been the birthplace of the confection. Similar assertions have been made by Columbus, Ohio (1904) and Davenport, Iowa (1906). The debate continues, though the Pennsylvania town is reported to possess evidence of the treat's earlier provenance in the form of an invoice Strickler received for the oval dishes. At this writing, the document appears to have gone missing.

GROWERS WERE SO BUSY MEETING DEMAND that they took little notice of a problem that was nipping at their heels. Beginning at the turn of the century, a malady, later identified as a fungus, started causing Gros Michel plants to wilt and die before they could bear fruit. Panama disease (it began to spread before it was given a name) was incurable and mysterious. It progressed slowly in some regions and moved with devastating speed in others. It wiped out every plantation in the South American coastal nation of Suriname in five years. In other parts of Latin America, the process spanned decades.

That bananas were endangered was as unknown to the typical American as the banana companies' political actions. (The same is true today, as disease spreads and banana companies attempt to win favor from local governments as part of a global trade war that has engulfed the industry). Another difficulty involving the fruit was far more public, however, and closer to home.

The downside to the banana's portability, according to historian Virginia Scott Jenkins, was that there was no place, other than the gutter, to discard what banana marketers had taken to describing as the "sanitary wrapper." A discarded banana peel quickly became a gooey mess. People actually did slip, fall, and sometimes injure themselves when they stepped on them. What we know as a movie gag was real enough that in 1909 the St. Louis city council passed an ordinance prohibiting persons from "throwing or casting" a "banana rind" on public streets or sidewalks (another regulation the official body passed that year forbid anyone from allowing a "bear to run at large"). In a 1914 letter to his troops, British Boy Scout commissioner Roland Philipps suggested that a youngster's daily good turn might "consist in moving a piece of banana peel from the pavement."

Such private efforts were of little help. It took a public agency to solve the banana peel problem. In New York, a former Civil War colonel named George Waring used his military experience to fashion the city's department of street sweeping. The wild pigs that once roamed the street, eating any organic matter they could find (this is not a joke), were replaced by uniformed workers, who tidied specific beats and deposited the waste they collected into public composting facilities. The program was the first large-scale recycling effort in the United States, with regulations strictly enforced by the New York Police Department. The system was eliminated during a post–World War I cash crunch; from that point on, banana peels—and anything else discarded in the city—were dumped into the ocean, burned, or sent to public landfills.

Over time, the sidewalk pratfall became less of a genuine hazard and more an essential element of slapstick comedy. Watching someone fly into the air and then go sprawling *was* funny, especially if it wasn't you. It appeared on the vaudeville stage first, then on the screen in 1921, in *The High Sign* with Buster Keaton. The gag was reprised dozens of times, to the greatest and most chaotic effect in *The Battle of the Century* (1927), featuring Laurel and Hardy. The mishap in that film launches what is generally considered the greatest pie-throwing melee in cinema history. Charlie Chaplin, who featured a slip in *The Pilgrim*, released in 1923, also understood that the joke got old quickly. A decade or so later, Charles MacArthur, writer of a film adaptation of *Wuthering Heights*, asked Chaplin how to make something so tired seem new: "How, for example, could I make a fat lady, walking down Fifth Avenue, slip on a banana peel and still get a laugh? It's been done a million times," MacArthur asked. "Do I show first the banana peel, then the fat lady approaching, then she slips? Or do I show the fat lady first, then the banana peel, and then she slips?" Chaplin's answer: "Neither. You show the fat lady approaching," he said. "Then you show the banana peel; then you show the fat lady and the banana peel together; then she steps OVER the banana peel and disappears down a manhole."

AMERICANS SAW FEWER DISCARDED BANANA PEELS, but they ate more and more of the fruit. In the decade following 1900, consumption of bananas nearly tripled—from about 15 million bunches to over 40 million. It was an amazing feat. Bananas so outsold apples and oranges that, in 1913, the U.S. government attempted to tax the fruit at a nickel per bunch. That would amount to $2 million annually at a time when bananas cost less than $1 a bunch at wholesale. (The proposed levy was part of the Underwood-Simmons Tariff Act, which was designed to raise funds by imposing taxes on the sale of dozens of items.)

The idea was greeted with outrage. United Fruit had worked to make the banana a "fruit of the people," positioning it as cheap, healthy, and convenient, according to historian Marcelo Bucheli. The company paraded executives before Congress, encouraged grassroots support—the National Housewives League, with 2 million members, made an impassioned plea—and convinced diplomats from banana-producing nations to protest directly to President Woodrow Wilson. On July 13, the *New York Times* weighed in: The banana was not only a staple food—and it was amoral to tax such comestibles—but also one of the few genuine pleasures available to the common man. "They are entitled to their little luxuries exactly because they are poor . . . [The banana] is not less a food because it is so toothsome and sweet." In October 1913, Congress passed the law with the provisions on bananas removed. The act's most significant and wide-reaching provision, however—the enactment, for the first time in U.S. history, of a true personal income tax—was kept in place.

The banana was certainly healthy and convenient—and to consumers it was a bargain. They were far cheaper than apples, often selling for a quarter per dozen, about the price of two single apples. That the tropical fruit was cheaper was considered to be a source of both wonder and pride. In a January 27, 1913, editorial, the *Houston Post* asked: "How does it happen that the home-grown apple is placed beyond the reach of the average consumer and that the foreign-grown banana has increased in quality and decreased in price? The banana is a perishable fruit. It must be marketed immediately on importation, and the business is one which requires millions in investment and the risks incident to fleet sailing in water menaced by hurricanes and northers."

The answer, the newspaper explained, was "no secret." Bananas were produced on a huge scale and sold directly to consumers. The magnanimous, efficient banana companies understood that "there is more money for them in selling a huge total of product at a low net profit than there is in extracting a high profit from small sales at prices prohibitive to the average consumer."

To the public, the banana companies weren't just smart or altruistic, they were heroic entities that uplifted every region they entered. A *New York Times* article published in 1924 implied that the reign of United Fruit would be remembered as a pinnacle of human achievement. The story, headlined "Lowly Banana Rebuilds an Empire," described the presence of U.S. enterprises in Central America as "the rehabilitation of an ancient empire . . . that flourished long before Columbus." The story continued: "The opening up of the humid lowlands of Central America by the new seaports, railroads, and banana plantations of the United Fruit Company is more than a story of business faith and commercial enterprise. It is a demonstration of empire building with a new ingredient capable of correcting the mistakes of the past."

There are some apt comparisons between Central America's Mayas, whose reign peaked between 250 BC and AD 900, and the fruit company. Both introduced revolutionary technology (the Mayas invented written language and the numeric concept of zero), and both carved immense habitations out of raw jungle. When the new empire encountered the old, United Fruit was deferential, even reverent. After rediscovering the ancient city of Quiriga while it cleared jungle in Guatemala, the fruit company paid archaeologists to restore the ruins; the site is now a protected national park.

Yet there was an irony to these seemingly positive works. Relics were restored, but the descendants of the Mayas, many of whom spoke (and still speak) the ancients dialects of their ancestors, were exploited. Frederick Upham Adams, the man who as a child had seen his first banana at the Philadelphia Centennial Exhibition, described the workers as "ignorant and physically deficient." (Adams's accounts are stirring and well written; they are also heavily slanted toward the point of view of the colonial-minded banana producers.) Life expectancies for banana laborers were decreasing, while United

Fruit's control over every facet of life in the region was reaching near-total levels.

The company rewarded those who cooperated, and began to behave with more and more brutality toward those who didn't. There was one clear way to distinguish between those who benefited from the company's growth and those who didn't. The lucky ones nicknamed the company *mamita*. Those who weren't so fortunate called it El Pulpo.

CHAPTER 12

Sam the
Banana Man

IF UNITED FRUIT WAS INVENTIVE, with Minor Keith figuring out how to draw profit from the jungle and Andrew Preston developing technologies that put a banana in every lunchbox possible, then Samuel Zemurray was a gold-plated tough guy. Though the immigrant—who was born Schmuel Zmurri in Kishinev, Bessarabia, Russia (now Chişinău, Moldova), arrived in the United States in 1892, and transformed himself into a banana tycoon in less than twenty years—wasn't a thug, he certainly knew how to use rowdies and persons of ill-repute to his advantage.

Zemurray's ambitious rise began with hard labor: His first job was selling household merchandise on his back, door-to-door, in Mobile, Alabama. He quickly found that there was more profit in fruit than pots and pans, carving a tiny niche in the banana market by buying bruised and too-ripe-to-transport bananas and selling them to local grocers. His first load, a full boxcar, cost him $150. His profit after selling that initial shipment of fruit: $35.

By 1910 Zemurray was importing fresh bananas to the United States, but his operation was nothing like United Fruit's. Instead of a gleaming fleet of white ships, Zemurray worked his way up to a pair of ramshackle steamers; instead of nation-sized chunks of land, Zemurray's cargo came from a modest five thousand acres of cleared forest in Honduras, alongside the Cuyamel River. Zemurray named his company Cuyamel Fruit Company after the waterway. He ran into trouble almost immediately and not with competing banana companies or reluctant local officials: The U.S. government objected to Zemurray's presence. Honduras was in debt, and the American secretary of state, Philander C. Knox, was working to have J. P. Morgan and Company take over the Honduran customs service. The scheme would have allowed any tariffs or duties collected in the Central American nation to be directly funneled to the U.S. bank. Zemurray was worried that Morgan would overtax him—his banana business ran on tight margins, just like United Fruit's—and appealed for an exception. Knox not only rebuffed the banana entrepreneur but warned Zemurray, who did not like to be warned of anything, to keep in line.

Today, Honduras is one of the poorest and least-visited countries in Central America; the countryside remains sleepy, and the banana plantations seem little changed from how they must have looked almost a century ago. The Honduras that Zemurray grew his first bananas in was more like a free-for-all. With no extradition treaty to the United States, the country became a haven for "people on the run," wrote Lester Langley and Thomas Schoonover in 1995, in *The Banana Men*. That meant an assortment of "Americans, Chinese, Syrians, and Turks; soldiers of fortune and tropical tramps," they explain, adding, "Honduras was especially attractive to bank embezzlers."

The country and much of the region was also filled with mercenaries—usually from the United States—who acted as police, militiamen, and enforcers; they'd played a huge part in the frequently violent relationship between the United States and Central

America in the nineteenth century. The soldiers-for-hire were known as filibusters, after a Dutch term meaning "freebooter" or "pirate." The most infamous of these was William Walker, who shot his way into the presidency of Nicaragua, where he tried to establish a slave state. After being deposed, he was captured in Honduras and executed by firing squad. Other privateers didn't simply escape Walker's fate—they prospered. Zemurray, whose nickname was the rather benign Sam the Banana Man, employed two of the most legendary of these Central American filibusters: Lee Christmas and Guy "Machine Gun" Molony.

The thirty-seven-year-old Christmas had lived in Honduras for several years. He'd worked as an engineer on the banana railroads— he'd been fired from a similar job in the United States because he was color blind and couldn't read the signals on the tracks—and happily jumped into an insurrection when a battle between government forces and rebels suddenly erupted around his train. Christmas already had grievances with Honduran officialdom, so he threw his lot in with the insurgents, acquitting himself by killing several soldiers and ending up as one of the region's most feared fixers— available and well used in multiple exploits and escapades, both domestically and in neighboring countries.

Molony was quite a bit younger than Christmas, but he made a good partner. At age sixteen, he ran away from his native New Orleans to fight in South Africa's Boer War, gaining an aptitude with his namesake weapon. On his return to the United States, Molony became a police officer but found the work uninteresting: not enough action. He resigned and set off for Central America, according to his personal papers, now archived at Tulane University, seeking "adventure . . . fame . . . or the hope of future material rewards."

Both Molony and Christmas had experienced plenty of both (and the rewards too) by the time Zemurray sought them out, as he searched for a way to outsmart both the U.S. State Department and the sitting Honduran government. (Knox, suspicious that Zemurray would ignore warnings to stay away from Honduras, had dispatched U.S. Secret Service agents to New Orleans, where Zemurray lived at the time, to monitor the banana entrepreneur.)

In the context of over half a century of American adventures in Central America, what Zemurray planned might have seemed commonplace, but it remains one of the most audacious escapades of the era. According to his United Fruit Historical Society biography, Zemurray and the two mercenaries met at a New Orleans bawdy house. While the Secret Service agents monitored the brothel's front door, the three men slipped out the back, making their way to a waiting boat. Laden with ammunition, the conspirators sailed south. On their arrival in Honduras, the trio—who'd also brought along former Honduran president Manuel Bonilla, who Zemurray had recruited for the plot—drummed up supporters and mounted an insurrection. Six weeks later, Bonilla was again in control of the country. One of his first acts was to sign a bill that allowed Zemurray to operate, tax free, across a broad portion of the nation. (After the fighting ended, Lee Christmas settled down, becoming a general in the Honduran army, and marrying Ida Culotta, the eighteen-year-old daughter of one of Zemurray's colleagues.)

UNITED FRUIT DIDN'T LIKE COMPETITION, and it usually dealt with rivals in the standard way: It crushed them in price wars. It had gained partial control of the British banana market by purchasing part of Elders & Fyffes, the company's largest rival in Jamaica (the company, now simply Fyffes, remains the United Kingdom's largest banana importer, though Chiquita sold it to an Irish conglomerate in 1986). In 1912, United Fruit drove Atlantic Fruit, its chief rival in Costa Rica, into bankruptcy, taking possession of the stricken company's land, workers, and railroads.

But Sam Zemurray was too small. Andrew Preston, the proper Bostonian, barely admitted to knowing who the foreign-born, Jewish Zemurray was when he testified at a congressional antitrust hearing in 1910. Even though United Fruit also had holdings in Honduras, it still didn't appear to regard Zemurray as a proper rival (and wouldn't, for at least fifteen more years). The company had other battles to fight. American soldiers were stationed on its behalf as police officers in Panama in 1918 and as union busters in Guatemala—where it was granted a hundred-kilometer-wide ministate—two years later. Troops were twice called on to "monitor" elections in Honduras and returned to Panama in 1925 to break up a plantation strike.

BY THE LATE 1920S, United Fruit was worth over $100 million. It had 67,000 employees and owned 1.6 million acres of land. It had business interests in thirty-two countries. It operated everything from churches to laundries. It had strung 3,500 miles of telegraph and telephone lines, including a system of ship-to-shore transmission it invented specifically for the purpose of making sure banana loaders were ready, at the docks, when cargo vessels came in. Time is of the essence with perishable fruit. As soon as the workers received the signal, they'd work, without rest, for up to seventy-two hours, harvesting and loading the fruit. The company was selling bananas as far away as Paris and was also becoming a market leader in sugar, cocoa, and coffee. In addition to running his fruit business, Andrew Preston was president of two banks, one insurance company, and a steel manufacturer. Minor C. Keith had become so powerful that he was called by many "the uncrowned king of Central America."

Bananas continued to change life in the United States. Items that we consider mealtime standards today didn't exist until United Fruit invented them. Company research found that mothers were feeding mashed bananas to their babies, for example. So United Fruit hired doctors to endorse the practice and launched advertisements to drive the point home. In 1924, writes Virginia Scott Jenkins, the company scored what would be its biggest culinary hit: The United Fruit test kitchens suggested that the perfect breakfast for a busy, modern family would consist of bananas sliced into corn flakes with milk. It wasn't just the recipe that broke new ground. It was also the coupons, pioneered by the company, packed inside cereal boxes (redeemable for free bananas that the cereal companies, not the fruit importer, paid for). The company made sure that children knew about bananas, too. It set up an official "education department," devoted to publishing textbooks and curriculum materials that subtly provided information about the fruit.

United Fruit also added a new element to its political strategy. If military action was impractical (U.S. troops might be unavailable or force precluded by situations on the ground), Central America's geography became an ally. The region's countries were small and easy to move between. There were plenty of natural ports on both the eastern and western coasts, and bananas could be grown just about anywhere land could be cleared and a railroad could be laid. If a government became particularly balky, the company would simply threaten to go next door.

But one thing United Fruit couldn't control was nature. Not long after bananas added themselves as a third party in cereal and milk, the troubles growers were beginning to have with an aggressive malady became public. One headline in *The New York Times* read: "Banana Disease Ruins Plantations—No Remedy is Available—Whole Regions Have Been Laid Waste and Improvements Abandoned by Growers." Fallow farms weren't just fallen stems and the dried-out remains of banana leaves. Railroad tracks were torn up, and boxcars sat unused and rusting. The houses banana executives lived in stood empty, and the villages where banana workers worked were turned into ghost towns. The *New York Times* article went on to compare the scene to "a leper colony."

CHAPTER 13

No Bananas Today

WITH LAND FOR THE TAKING in Central America, there were few signs at home of a banana shortage. The fruit had become so beloved that—as in Uganda today—people began to sing songs about it.

It began in New York City's Tin Pan Alley. The district was more than just a place where music was created. It was, said a 1983 article in *American Heritage* magazine, where the *idea* of a pop hit came into being. (The historic song-writing zone, whose name came from the clattering din that filled the streets surrounding it, was actually a moving melodic marketplace. It started in downtown Manhattan but by the 1950s had migrated north to Times Square, where it finally vanished at the dawn of the rock-and-roll era.) Thousands of ballads, show tunes, and novelty ditties were churned out in the Alley by ambitious lyricists, up-and-coming composers, and reprobate vaudevillians.

As with the banana industry, Tin Pan Alley was powered by revolutionary technologies that brought the general public items once available only to the rich. The first commercial radio station opened in Pittsburgh in 1922. Prices for the Victrola "talking machine," a record player, had dropped to as little as $15 for compact and stylish units (in current dollars, about the same price as today's basic iPod). Americans were developing a nearly insatiable appetite for musical entertainment, cut in spiraling grooves on flat discs and cylinders made of shellac (and later of vinyl). "The consumption of songs in America is as constant as the consumption of shoes, and the demand is similarly met by factory output," wrote the *New York Times* in 1923.

Most of the tens of thousands of songs produced by Tin Pan Alley are long forgotten. Those that remain in memory are classics: Irving Berlin's "God Bless America" and "White Christmas" along with George M. Cohan's "Give My Regards to Broadway."

"Yes, We Have No Bananas" will never be viewed with such piety. But it was a much bigger sensation.

The song was churned out in the spring of 1923 by composers Frank Silver and Irving Cohn. It first became a hit on sheet music, designed to be performed at home (printed songs were the karaoke of their time). During the following months, at least four different recordings of the song emerged, most famously by the hugely popular comic singer and actor Eddie Cantor. "There is a calm and deliberate, even a scientific, inquiry into why 97.3 percent of the great American Nation, at the present advanced state of civilization, devotes itself zestfully and with unanimity to singing 'Yes, We Have No Bananas,' " the *New York Times* article went on to say. The news story offers several possible causes, including vapidness, a national inferiority complex (manifested in a preference for lowbrow music), "infantile regression," and "mob psychology."

The origins of the song that led to this alarming state of affairs are somewhat cloudy. The melody was adapted from an 1860s sheet-music hit called "When I Saw Sweet Nellie Home," which in turn was derived from, of all things, Handel's "Hallelujah Chorus" (you can actually hear traces of the classical work in the banana song if you hum one, then the other, in the same key: *hal-le-lu-jah* . . . *yes-we-have-no*). But there are several variations on the origin of the final singsong hit.

The most widely accepted version puts Frank Silver on a date; while visiting his girlfriend's home, he's bemused, then perturbed, by an underfoot kid brother who keeps repeating the title phrase, explaining that the amusingly mangled verbiage was something he'd heard uttered by an immigrant fruit vendor. A second starting point places Cohn and Silver at a speakeasy called the Blossom Heath Inn, forty minutes by train from Manhattan in Lynbrook, Long Island. In that account, the title is coined by a Greek grocer named Jimmy Costas, who used the phrase as a sort of verbal shoulder shrug when his shelves were fresh out of the tropical fruit. A 1931 account of the song's beginnings, published in *Harper's Magazine* editor Frederick Lewis Allen's *Only Yesterday*, mixes the two yarns: The keynote phrase was coined by an Italian fruit seller, repeated in a newspaper cartoon, and test-marketed by the songwriters in the Long Island suburbs before it finally made it to Broadway.

The song's symbolic origins, however, lie not in specific people or places, but in the question it suggests: Are bananas available?

The answer was yes—they're not.

Why would a grocer with plenty of supply—the song mentions onions and cabbages as well as "all kinds" of fresh produce—be unable to meet demand for what had, in the previous two decades, become America's favorite and most widely available fruit?

The malady that turned banana plantations into dust was beginning to have an effect on supply. These occasional shortages were barely noticed by shoppers, because banana companies were continuing to acquire land and plant new crops. But that process was accelerating to the point where a few public blips began to appear. It didn't mean an overall slowdown in banana consumption or an increase in prices. Instead, Americans got a happy song. Yet in the banana-growing nations, the results were increasingly harsh.

Man Makes a Banana

I T WASN'T THAT UNITED FRUIT was ignorant of Panama disease. A few executives warned of an impending disaster, but since the disease was relatively slow-moving, compared to today's banana maladies, they generally went unheeded.

The banana barons might have adopted a resistant banana if they knew of one exactly like the Gros Michel, requiring no change in consumer tastes or in growing, ripening, and shipping. While the Cavendish was grown as a minor commercial variety in a few places, the idea that it would replace the best-known banana was unthinkable. The lesser-known fruit was smaller, more fragile, and didn't taste as good as the Gros Michel. Though the banana industry had shown, repeatedly, that it knew how to innovate, it no longer seemed to want to—not when it could simply level some virgin forest and start new plantations to replace the dying ones.

The first efforts to breed stronger bananas were conducted by academics, who had a daunting task: they had to, for the first time, find out what bananas actually were, and they had to determine the genetic makeup of the fruit at a time when such structural studies were barely heard of. Almost nothing was known about bananas. With just a single variety, and it so easy to grow, an advanced understanding of the fruit, until then, seemed pointless.

The Gros Michel crisis made the work seem absolutely urgent—at least to the scientists tracking the path of the disease. In 1922 the British government founded the Imperial College of Tropical Agriculture, with solving the Panama disease riddle as the institution's primary task. The key to finding a solution, the early banana scientists believed, was in creating hybrid fruit, crossing the Gros Michel with some kind of wild banana, hoping that the resistant qualities of the latter would combine with, but not significantly alter, the taste and shipping characteristics of the former. A botanical research station in Trinidad was opened so that whatever resulted from the college's experiments could be tested in the field. Much of this work was independent, though some was commissioned by United Fruit. Scientists frequently moved between the public institutions and the private employer.

The results were maddening. E. E. Cheesman, who directed the facility, described the frustrating nature of the search for a new banana in a 1931 report: "The existence together in Gros Michel of many characters desirable in a commercial banana, such as compactness of bunch, a fruit skin not abnormally sensitive to bruising, ability to stand up well to conditions of bulk transport, and an attractive appearance on ripening, would appear at first to render the problem a simple one. All that is immediately required is to 'build in' to this type resistance to Panama Disease."

Noting that there were several other banana breeds that had that resistance, he concluded that "in many crops, the solution would be a comparatively elementary exercise in plant breeding."

Not with sexless, sterile bananas.

Unlike the Cavendish, seeds could occasionally appear in the Gros Michel—one or two for every ten thousand plants. Finding

one meant manually examining each individual fruit. Even if a seed
was discovered and bred, the odds of it actually growing into something were slim. If growth did occur, the problem reversed itself:
the new bananas would often have seeds, making them unacceptable
as an edible product. "To start with a plant almost completely sexually sterile, raise progeny in sufficient numbers to make a breeding
problem possible, combine desirable characters and end with another
sterile plant, is very nearly unique in plant breeding," Cheesman
noted.

A worldwide search for wild bananas—blind-date candidates for
marriage with Gros Michel—began. Scientists and explorers searched
Africa, Asia, and the Americas for wild species; these were then transported back to Trinidad and Jamaica, where they were stored and
tested. Many of the collected bananas, along with the processes they
started, form the basis for today's banana-breeding experiments.

In 1925 a wave of excitement swept through the small world of
banana research. A hybrid emerged, growing to full fruit, which
seemed to have the desired characteristics. Most importantly, the
plant, unlike every other hybrid the Imperial College produced,
was resistant to Panama disease. The new fruit was significant
enough that researchers felt they could give it a name. IC1 was
the first hybrid banana to come from the Imperial College; the
naming convention—an abbreviation for the breeding facility,
followed by a sequenced number—is still used in banana research
today.

But subsequent generations of IC1 turned out to be less perfect.
Each time a new crop was harvested, the fruit moved further and
further from the ideal. The hybrid's status was downgraded from
candidate to raw material for future experimentation. Those successor bananas were equally inconsistent. Fruit that bred well in the
lab failed in the field. Many even contracted Panama disease.

Humans had been breeding bananas for millennia, with spectacular success across the globe. But they'd never tried to create a

fruit that was meant to be grown by the billions and feed people thousands of miles away. For years the effort was a dismal failure. Yet a world search for new bananas had begun. The fruit was better understood. And scientists, from then on, would grow more and more savvy about breeding bananas.

CHAPTER 15

The Banana Massacre

I REMEMBER THE FIRST TIME I ever understood that the retelling of ordinary events could become magic. I was a teenager, just beginning to write, searching for inspiration. I'd always loved books about other worlds—science fiction, Edgar Rice Burroughs's Tarzan series, even old pulp novels I bought at a local junk shop. But it had only recently begun to occur to me that the greatest constructed worlds could be found in works that were considered to be "true" literature.

That point was made most sharply with Gabriel García Márquez's *One Hundred Years of Solitude*. I spent half a summer reading it, staying up late to follow the epic story that chronicled six generations of a single family living in a fictional village in Colombia. I was so enthralled by the characters, by the way they were swept up in events that seemed to be not of this world, that I hardly noticed the more earthbound events that actually formed the novel's story.

The book plays out against a backdrop of bananas. The climax comes during a plantation strike, when martial law is declared. The workers gather in their town square amidst ominous signs. "Around twelve o'clock," Márquez writes, "more than three thousand people, workers, women, and children, had spilled out into the open space in front of the station and were pressing into the neighboring streets, which the army had closed off with rows of machine guns." The crowd remains in the square, even after they are ordered to disperse. A second warning is met with defiance. Eventually, time runs out: "Fourteen machine guns answered at once. But it all seemed like a farce. It was as if the machine guns had been loaded with caps, because their panting rattle could be heard and their incandescent spitting could be seen, but not the slightest reaction was perceived, not a cry, not even a sigh among the compact crowd that seemed petrified by an instantaneous vulnerability. Suddenly, on one side of the station, a cry of death tore open the enchantment: 'Aaaagh, Mother.' A seismic voice, a volcanic breath, the road of a cataclysm broke out in the center of the crowd." Three thousand striking banana workers are killed; their bodies, one by one, are thrown into the ocean.

In rereading the book a few months ago, I was once again moved not just by the author's language but by the way it created, in just a few words, both a sense of sorrow and a photographic depiction of the events surrounding it.

But what I also understood, after spending several years researching the book you're reading now, was that this wasn't fiction. Márquez had woven a story, for sure, but the event he was talking about—the Colombia banana massacre of 1929—was real.

WITHOUT A NEW BANANA, a vicious cycle emerged: Fruit was grown then stricken; plantations were abandoned and new ones founded; disease would strike again. Unlike the apple industry, banana growers couldn't afford to market multiple varieties of their fruit. If the uniformity of bananas was what made them so powerful and popular, it also brought about the emergence of the first monoculture—dependence on a single variety of crop, creating huge economies of scale and huge susceptibility to catastrophe—in the history of commercial agriculture. The system worked when Keith was building railroads and when it took just a few hoodlums and good timing to take over a country. But by the late 1920s, as the banana industry became larger, people in the countries where the fruit grew became more aware of just how valuable the product they were providing to American consumers was—and how little of that value they were receiving. They were underpaid and treated poorly. To add insult to injury, their land was being stolen. At the same time, a powerful wave of workers' movements—inspired by the founding of the Soviet Union in 1917—was reaching Latin America.

The banana industry—rightly—saw this as a huge threat. It couldn't survive without cheap fruit, which meant cheap labor. Because Panama disease was permanently making fallow so much of its existing holdings, the fruit companies had a continuous need for new land, according to John Soluri, author of *Banana Cultures: Agriculture, Consumption, and Environmental Change in Honduras and the United States*. To keep bananas affordable, that territory needed to be acquired, and cultivated, as inexpensively as possible. Controlling labor and terrain couldn't be done without cooperative governments (or military intervention, if they weren't). But Latin American leaders also had to pay some attention to their constituents. Sometimes, the general public would be appeased; other times it was repressed. In either case, the banana industry had to work constantly to stay ahead and in control of an ever-deepening cycle of exploitation, violence, and revolution.

But even in a region that had seen dozens of interventions and takeovers, what happened in Colombia, beginning in December 1928 and climaxing just after the start of the new year, was exceptional.

United Fruit had been in Colombia since 1899, operating plantations in the Magdalena region of the country. Colombia was different from the other United Fruit nations. With large exports of coffee, it was not exclusively a banana land. Intense political conflict had been part of Colombia's history long before the fruit was planted there: At the turn of the century, conservatives and liberals had fought the brutal War of a Thousand Days, which cost as many as 100,000 lives. The hostilities had also cost the country Panama—which had been a territory of Colombia—and brought a conservative and ultimately banana-friendly government to power.

But the sweetheart deals banana companies received on land, taxation, and worker conditions had a backlash. The plantation operators became a target for liberal and social activists. By the early 1920s, Colombian workers began feeling confident enough to strike. Even some local growers attempted to loosen the American produce giant's grip on the nation by opening their own independent export operations (they were defeated by generous "grants" United Fruit gave to plantation operators who remained in the fold).

By 1927 Colombia's political system seemed to be leaning against the banana conglomerate. The national assembly ordered an investigation into United Fruit's land-acquisition policies. The conservative party's thirty-year grip on power seemed to be loosening, with liberals making gains, especially in the countryside. Banana workers, who were without even the most basic rights, felt emboldened.

The biggest labor action ever faced by a banana company began in October 1928, when 32,000 workers went on strike. They demanded to be granted medical treatment and proper toilet facilities; they insisted on being paid in cash rather than company-issued scrip only redeemable in United Fruit–owned stores. They asked that they be considered true employees rather than subcontractors who weren't even afforded the minimal protection of Colombia's weakly drawn labor laws.

The strike panicked United Fruit. Even after the government sent troops to occupy Magdalena, effectively usurping liberal power, the nation was too volatile for anything to be guaranteed.

The conflict made headlines in the United States. A *New York Times* article, published in December 1928, laid out the company position on the strike. Eight decades later, and in light of what happened next, United Fruit's statements seem beyond cruel. Banana company spokesmen attributed the strike not to a genuine need to improve conditions for exploited workers but to a "subversive movement" and "not representatives of any established body of laborers." In fact, the article quoted the company as saying, "no complaints have been received by our employees."

United Fruit reported that in response to the strike, the Colombian government had suspended the rights of free assembly and free speech. "We are convinced," a spokesperson said, "that only this prompt action by the government prevented great loss of life." The clampdown was also celebrated by the U.S. ambassador to Colombia, Jefferson Caffery. In a telegram sent to U.S. Secretary of State Frank Billings Kellogg, he wrote: "I have been following the . . . strike through United Fruit Company representative here; also through minister of Foreign Affairs who on Saturday told me government would send additional troops and would arrest all strike leaders and transport them to prison at Cartagena; that government would give adequate protection to American interests involved."

Martial law was declared on December 5.

On December 6, in the town of Ciénaga—just as in Márquez's fictional Macondo—banana workers gathered in the town square. The city hall stood at one end and the main church at the other. The workers were not there, specifically, to protest. December 6 was a Sunday; they'd attended mass and were waiting to hear a speech by the regional governor. Because the address would follow church services, the workers were accompanied by their wives and families.

General Cortés Vargas—the military official in charge of the region, who claimed he acted only to prevent an even worse intervention by the U.S. military—had given his commanders these orders: "Prepare your mind to face the crowds of rebels . . . and kill before foreign troops tread upon our soil."

Four machine gun positions surrounded the square, on rooftops, one at each corner.

An order was given. The area was to be cleared in five minutes. The countdown had begun. The crowd didn't—and couldn't, packed into the square as they were—disperse. The troops opened fire.

As he had throughout the early stages of the crisis, U.S. ambassador Caffery reported the events to his superiors in Washington. The tone and language of the memo are beyond chilling. They are as clear a manifestation of terrible indifference as you will ever read: "I have the honor to report," Caffery wrote, "that the Bogotá representative of the United Fruit Company told me yesterday that the total number of strikers killed by the Colombian military exceeded one thousand."

CHAPTER 16

The Inhuman Republics

THE EFFECTS OF THE COLOMBIA MASSACRE were beyond wide-reaching. Initially, the event was so outrageous that the liberals were able to use it to take power; they instituted land reforms and attempted to try the culprits for the massacre. The result was even more polarization. United Fruit attempted to maintain its position, but this time the company seemed to have gone too far. As operations in the South American nation became more difficult, the banana grower began closing plantations and shipping equipment to Costa Rica. This time United Fruit used the advance of Panama disease as an excuse, though the *New York Times* reported that "labor troubles and difficulties with the government are responsible for the new policy."

In hindsight, the departure of the banana industry was one of the country's smaller problems. The liberal who'd demanded an investigation into the banana massacre was Jorge Eliécer Gaitán, a politician and lawyer who'd come from an impoverished background himself.

Using the country's radio network—which had partially been built by United Fruit—Gaitán made fiery speeches advocating the interests of "the people" and denouncing the "oligarchy" that he saw as dominating them. Gaitán formed his own political party in 1933 and was a dominant force in Colombian politics until 1948. He was poised to win the country's next scheduled elections when he was assassinated at a campaign rally in Bogotá.

Like the Kennedy assassination in the United States, the truth about Gaitán's murder will probably always be in dispute. The man who pulled the trigger, Juan Roa Sierra, was immediately beaten to death; in the years following, everyone from U.S. and Soviet agents to political rivals and Fidel Castro were accused of ordering the killing. What is known is that a period known as *la violencia* followed, during which rival political forces in Colombia would launch a brutal and deadly guerilla war. From the late 1940s through the 1950s, as many as 180,000 Colombians died; a military dictatorship seized control of the nation in 1953. The dominos continued to fall. Rebel groups began operating against the military forces ruling the country; paramilitaries were created as a response. With chaos throughout the country, drug cartels were able to establish domain over huge swaths of the countryside. Today, Colombia is a nation of kidnappings, murder, and violence; several insurgent organizations control different parts of the country; the cocaine trade mingles with both sides and is believed to finance at least part of the operations of the FARC, the guerilla faction that began as the military arm of the Colombian communist party, an offshoot of the liberal movement that fractured when Gaitán was assassinated.

It isn't fair to blame the banana industry for all of Colombia's problems. But it is important to point out that in that country and throughout Latin America the destabilization resulting from banana-related interventions created a tradition of weak institutions, making it difficult for true democracy and fair economic policies to take hold. The Latin American tradition of governments not supported by the general population, and propped up by overseas commercial interests, was created under the authorship of United Fruit.

There was even a name for such puppet-string governments. The term was first used by O. Henry in *Cabbages and Kings*, a 1905 collection of short stories that took place in a mythical Central American country called Anchuria. (The appellation is a play on words for Honduras, where the writer briefly sought refuge from U.S. officials pursuing him on a fraud conviction. In Spanish, the word for the real nation translates as "depths." The name of the author's mirror land comes from the Spanish *ancho*, meaning "width.") But the term coined by O. Henry didn't come into popular vogue until after the Colombia massacre, when it appeared in a 1935 *Esquire* magazine story that chronicled American adventures in the region. The article described the actions as "inhuman," and termed the nations that so readily acquiesced to the fruit companies and the U.S. government as "banana republics."

CHAPTER 17

Straightening Out the Business

THE EVENTS OF EARLY 1929 came at a desperate time for United Fruit. As physically violent as its affairs were overseas, it was facing an opponent at home that was, from a business standpoint, even more aggressive. For years, the company had been able to steamroll competitors, forcing them into withering price wars. Of its early rivals, only Standard Fruit—the future Dole, started by Joseph Vaccaro, the entrepreneur who bought up all of the ice factories along the Gulf Coast in the late nineteenth century— was left standing, mostly because United Fruit had once been a partial owner of the company but was forced to divest by antitrust investigators. The larger banana company didn't dare attempt to squeeze its legally designated rival from the market.

But United Fruit did battle another company: Sam Zemurray's Cuyamel Fruit. Fifteen years after it was founded, the smaller company owned an extensive steamboat fleet and had its own record of technological innovation—creating superior irrigation systems at the Honduran plantations it operated. Zemurray even competed with United Fruit to buy up regional competitors, and frequently won. Just after the Colombia intervention, Cuyamel's stock began to rise. United Fruit's shares plummeted.

The larger banana company, just as it did when faced with worker challenges—or spreading blights—responded by rote. It started a price war.

At first, the result seemed like little more than a draw. But as the world's largest banana grower's stock price fell further, it decided that rather than continue the battle it would buy Cuyamel, even if it had to pay a huge premium. In 1930 Zemurray sold his company, receiving 300,000 shares of United Fruit stock and a seat on the banana giant's board of directors. The erstwhile banana baron's intention was to retire and enjoy the $50 million fortune he'd acquired. But United Fruit's stock continued to plunge. The situation was worsened by the crash of the U.S. stock market in October of that year. Prior to that, a single share of the banana company sold for $158. By 1932 it had declined to $10, taking Zemurray's riches along with it.

Enough was enough. At a directors' meeting that year, Zemurray loudly voiced his concern.

Zemurray, according to his United Fruit Historical Society biography, was never made to feel terribly welcome at United Fruit. After the deaths of Preston, in 1924, and Keith, in 1929, control of the company had fallen to shareholders, the largest being the Bank of Boston. The bank's president, Daniel G. Wing, was a legendary old-money financier with decidedly patrician sensibilities. Like U.S. Secretary of State Philander Knox two decades earlier, Wing made the mistake of underestimating the up-by-his-bootstraps immigrant, who had uttered his protest in the thick Russian accent he'd never even remotely banished.

Wing's reply: "Unfortunately, Mr. Zemurray, I can't understand a word of what you say."

An enraged Zemurray did what he always did—and what he believed banana men always had to do. He took matters into his own hands. Investor by investor, he convinced United Fruit's share-holders that current management was destroying the company. At the next board meeting, Zemurray had gathered enough support to oust Wing and the rest of the company's old guard. His final words to the departing executives: "You gentlemen have been fucking up this business long enough. I'm going to straighten it out."

Sam the Banana Man, who'd launched the banana industry's first audacious seizure of power, had pulled off another one, this time in the boardroom, taking over the company responsible for the bloodiest and most recent of those interventions. But as terrible as the aggression in Colombia had been, it would soon be exceeded by actions of Zemurray's own design.

PART IV

NEVER ENOUGH

CHAPTER 18

Knowledge Is Powerless

T HE BANANA INDUSTRY weathered stock market crashes and price wars. But Panama disease had turned an enterprise that relied on tight controls and stability into a bizarre and treacherous roller coaster ride. Not only did the number of bananas being grown in Central America swing wildly during the first decades of the twentieth century, but the places they were grown also began to shift at an alarming rate. "In some localities," writes historian John Soluri, "production plummeted and economies all but collapsed, even as regional exports were rising." In Honduras the output of Standard Fruit dropped from 4.5 million to 1.9 million bunches during the first half of the 1920s. The number rose the following decade but only because new plantations were opened in areas of newly cleared forest.

A few attempts to research the banana out of its problems continued. In 1931 Scottish agronomist Claude Wardlaw, working at Trinidad's Imperial College of Tropical Agriculture, conducted a Panama disease survey and found devastation: 15,000 acres infected in Jamaica and 50,000 in Panama, with the entire Atlantic coast of that nation now unable to sustain banana crops. Even the figures for countries with seemingly low levels of the blight were ominous, since the numbers didn't count land that was completely out of service. Honduras, for example, showed only 5,000 acres of loss (just a fraction of the country's total production), but adding the written-off acres would have boosted the total close to Panama's.

Wardlaw was also one of the first to unlock the mystery of how Panama disease spread. It wasn't something in the air that appeared out of nowhere or even something that had lurked in the soil for ages. The banana industry itself, Wardlaw said, was responsible. When he visited United Fruit's Costa Rica plantations in 1929, he was astonished at the poor agricultural practices he encountered. The reason the disease moved so quickly, Wardlaw surmised, was that it was being transported by people—even to the very plantations that were being cut *in order to grow disease-free fruit*. "The amazing thing," the scientist wrote, "is that very few [banana producers] . . . possess even a smattering of real agricultural knowledge, and if they do, it probably does not help them in the least." Proper in-the-field husbandry seemed to be the one technical skill United Fruit was unable to master. It was easier just to pull up their stakes on ruined plantations and move on. The same problem exists today. At the Chinese banana plantation I visited, I watched as farmers and families came and went, transferring infected soil acre-by-acre via footprints and bicycle tracks. Houbin Chen, the scientist who accompanied me, took care to change his shoes every time he moved to a new plantation, keeping several pairs in the trunk of his car. The effort seemed futile, I noted, given what was going on around us. "I know," he sighed. "But I need to set a good example."

The banana industry did fund some research. Scientists backed by United Fruit determined that Panama disease was probably spread via water, running through the banana's root systems. They identified the malady as a fungus in the fusarium family. When breeders created IC2, the second human-bred banana resistant to the blight, by crossing Gros Michel with a wild Asian species, banana companies agreed to grow it in Honduras. But the fruit lost resistance before it was able to be put into large-scale production.

The problem was that the programs banana scientists came up with were largely ignored by growers working for the same companies. Even if a new banana couldn't be found, even if the disease couldn't be cured, plantation managers could adopt practices that would extend the life of existing growing areas and slow the malady's advance. They could quarantine infected areas and make sure that workers, trains, vehicles, and tools were cleaned and sanitized so they'd be prevented from spreading contaminated soil. For the most part, they didn't do any of this.

Wardlaw also was one of the first to see that banana growing was throwing the entire Central American ecosystem out of balance. "Virgin forest," he wrote, "is the raw material of the agricultural pioneer. Before it can be exploited to advantage, its value must be truly assessed, otherwise the exploiter may find himself bankrupt while posterity is left with an infinitely poorer heritage." Wardlaw believed that Panama disease was the product of willful disregard of the laws of nature. Bananas were growing in a place where they never belonged, and—like many biologic newcomers—came under attack from pathogens they couldn't resist.

Banana growers did find havens where the Gros Michel seemed to be the stronger force. For years, the Santa Marta district of Colombia—a focal point of the 1929 strike—remained free of the blight even as surrounding areas succumbed. The region became a key source of the clean, disease-free plants needed to jump-start new plantations. Why Santa Marta was resistant wasn't clear—it might have had something to do with climate or soil conditions—but in 1948 the disease arrived there, and the plantations quickly succumbed.

In the 1950s, Wardlaw and his colleagues reprised the 1931 survey. By then the blight had gone global. Eight nations in Asia were infected, five in the Pacific, twelve in Africa, and twenty-two in the

Americas, including the entire Caribbean. Even the United States was struck. A few nascent—and probably ill-fated, with or without a fungal attacker—plantations were hit in Florida, and promptly shuttered. In every case, the failure of the banana companies to enforce proper quarantine and isolation practices hastened the spread of the disease.

The banana moguls knew what Panama disease was. They knew what it did. They knew how it spread. But they refused to use any of this knowledge for positive change. It was as if the power of the banana, which had changed both the nations that consumed it and those that grew it, had addicted United Fruit and its rivals to just one method of growth: blunt marauding through the tropics without considering the consequences of, or alternatives to, standard procedure. Now that nature had answered back, the banana companies seemed deaf and baffled.

CHAPTER 19

Pure Science

WILSON POPENOE WAS DETERMINED that his voice not be ignored. He'd become obsessed with plants as a boy, while working in his father's greenhouse near Pasadena, California. By the time he was twenty, he was an agricultural prodigy, with an encyclopedic knowledge of nearly every fruit and vegetable grown in the United States and an intense desire that his understanding should encompass the entire world. When Cornell University offered him a full scholarship, Popenoe turned it down, deciding instead to travel the Americas and Asia for the U.S. Department of Agriculture, where he was given a title never before bestowed on anyone: plant developer. The self-taught scientist literally changed landscapes wherever he went. In 1913 he helped establish orange crops in Brazil. In Brazil, Ecuador, Honduras, and Guatemala, he planted coconuts, olives, figs, and Thai rambutan. In 1923 he married archaeologist Dorothy Hughes, and the two continued to travel—with Dorothy providing pen-and-ink drawings to accompany Wilson's photographs and written reports.

The couple's wanderings made them especially aware of the desperate conditions plantation and farm workers faced across the world. In one of his reports, Wilson Popenoe noted the mistreatment of black laborers on South African farms. When Dorothy Popenoe took a solo trip to Panama, she attempted to take a picture of a local woman kneeling by a stream but was rebuffed. "She didn't like Americans," she wrote in a letter to Wilson. "I was reminded of your tale of the Guatemalan Indian, who wanted nothing but to be left alone." Instead, the "Indians" of Central America were picking bananas.

In 1925 Popenoe was hired by United Fruit to open a research station in Lancetilla, a few miles from the company's Honduran headquarters in Tela. It was a curious job for someone who'd expressed so much sympathy for the exploited, but the scientist was determined that his work could aid people working at both the highest and lowest levels of the banana industry. His primary assignment wasn't to breed a resistant banana, it was to collect them, gathering samples of both wild and local fruit from around the world, and return them to Honduras for experimentation. As a hedge, the self-made plant expert was charged with a secondary task: determining what crops might be grown on land ruined by Panama disease—or even in the entire region, if bananas completely vanished. His proposed replacement crops included rubber, a dozen kinds of timber, the oil palm, and cocoa, all of which are now grown across wide stretches of Central America.

Some of Popenoe's projects benefited United Fruit at the highest—and most personal—levels. When Sam Zemurray wanted to curry favor with Honduran president Tiburcio Carías Andino, he ordered Popenoe to develop a local breed of tobacco that could compete with product from Cuba. Whether Popenoe succeeded is still debated, but what is certain today is that any American connoisseur who wants to stay within the law is indebted to Popenoe: The Honduran product is as close as one can get to a Havana stogie. Popenoe also collected poisonous snakes—but not for fun. He knew that snakebites were common, especially among banana workers, and developed one of the world's largest collections of antivenin.

Popenoe left multiple legacies. The descendants of the fruit from his banana collection are still used as basic stock in the attempt to create resistant breeds. And North Americans owe Popenoe a debt every time we scoop up a chip with guacamole. He planted the first successful avocado crops in the hemisphere (though they remained largely an expensive import until after World War II, when California finally caught up. Even then, said a 1950 report by the state's Avocado Society, growers remained "dependent on Wilson Popenoe"). Popenoe made huge strides in advancing native control of Latin America's agricultural destiny. The scientist managed to convince United Fruit to donate $3 million in order to found the Pan-American School of Agriculture (and even more amazingly, he got the fruit company to agree *not* to hire the institution's graduates, ensuring that the locally trained plant experts would serve public, rather than corporate, interests).

The final thing Popenoe left behind is the most problematic. The botanic gardens he planted at Lancetilla are still open today. One of the more pleasant ways to get to them is to rent a bike in Tela and pedal to the facility along dirt roads, through deeply shaded bamboo forest. Guest cabins can be rented there, and though they aren't air conditioned, a visitor can cool off with a quick dip into the Lancetilla River. The gardens are gorgeous and quiet. They're Popenoe's most lovely creation, and it is hard to imagine that anything malicious—even if it was not intended to be so—could have been created there.

In many ways, Popenoe was a pure scientist. As sympathetic as he was to native causes, his job was to solve problems. Sometimes that meant not being able to see that immediate success might do long-term harm. The oil palm is a good example of that. Though it initially helped revitalize land left fallow by Panama disease, it has now become so widespread in Central America that it is responsible for much of the region's deforestation. For bananas, Popenoe helped create an even more controversial legacy: It is called Bordeaux mixture.

CHAPTER 20

A Second Front

I T WASN'T JUST THAT Panama disease was so virulent that any attempt to control it seemed futile. Banana growers were soon finding other things to worry about. In 1935 a new banana-killing pathogen appeared. In many ways, Sigatoka, which was first described in Fiji (the disease is named after a river on that South Pacific island), was even more insidious than the better-known fungus that had been spreading across Latin America for over three decades. Though it killed plants outright, just as Panama disease did, it could also—if fruit was harvested at the earliest, invisible stages of infection—strike while the fruit was in transport. Bananas loaded unblemished would arrive at market in various states of rot, ranging from mild softness to massive discoloration, along with a foul taste and odor. Even worse, Sigatoka was not spread on shoes and tools or in soil and water.

The pathogen was airborne. That meant it moved at a pace much quicker than Panama disease. From a single Honduran plantation, Sigatoka expanded through the region's entire banana crop—

vulnerable, as always, because each fruit was a clone of the other—with astonishing rapidity. The banana industry had recently begun to open huge operations in the virgin, Panama disease–free soil along the canal nation's Pacific coast. The project went well, and several years later the earlier infection had yet to arrive. But when Sigatoka appeared, the entire region was wiped out in a matter of weeks.

But faster and more toxic as it was, Sigatoka was different from Panama disease in one critical respect: United Fruit was able to find a cure. Copper sulfate—you might have used it in a high school science experiment, growing blue crystals from the substance in a baby-food jar—was quickly found to stop the new malady in the lab. The technical problem was how to apply it to the banana fields. Ordinary crop-dusting didn't provide enough coverage. Instead, the company—in a research effort led by Wilson Popenoe—was able to modify a formula used by French winemakers, mixing the powerful chemical with lime and oil so it could be turned into a fine spray. Even then, applying it was a huge technological challenge, but it was the kind of task United Fruit had always been good at.

The substance known as Bordeaux mixture led to a chemical retaking of the tropics. "To deliver the necessary enormous quantities—250 gallons per acre, twenty to thirty times a year—United Fruit created a fungicide infrastructure of phaeronic scale," wrote Steve Marquardt in a 2002 issue of the *Latin American Research Review*. The company had to install miles and miles of piping, thousands of pumps, and reel after reel of firehoses and nozzles. A quarter of United Fruit's workers were pulled from picking and packing, and turned into pesticide sprayers. "Fields," Marquardt notes, "turned into factories." Pesticides have been used for thousands of centuries, but United Fruit's industrialization of the process was the final part of an infamous trio of "innovations" that, in less than two decades, transformed the way people controlled—and reacted to—agricultural maladies. Aerial spraying was invented in 1922. It was followed, ten years later, by the first crop experiments with DDT. The use of

Bordeaux mixture became widespread in the years just prior to World War II.

THE CAMPAIGN TO CONTROL SIGATOKA had an unexpected fringe benefit for the banana company: Such an effort was too expensive to be mounted by small plantation owners. The disease, and the "cure," helped United Fruit squeeze most of its last few remaining competitors out of business, leaving the Central American banana market to itself and the much-smaller (and untouchable, thanks to antitrust laws) Standard Fruit.

The bananas benefited. The banana growers benefited. American consumers benefited. The only people in the fruit's supply chain to be harmed by the disease were the banana workers themselves. Already burdened by near-indentured status, with substandard housing, poor medical care, and no ability to organize, they now faced a much more insidious threat: Bordeaux mixture made them sick. Workers would return from the field with their skin literally turned blue by the heavy spraying (a nickname for a Bordeaux mixture–stained *bananero* was *perico*, or "parakeet"; they were as brightly colored as the common tropical bird). No longer was the biggest immediate health risk faced by banana workers an industrial accident—a wound from a machete or a mishap on a loading dock. After a few months of exposure, workers could no longer scrub the blue tint from their flesh. They'd lose their sense of smell and their ability to hold down food.

Then they died.

"Pervasive fear of the respiratory effects of Bordeaux inhalation fostered an enduring trope in Central American anti–United Fruit literature and journalism: the skeletal, tubercular former *perico*, dying alone in an urban slum or on the fringes of the plantation zone," Marquardt writes. It was, he notes, a "macabre exchange": human lives traded for bananas. The misery was hardly abated by the fact that United Fruit paid the workers applying the fungicide much more than an ordinary banana worker would earn. Many poor workers took up the offer—with fatal consequences.

THE FIGHT AGAINST PANAMA DISEASE wasn't going nearly as well. Convinced that irrigation was the key to sweeping the fusarium fungus out of the fields, United Fruit engineers began constructing extensive hydraulic systems—moats and dams, canals and levees—powered by gigantic pumps.

There was great optimism about these efforts, and, combined with the Sigatoka spraying apparatus, it seemed that the war against the jungle had finally, permanently been won. A company newsletter, Marquardt notes, boasted that control had at last been asserted over "creeping, progress-consuming, tropical Mother Nature."

Once again, the company's most powerful enemy punished that overconfidence. Irrigation did provide a brief respite from Panama disease—then it boomeranged. Water *spread* the fungus. By 1950 Panama disease was moving faster than ever before. (An inconvenient truth, if there ever was one.) Even so, company managers continued to cling to their miracle cure. The failures, they believed, were only because not enough water was being applied.

What began as drenching became torrential. The technique was called "flood fallowing." It was nothing less than creating huge, artificial lakes—building earthen sluices around entire plantations and filling them three feet deep in an attempt to swamp the fungus. It was expensive, scarring to the land, and more than ineffective: All that water *did* kill large amounts of the Panama disease fungus, but it also destroyed almost everything else—including other fungi and bacteria—along with it. The scrubbed, drained fields would then provide a clean, competition-free vacuum for any malady strong enough to colonize quickly.

Panama disease fit the bill.

Whether victorious—as in the conquest of Sigatoka—or vanquished, the banana industry's attitudes seemed unchanged. From

Minor Keith's conquest of the Panamanian jungles, through the overthrow of Honduras just before the First World War, to the harsh lesson taught to Colombia's workers in 1929, the Octopus knew only one way to wield power: bluntly, with brute force. Soon—once again at the behest of Sam Zemurray, the rough-and-tumble self-made billionaire who sat at the center of the business during its most turbulent and aggressive years—the banana industry would embark on its most complex, angry, and ultimately futile application of that philosophy.

CHAPTER 21

No Respite

tregua
respiro

O CALL THE SS *SIXAOLA* a banana boat is like calling the Grand Canyon a big ditch. Built in 1911, less than forty years after Lorenzo Dow Baker brought his first shipment of fruit from Jamaica aboard a ship powered by sails, the vessel was enormous: It was half as large as the *Titanic*, capable of holding five hundred railroad cars full of bananas. The *Sixaola* wasn't the only ship in the Great White Fleet that indicated how huge the public's appetite for bananas had become. Bigger vessels were being constructed at shipyards across America. Even the smallest of United Fruit's ships could carry thousands of times more fruit than Baker had.

But the *Sixaola* was United Fruit's seafaring pride. The vessel was named after a Panamanian river that emptied into Bocas del Toro, the natural harbor that was United Fruit's primary shipping point for much of the early twentieth century. For nearly thirty years following its launch, it had mostly plied the same route: from Panama to New Orleans, a journey of just a few days, through seas that were—except during hurricane season—nearly always calm.

All that changed in 1942.

When World War II broke out, American banana consumption was at an all-time high. It had grown every year since 1900. Desire for the fruit became even stronger in the 1930s: Unemployed workers might have sold apples in the street, but they still preferred to eat the cheaper banana. United Fruit had weathered the depression nearly unblemished. Under Sam Zemurray, the company gained nearly full control of the global market for bananas, even as the amount of work it had to do to evade Panama disease increased. When one plantation failed, another was built, a task that meant forging an entire settlement from scratch. Land needed to be cleared, railroad lines and telegraph lines needed to be extended. Housing, schools, and hospitals for workers had to be built, and infrastructure, including cattle ranches to breed livestock for food and donkeys for banana-field transport, sawmills and machine shops, water transport systems and power-generating stations all needed to be put into place. Executive perks were also carried over—sometimes literally, with structures disassembled, transported, and rebuilt so that each plantation had the golf courses, churches, restaurants, and, for single executives, brothels, often filled with underage girls, needed to create lifestyles most of the officials could neither have afforded nor gotten away with at home. United Fruit's minicolonies were a huge incentive when it came to bringing skilled managers to the otherwise less-than-comfortable-for-gringos tropics. They were also planning centers for some of the company's most terrible actions. When I sat with a former company executive in the dining room of what was the banana giant's country club outside San Pedro Sula, Honduras, he told me how he'd grown up—his father also worked for the company—in a United Fruit compound and how, at these very tables, "governments were made and broken in between rounds of golf."

Some of the abandonments seemed to happen as rapidly as in places like Pompeii or the mysteriously empty Maya outposts in the jungles. Though Panama's Bocas del Toro still served as a shipping point, plan-

tation operations were completely halted. Thousands of acres were left
bare, and thousands of workers lost their jobs. In Honduras the huge
shipping terminal of Puerto Castilla became a ghost town (a military
base now occupies the area; the only remnant of United Fruit's reign is
a falling-down former hospital surrounded by a high fence).

The oddest desertion of all was at Sosua in the Dominican
Republic. After the village was left empty in 1940, President Rafael
Trujillo offered it as a Jewish homeland—a safe zone at the beginning of the Holocaust. Plans were made to house 100,000 refugees.
But the logistics of the plan were never worked out: Only five hundred families actually relocated to the island. Today, twenty-five
remain, operating an active synagogue and the country's biggest
dairy operation. Holstein and Jersey cows graze on pastureland that
was once United Fruit plantations.

The first drop in banana demand since the founding of the industry came at the start of World War II. Fuel, milk, and meat were
rationed, but some supplies were always available since they were
produced within U.S. borders. Not bananas. They had to be shipped.
Though Central America was free of hostilities, and the plantations
could have kept operating at their normal pace, there were no vessels
to bring the fruit back home. Most of the Great White Fleet was
commandeered by the military. Those ships that continued in private service were forced to make a treacherous journey. German
submarines patrolled the area. Cargo vessels traveled in convoys
through what had been declared the Eastern Sea Frontier.

The *Sixaola* had already survived a near-fatal accident. Three
years after it was built, it was drafted into service for World War I.
The ship could carry 3 million tons of beef on a single transatlantic
voyage. In February 1917, as she was being loaded in New York, the
Sixaola caught fire. Two crewmen were killed, and the boat half-
capsized in its Hudson River berth. After the war, the vessel was
raised, refurbished, and returned to transporting bananas.

The *Sixaola* remained in United Fruit service as World War II
began, making voyages from the United States to the Caribbean,

and across the Atlantic. The ship's crew was constantly on edge during these voyages. Twice, the *Sixaola* was shadowed by German submarines.

The first incident occurred near Cape Race, at the tip of Newfoundland's Avalon Peninsula. Even in peacetime, the promontory was a place sailors tried to keep away from. It was shrouded in nearly perpetual fog and jutted far into the Atlantic. (A radio beacon at the Cape Race lighthouse was the first to hear a distress call from the *Titanic*.) Just off the cape, on the night of February 4, 1942, as it traveled from England to New York, the *Sixaola*'s lookouts spotted a German craft. The U-boat followed the cargo vessel for several hours before veering off. A few days later, the ship—now heading south, along the coast of North Carolina—was chased again. This time, a pair of subs tailed the *Sixaola* for four hours, finally breaking away just after dawn.

Sinkings of cargo vessels had risen to several a week by the middle of the war. On June 12, 1942, the *Sixaola* set out from Panama filled with bananas, a shipment of trucks for the U.S. Army, and 201 passengers and crew. It had barely reached the coastline of Guatemala when a pair of German torpedos ripped into the ship's hull. The banana boat's captain, William Fagan, gave the abandon ship order two minutes later. Before everyone aboard could get into the lifeboats, the *Sixaola*'s boilers exploded. Twenty-nine crew members died, including stewardess Edna Johansson; for her sacrifice, she became the first female recipient of the Merchant Marine Combat Bar. Forty-nine survivors not found during the initial rescue were lost at sea for four days before they finally drifted ashore.

"It was terrifying," the ship's purser, Emmanuel Zammit, told the Cyber Diver News Network, "with all this debris flying over from the blast in the bow of the ship." As he waited aboard the lifeboat for rescuers, Zammit heard the rumble of diesel engines; one of the German submarines surfaced directly in front of him. The U-boat's commander emerged on deck and asked whether the *Sixaola* was carrying only bananas or whether it was also transporting military cargo. The survivors refused to answer, and the subs were quickly chased away by approaching U.S. military vessels.

NINETEEN GREAT WHITE FLEET SHIPS were sunk during the war. The human cost was high, but for a company as large as United Fruit, the damage was an opportunity to build even larger banana boats. A new *Sixaola* was christened two years after the war ended. It was painted white, but it was also emblazoned with a new symbol: an emblem that helped ensure the company's survival, dominance, and place amidst the mainstays of American culture. It was a blue oval, with the name Chiquita at the center.

CHAPTER 22

Brand Name Bananas

BANANA COMPANIES STILL HAD TO SELL BANANAS, and in a world with thinning supply it was important to each to sell more of *its* own bananas. There were several banana growers, but once the fruit arrived in markets, there was no way to distinguish whether a particular banana came from United Fruit,* Standard Fruit, or a smaller rival. The largest banana company's method of increasing sales was to turn the fruit it sold into a brand name. The invention of "Chiquita" involved more than just a simple name. (Initially, the logo was placed on a band that held bunches together. Stickers didn't come until later.)

In 1944 the company introduced the Chiquita banana jingle, arguably the most well-known advertising melody of all time. The tune was written by the banana company's advertising agency and was presented by an animated banana, who sang with an exotic

---

* While Chiquita had become the company's brand name, officially it was still called United Fruit.

accent and wore a bowl of fruit on her head. Miss Chiquita was pat-
terned after Brazilian bombshell actress Carmen Miranda, who had
worn a similar costume while she danced seductively amidst a troupe
of man-sized bananas in the 1943 musical film *The Gang's All Here*.
Miranda was frequently addressed in her movies with the Spanish
diminutive that the banana company adopted. Chiquita's tuneful
mascot didn't turn into a "real" woman until a 1967 redesign.

The original Chiquita theme is not the one you hear today. It
was performed in a sultry, salsa-influenced style, with lyrics that
provided another measure of consumer education:

> *I'm Chiquita banana and I've come to say*
> *Bananas have to ripen in a certain way*
> *When they are fleck'd with brown and have a golden hue*
> *Bananas taste the best and are best for you*
> *You can put them in a salad*
> *You can put them in a pie-aye*
> *Any way you want to eat them*
> *It's impossible to beat them*
> *But, bananas like the climate of the very, very tropical equator*
> *So you should never put bananas in the refrigerator.*

The catchy tune was an instant hit, even if the information it
provided was wrong—and a sly way to boost sales: As historian
Virginia Scott Jenkins points out, the company that ran dozens of
cold-storage rooms across the United States knew that bananas
actually last longer when refrigerated.

Today, that little bit of misinformation has been replaced, along
with the rest of the song's lyrics.

> *I'm Chiquita Banana and I've come to say*
> *I offer good nutrition in a simple way*
> *When you eat a Chiquita you've done your part*
> *To give every single day a healthy start*

Underneath the crescent yellow
You'll find vitamins and great taste
With no fat, you just can't beat 'em
You'll feel better when you eat 'em
They're a gift from Mother Nature and a natural addition to your table
For wholesome, healthy, pure bananas—look for Chiquita's label!

The jingle's melody has been rearranged as well. It is far less sexy, less Latin. If the Gros Michel was a banana with spectacular taste and personality, then the new tune is as plain—and ubiquitous—as the Cavendish that would soon replace it.

The original sexy singing banana
teaches you to cook (1947).

CHAPTER 23

Guatemala

S AM ZEMURRAY had retired in 1951, and as with many industrial titans, had turned—perhaps out of conscience—to philanthropy. He helped Wilson Popenoe found his Honduran training facility. With his wife, Zemurray funded a women's studies professorship at Harvard. He worked to preserve Mayan ruins throughout Central America (Zemurray's daughter, Doris, was an archaeologist who directed Costa Rica's national museum in the 1960s). The bootstraps immigrant provided cash to support *The Nation*, the weekly liberal newsmagazine.

But Zemurray was not quite a former banana baron. He continued to chair the company's executive committee, and old Sam—the street fighter who, upon taking over United Fruit more than two decades earlier, became known to Wall Street as "the fish that swallowed the whale"—would emerge one final time.

It was 1954. Guatemala.

The small country—Central America's northernmost, sharing a border with Mexico—was deeply impoverished, with an average life expectancy of under forty years, and deeply dependent on bananas. More than half of the country's economy was tied to growing, harvesting, and transporting the fruit. Zemurray's company controlled 75 percent of that trade.

Guatemala had been one of the most important centers of the Mayan empire, and most of the country's 3 million people were descended from that culture, which had hidden treasures in sacred caves and filled the jungles with towering, intricately carved pyramids. More than just about any other Latin American nation, Guatemala's native population had suffered since the arrival of the Spanish in the early sixteenth century; for hundreds of years, Mayas—many of whom spoke no Spanish, using instead one of over twenty native dialects—had no civil rights and lived in conditions that were among the most primitive in the Western Hemisphere.

It was a perfect place to grow bananas. United Fruit arrived in the country in the early 1900s, building the town of Bananera near the Caribbean port of Rio Dulce. (Bananera's are among the oldest continually operating plantations in the world, though they were taken over by Del Monte in 1972. That company still both harvests and funds an agricultural research center there.) Part of the country's suitability was its terrain and climate. But even more important was the nation's government—or lack of it. The first Guatemalan president to encounter United Fruit was Manuel Estrada Cabrera, who ruled from 1898 through 1920. Estrada believed his country needed to modernize and invited United Fruit to build the nation's entire infrastructure; the banana giant constructed telegraph lines, railroads, and seaports. (The only thing the company didn't build was roads, since highways might be a threat to the train lines that ensured dominance in the banana industry.)

None of these "improvements" benefited the descendants of the Mayas. The country's ruling Ladino class—those with Spanish lineage—became richer; the poor probably didn't get poorer (they were already beyond destitute), but village life declined as the plantations were built. Estrada was a modernizer, but, like most absolute

rulers—and he soon became one—he also exhibited streaks of impe-
riousness and ruthlessness. Freedom of the press was abolished.
Enemies were executed. The Guatemalan president's most bizarre
caprice was his admiration for Minerva, the Roman goddess of wisdom. During his rule, he built, with banana money, several Greco-
Roman-style temples to her, including one in Guatemala City with
the inscription: "Manuel Estrada Cabrera Presidente de la Repub-
lica a la juventud estudiosa" (Manuel Estrada Cabrera, President of
the Republic, to studious youths).

Estrada was overthrown in 1920. Five more rulers followed,
until 1931, when General Jorge Ubico took office. Ubico had won an
election but instantly assumed absolute power, changing the country's laws to give him an unlimited term in office. Ubico's attitudes
toward Guatemala's peasants were practically schizophrenic. He
nursed the country through the Depression, holding town meetings
in the indigenous villages and listening so patiently to complaints
that people living in the places he visited began to call him "father."
At the same time, Ubico issued edicts that made him, even today,
one of the cruelest rulers in Latin American history; he required
most Indians to work for landowners—United Fruit owned or controlled the vast majority of Guatemala's cultivated terrain—for a
minimum of one hundred days annually. He created a secret police
force. Most notoriously, Ubico passed laws that imposed the harsh-
est penalty on any non-Ladino who failed to follow orders when he
was working: The offender could be murdered on the spot.

Like Estrada, Ubico's ego was tied in with his might—and
expressed in bizarre fashion. He imagined that he was the heir, or
even the reincarnation, of Napoléon, commissioning paintings and
busts of himself for civic buildings and even dressing Guatemalan
soldiers in uniforms that resembled those worn by eighteenth-
century French troops. He was a believer in numerology: A star
with the number five at the center was displayed above the presidential palace on holidays. The pentagram's points and the numeric
symbol were representative of the letters in the dictator's first and

last names. Tomás Borge Martínez, cofounder of the Nicaraguan San-
dinista movement, said that the dictator was "crazier than a half-
dozen opium smoking frogs."

Ubico's rule came at the time Panama disease was hitting Guatemala hardest. As the malady spread into the countryside, United
Fruit took possession of so much land that many of its tracts were
considered nations within a nation. The fruit company was allowed
to undervalue the land it owned, and the stated worth of its holdings were so low that it didn't have to pay taxes.

Ubico's biggest enemy was Communism. He "saw Communist
conspiracies everywhere," historians Marcelo Bucheli and Geoffrey
Jones observe. In addition to detaining and sometimes killing anyone perceived as having connections with a labor movement, Ubico
also banned—meaning they couldn't be written or spoken—words
and phrases like *trade union*, *strike*, and *petition*. Ubico's attempt to
control his nation's vocabulary climaxed when he banned the word
workers. From that point on, whether you were a street sweeper
or a banana picker, you were to be called—and only called—an
employee.

Guatemala, wrote the *New York Times*, was a "big, private madhouse." The residents of that madhouse were a banana company
desperate for new land, a dictator who opposed any form of organization for impoverished workers, and a world that, by 1944, was
quickly polarizing into West and East, capitalist and Communist,
American and Soviet. Guatemala was about to explode.

IF THE COUNTRY WAS A TIME BOMB, the fuse was lit in an unexpected way. Since Ubico took power, a new group had emerged
in Guatemala: a middle class. Though they had comfortable lives,
they resented the fact that their nation was, in most respects, little
more than a giant, foreign-owned banana plantation. The first strikes
began with schoolteachers. Throughout 1944, more and more ordinary Guatemalans filled the streets of their cities despite Ubico's

attempts to banish even the language of rebellion from his citizens' minds. The government response was typical. Soldiers were called in, and the demonstrators were fired upon. But this time—in a world that was successfully beating back the forces of fascism—the violence turned into a catalyst: The strikes and protests expanded. In July, Ubico attempted to maintain his grip by "resigning," naming a loyal crony as his successor. The puppet regime was forced to call for elections but held on to power by jailing opposition candidates and reserving control over the military. As long as it maintained that grip, Ubico and his allies would remain in power, and Guatemala would remain a banana republic.

THE GUATEMALAN GENERALS DIDN'T CRUMBLE. They succumbed to a surprise attack. The army's junior officers had been discontented since late June, when forces loyal to Ubico fired on protesters in Guatemala City, killing María Chinchilla, a grade school teacher. The battle began in October, at Fort Matamoros— the headquarters of the nation's military, located at the geographic center of Guatemala City. A pair of young soldiers, Captain Jacobo Arbenz (a former schoolteacher) and Major Francisco Arana, spearheaded the effort. Seventy students were surreptitiously brought into the military base. Within minutes, they'd killed the high-ranking officers who supported the government and gained control of much of the base's heavy artillery. A battle between loyalists and the rebelling soldiers and students ensued; twelve hours later, Fort Matamoros had been completely destroyed, 1,800 loyalists and rebels were dead, and the government had fallen. Ubico's handpicked replacement, General Francisco Ponce, resigned. He left, along with his patron, for exile in Mexico. Arbenz and Arana quickly called for elections; a university professor named Juan José Arévalo gained the presidency in 1945. It was the beginning of what Guatemalans call Los Diez Años de la Primavera, "The Ten Years of Springtime."

Despite Arévalo's reforms—he allowed political parties and press freedom, and for the first time term limits were imposed on elected officials, including the president—the lives of banana workers changed little. United Fruit controlled the countryside, and changes in labor practices, such as the legalization of trade unions, specifically excluded those working on plantations. Arévalo attempted to improve living standards nationwide by building schools, hospitals, and enacting social welfare programs. He had already attracted the suspicious attention of the United States by describing himself as a "spiritual socialist," which meant that he hoped to liberate the minds of the peasants, even if their physical lives were still, for the moment, tightly controlled by outside interests. It hardly mattered that Arévalo also listed his idols as Abraham Lincoln and FDR.

The Arévalo regime came under near-constant attack. Arbenz helped put down a coup against the leader in 1949, and, facing constant opposition—over two dozen plots against Arévalo were foiled—the president's term expired without major land reform. That left Guatemala's big problem unsolved, according to Stephen Kinzer and Stephen Schlesinger, authors of *Bitter Fruit: The Story of the American Coup in Guatemala*.

In 1950 Arévalo was the first president of Guatemala ever to finish a term—and leave, as the law dictated. Though he was viewed as a hero by the Guatemalan people, his own self-critique was more pessimistic: "When I ascended to the presidency of the nation," he said, "I was possessed by a romantic fire . . . I still believed . . . that the government of Guatemala could rule itself, without submission to external forces." He blamed his disappointment directly on United Fruit and the United States: "The banana magnates, co-nationals of Roosevelt, rebelled against the audacity of a Central American president who gave his fellow citizens a legal equality with the honorable families of exporters."

Whatever Arévalo couldn't, or didn't, accomplish was left to his successor, Jacobo Arbenz. The former junior officer would go on to become the biggest enemy in United Fruit's history.

What bothered Arbenz most wasn't even that the banana companies owned so much land in the country—4 million acres, or 70 percent of the nation's arable territory—but that they weren't using it. More than three-fourths of it was fallow. In his inaugural speech, Arbenz, according to Kinzer and Schlesinger, said he wanted to convert Guatemala from a "dependent nation with a semi-colonial economy to an economically independent country." The new president had been warned to temper his remarks, so he chose not to mention specific targets by name when he called for land reform, saying only that his goal was only to rid the nation of its *latifundios*.

The term means "private farms." Nobody could mistake who the thirty-eight-year-old president was talking about.

THERE WERE COMMUNISTS IN GUATEMALA. The party was active, and Arbenz saw them as part of his coalition. Many of the country's workers supported the party. Arbenz was eager to listen to their ideas. Some party members were appointed to cabinet posts. Arbenz knew that he had to rule by coalition, and though he saw the party as a valuable ally—and even had Communist advisors as he planned land reform—his partner in rebellion, Francisco Arana, maintained control over the military, where there were no Communist influences, and expanded the press freedoms originally enacted by Arévalo. Arbenz may not have possessed entirely clean hands. Arana was murdered in 1949. The theory, never confirmed and often disputed, is that Arbenz, frustrated by his compatriot's failure to fully support the new policies, engineered the killing.

IN OCTOBER 1951, Arbenz had his first hostile encounter with United Fruit. A company official had arrived at the presidential palace with a series of dictates: The banana giant's current contracts would be extended. Taxes would not be raised. As Sam Zemurray had once done from the other side of the table, Arbenz, according to

Schlesinger and Kinzer, "replied . . . in a manner to which the Boston executive was not accustomed." The Guatemalan asked for payment of export duties; he asked that the company offer fair prices for land it acquired; and, most audaciously, he asked that United Fruit obey the Guatemalan constitution.

It was the beginning of the end for Jacobo Arbenz.

United Fruit had taken a two-prong approach during the first five years of La Primavera. It didn't absolutely oppose improving workers' conditions—it was willing to negotiate—but it was dead set against any reform that would cost it territory. The company's image-making machine campaigned, in both overt and subtle ways, against Arévalo, but initially did little resembling the ugly tactics that had led to the killing of thousands in Colombia less than two decades earlier. But Arbenz's election, and his rhetoric, alarmed Sam Zemurray. A similar democratic transformation in Iran earlier that year had resulted in the nationalization of that country's American-owned oilfields. That wasn't going to happen in the bananalands Zemurray pioneered. He asked one of his closest advisors what to do. Edward Bernays is considered by many to be "the father of public relations." He was a nephew of Sigmund Freud and was more than just a spin doctor—he perfected the modern art of information management, authoring scientific papers on how influence could be gained and how public opinion could be manipulated. In his 1928 book, *Propaganda*, Bernays spelled out his methods: "If we understand the mechanism and motives of the group mind, is it not possible to control and regiment the masses according to our will without their knowing about it?" Bernays's favorite means of accomplishing this was not to attempt to influence the masses directly but by "engineering of consent," finding a key group of leaders involved in a certain issue, changing their opinions, and letting them do the rest of the work. (Bernays famously conducted a survey of five thousand doctors, who almost unanimously agreed that people should eat a "hearty breakfast." He then took the results to newspapers around the country, adding as an aside that bacon and eggs were just such a morning meal. His client was the pork industry.) According to former United Fruit executive Thomas P. McCann, writing in *An American Company: The Tragedy of United Fruit*, Bernays recommended, and Zemurray agreed to, an aggressive campaign. It was, in a way, just like bacon and eggs: the goal was to convince America's elite that Arbenz was a Communist. The result would not be well-fed families. Instead, Zemurray hoped, showing the "truth" about Arbenz would lead to strong government action.

Bernays flew journalists into Guatemala, taking them on luxurious "fact-finding" junkets. Over two years, the media advisor managed to get dozens of articles published—in *Time*, *Newsweek*, the *New York Times*, the *Christian Science Monitor*, the *Miami Herald*, and in local papers across the United States—that portrayed the rulers of the Central American country as a dangerous threat. One wire service report stated that the goal of the new Guatemalan regime was to "engender hatred" of American business. As told by Schlesinger and Kinzer, Bernays planted stories that implied that Russia was training Latin American revolutionaries somewhere behind the Iron Curtain.

Arbenz was undeterred.

In 1952 he issued Decree 900. The law would redistribute land to local peasants; it allowed the government to confiscate any farm over 223 acres, with a key condition: The land had to be unused. Many of United Fruit's plantations had been abandoned because of Panama disease. That made them seemingly useless to the fruit giant, but it remained hostile to the idea of giving up the property, since it was still believed that flooding or some as-yet-undiscovered technique could restore the soil.

The result of the Arbenz decree was a spectacular change in Guatemala's balance of power: Nearly a quarter million acres were divided among 100,000 families. The new rule mandated that the former landholders receive compensation based on the declared worth of the confiscated territory. According to the formula, United Fruit was to receive $600,000. When the company protested that the sum was just a fraction of the true value of its holdings, which was true, Arbenz countered that the amount was based on tax returns submitted by the banana company itself. The company had been cheating on its taxes, and Guatemalan authorities simply chose to take United Fruit at its word. In 1954 a demand for the actual value of the land, about $16 million, was made. The appeal was not delivered by United Fruit, even though the company's executives had maintained contact with the Guatemalan government. Instead, it arrived via the U.S. State Department. It was an ominous sign: Guatemala wasn't just fighting a fruit company. It was fighting America.

United Fruit launched a second public relations campaign—this one aimed directly at the U.S. government. Zemurray hired a newspaperman named John Clements to write a study that would "investigate" the links between Arbenz and the Soviet Union. The "Report on Guatemala—1952" was sent to eight hundred influential Washington lawmakers and staffers. The "hastily written study," Schlesinger and Kinzer explain, "came up with a panorama of scheming Guatemalan communists . . . the document's account of a supposed Soviet intrusion in the small nation was full of unsubstantiated 'facts,' exaggerations, scurrilous descriptions and bizarre historical theories."

It wasn't difficult, in a Washington deep in the throes of McCarthyism, to sell the idea that Arbenz was a Soviet dupe. But at the highest levels, the company didn't even need pretense. The U.S. secretary of state, John Foster Dulles, had been a partner in United Fruit's New York law firm. Dulles's brother, Allen, was head of the CIA and a former member of the banana company's board. Ed Whitman, United Fruit's internal PR head, was married to President Eisenhower's private secretary. Whitman's contribution to the effort was a film equating the fate of United Fruit with that of the free world. It was called *Why the Kremlin Hates Bananas*.

In mid-1953, President Eisenhower authorized the CIA to oust Arbenz.

THAT DECEMBER, the team that would execute Operation PB Success—the first two letters of the code name stand for Presidential Board—was assembled. The plan involved several CIA field agents, including E. Howard Hunt, who would later be jailed for his role in the 1972 Watergate scandal. The operation was multifaceted. Psychological warfare would weaken the resolve of Arbenz and his army. U.S. military advisors would train and arm a force of Guatemalan "liberators," led by an exiled former Arbenz colleague, Colonel Carlos Castillo Armas. The template for the action came from an operation in Iran four months earlier. There, American-backed forces had successfully overthrown that country's democratically elected prime minister, Mohammed Mossadegh, returning the oil companies to U.S. control and installing Shah Mohammad Reza Pahlavi as the country's monarch.

Arbenz knew what had happened in Iran and, according to Schlesinger and Kinzer, panicked, making what would prove to be a fatal mistake. His undersupplied army would be no match for a U.S. invasion, so Arbenz contracted to buy a load of decade-old German weapons—captured during World War II—from Czechoslovakia. The CIA learned of the deal and tracked the Swedish-flagged ship carrying the arms across the Atlantic, allowing it to arrive in Guatemala. When the news was released in the United States, it was seen as proof of Arbenz's Soviet connection. (In fact, the deal was more of a quick purchase, through several middlemen, rather than a high-level operation. Prior to contacting the Czechs, Arbenz had attempted to purchase weapons from Denmark, Mexico, Argentina, and Switzerland.)

A naval blockade was imposed on Guatemala. The Arbenz government appealed to both the Organization of American States (OAS) and the United Nations, with no success. In neighboring Honduras—where United Fruit–friendly governments had ruled for nearly fifty years—U.S. intelligence operatives set up a training camp for Castillo-Armas's invasion force. Four hundred fighters were transported to Central America from the United States aboard a United Fruit cargo vessel. A radio station called La Voz de la Revolución featured music, comedies, and propaganda from "deep in the jungle," according to its broadcasts. The station was actually beamed from Miami along United Fruit's tropical radio network. Fake obituaries claiming that Arbenz had committed suicide were published in banana-friendly newspapers. Rebel planes flew low over the capital.

The Guatemalan army numbered nearly five thousand men. It seemed impossible that it could be defeated by the few hundred fighters who crossed the border on the night of June 18. The rebel radio stations began reports that "thousands" of soldiers and citizens were joining the liberators as they marched toward Guatemala City.

In fact, the lopsided battle was having the expected result. In Zacapa, 30 members of the Guatemalan military encountered 122 rebels. Only 28 insurgents survived the battle. The remaining 170 rebels were sent to take Puerto Barrios, United Fruit's primary export point, and were defeated by local dock workers. The surviving members of Castillo-Armas's forces retreated back to Honduras.

Arbenz lost the war anyway. It didn't matter that the rebels had failed. In fact, it was the failure that ultimately defeated the Guatemalan president.

Rumors began to spread. Now that the Guatemalan army had proved itself more capable than the usurpers, Eisenhower was preparing an all-out invasion. Even Arbenz believed the stories. The rumors were encouraged by the United States, which sent air force bombers to fly over Guatemala City. The Miami radio broadcasts began issuing accounts of Guatemalan soldiers being defeated in the jungles. The American news media was kept away from the sites of the "battles." Instead, they were given accounts, provided by U.S. ambassador to Guatemala John Peurifoy, of atrocities committed by Arbenz loyalists, backed up, Schlesinger and Kinzer say, with photographs of mutilated corpses thrown into mass graves (a former

United Fruit public-relations executive later admitted that the pictures were of earthquake victims).

FOR THE NEXT SEVEN DAYS, Arbenz remained in the presidential palace, unable to sleep, drinking constantly. Rebel radio began reporting that thousands of Guatemalan citizens were taking refuge across the border. The Miami studios even produced accounts of inch-by-inch battles, complete with sound effects. Those broadcasts were followed with news that Guatemalan army regulars were switching sides. When Arbenz ordered the military to open its arsenals and arm peasants, the field commanders—unable to tell what was real and what was propaganda—refused.

Arbenz had lost the army. They weren't against him—but they weren't with him. Like him, they'd been paralyzed and confused by the covert campaign. One witness to the events was a twenty-six-year-old former medical student named Che Guevara. The future revolutionary, living in Guatemala at the time (and making a living selling religious paintings), was dismayed by what he saw. When "the U.S. invasion took place," he recalled, "I tried to muster a group of young men like me to fight against the United Fruit adventurers. In Guatemala it was necessary to fight but hardly anybody fought. It was necessary to resist and hardly anybody wanted to do that."

On June 27, 1954, Arbenz resigned. At the airport, he was stripped to his underwear and paraded before the press as he boarded a plane to Mexico. For the rest of his life, he'd wander, stateless. The Americans had won; United Fruit too. But this time, victory for the banana company would be short-lived.

PART V

GOOD-BYE, MICHEL

CHAPTER 24

Cavendish

CHARLES EDWARD TELFAIR probably didn't recognize how important his bananas would become. But the British physician and amateur explorer certainly understood how easy the fruit was to grow. Telfair, born around 1777 (no exact record of his birth exists), was about three decades older than Darwin and one of many explorers who preceded the father of evolution into the tropics. Like many of his contemporaries, Telfair had collecting fever. As a surgeon with the British navy, he gathered hundreds of different animals and plants while traveling with the nation's colonial fleet. In 1810 Telfair was part of the force that conquered the island of Mauritius, centrally located along the Indian Ocean banana complex, 560 miles east of Madagascar. Since 1638 the island had been occupied by the Dutch, whose East India Company controlled much of the Pacific (and whose hold later would be compared to United Fruit's twentieth-century grip on Latin America). The most notable and sad achievement of the Dutch tenure on Mauritius was the elimination of the dodo. The island was uninhabited until westerners arrived. As on the Galápagos Islands, the animals on Mauritius possessed no protective instincts against human predators. The dodo was among the easiest to catch: With nowhere to go, and no natural enemies, it was not only tragically fearless but also flightless—and nutritious.

The dodo, along with many of the island's endemic species, was long gone by the time Telfair arrived. Upon taking control of Mauritius, the naval officer resigned his commission and became a state official, helping to orchestrate the island's role as part of the British realm. (Mauritius became independent in 1868 and has since become one of the richest African nations, with a stable democracy and a pro-business climate.)

British control over vast portions of the globe gave Telfair the ability to pursue his primary passion. The naturalist's wife, Annabelle, became his cataloging partner, painting the species her husband gathered (just as Dorothy Popenoe would fifty years later). Telfair purchased several parcels of land and began populating them with samples that he accumulated through an empire-wide tangle of zoos, horticulturists, and collectors in every corner of the earth.

Telfair was, in particular, a prodigious horticulturist, and not just for show: Since Dutch times the island had been used for sugar production, but Telfair industrialized the plantations, turning cane into Mauritius's most valuable export. Many of the chimneys from the mills Telfair designed still dot the island, though just eleven of the three hundred facilities that operated through the nineteenth century still function. On his private estates, Telfair built elaborately landscaped botanical gardens. In one of them, he developed the plant that earned him topiary immortality: The ornamental hibiscus, more commonly known (to fanatic growers of the plant, and there are many of them) as the tropical variety of the plant, made by crossing an ordinary hibiscus with an older line of *rosa-sinensis*, or Chinese rose. Tropical hibiscus is ideal for topiary.

It was an era when transportation was modern enough to slowly immerse the world in new and exotic plant and animal species, though commerce, which would require speedy cargo vessels, was decades away. Instead, overseas naturalists would carefully package their specimens and send them back to England or elsewhere in the empire via a coordinated network of colonial naval and merchant vessels. Many times, the samples didn't arrive intact. If not lost, they were often so disturbed that their point of origin, along with other identifying documentation essential for taxonomic work, was forever lost.

How Telfair received what would become known as the Cavendish banana—as *the* banana—isn't exactly known. Records only give the fruit's arrival date, 1826, and a vague origin in China (the Cavendish is still known, in a few places, as the "Chinese" banana). He might have received it through his trading network, or it could have been brought over by Chinese workers, who were being lured, under indenture, to the island's sugar industry. Mauritius shared a climate with coastal East Africa. It was ideal for bananas, though just how much of the fruit Telfair grew, or whether he considered it as anything but a botanic curiosity, is a mystery.

Three years after he received his first banana plants, Telfair sent several living samples back to England. One of the minor puzzles of banana history is who received them. Philip Keep Reynolds's 1927 book, *The Banana: Its History, Cultivation, and Place Among Staple Foods* (published in Boston, with the assistance of the United Fruit education department), identifies the receiver of the fruit as "Barclay of Burryhill" and the date of the fruit's arrival as 1829. Other accounts list the town as Berryhill. Those tracing banana history have never been sure exactly who Barclay was. And there is no town in England that goes by either version of the name. But there is a place called Bury Hill in Surrey, not a village, but an estate, once sprawling, covered in gardens and statuary. Bury Hill was owned by a beer magnate, a Robert Barclay, who had a penchant for funding global plant-collecting expeditions and who is known, even today, for introducing several tropical floral varieties—notably, the azalea and rhododendron—to the gardening public. There is no written record of him ever having received a banana from Telfair, so historians of the fruit never made the connection. But according to historian Marina Carter, who is writing a biography of the colonizing plant collector, a more general link does exist in Telfair's records, still housed on Mauritius. In 1820 Telfair noted the shipment of a parcel to a horticultural correspondent in southeast England. The package, which contained hibiscus (not bananas), was delivered to the Bury Hill estate. This earlier link between Telfair and Bury Hill makes it likely that the Cavendish sent to the unidentified Barclay and nonexistent Burryhill were in fact received by the flower-loving brewery magnate.

ROBERT BARCLAY NEVER HAD A CHANCE to distribute or grow the strange plant he'd received from his distant correspondent; he died one year after the banana arrived. His son, Arthur, took over the estate and the family business. Though the gardens were maintained, they stopped being a hub for exotic horticultural interchange. (The Barclay gardens continued to operate until the 1930s, when the estate, like many in England during the Depression, was broken up. Recently, local homeowners have found vestiges of Barclay's greenhouses and are attempting to restore some of them.) Following his death, Barclay's plants were purchased by the sixth Duke of Devonshire, who had his own affinity for exotic fauna, growing specimens in his private greenhouses at Chatsworth, a sprawling landholding in Derbyshire that is now part of Britain's Peak District National Park. The property has been occupied by the family since the sixteenth century, and today is home to the twelfth duke. He shares a name with Chatsworth's fifth master: Cavendish.

The Derbyshire property and the people who lived there are famous for many things. Mary Queen of Scots was imprisoned on the estate grounds during the sixteenth century. The fourth duke was a prime minister of England. The current occupant, Peregrine Cavendish, is the Queen's official representative at the Ascot Racecourse. His father was well-known for heaping scorn on animal rights activists seeking to ban fox hunts.

But William Cavendish, the nobleman who oversaw the construction of the property's magnificent rock gardens, nurseries, and arboretums, is better known for his lusty lifestyle—he was nick-named the Bachelor Duke—than as the namesake of the single most cultivated fruit on the planet. In 1836 botanist Aylmer Bourke Lambert, a former Cavendish employee, presented an antique Chinese drawing of a banana to a London meeting of the Linnaean Society, the natural history conclave—still functioning in both Britain and the United States—that took its name from the Swedish taxonomist who first classified bananas. Lambert believed that the fruit in the illustration was the same one he'd seen at the duke's estate. Lambert proposed to name the plant after the duke: *Musa cavendishii*. A society endorsement of a plant or animal's proposed nomenclature made adoption of that name almost a sure thing; the banana we eat—the endangered banana—was officially titled a year later, when a color painting and a scientific description of the "Cavendish Banana" was published in the *Magazine of Botany*.

TODAY, CHATSWORTH IS A TOURIST ATTRACTION. While the duke and his family live in private quarters (if they're home; they own eight other residences throughout the world), the public pe-ruses the visitors shop's fine china and garden furniture, and brings picnics to free concerts held on the grounds every summer. They also visit the gardens—a fifteen-foot-high bronze rabbit, a recent acquisition, is currently the facility's nonhorticultural centerpiece. That this is the adoptive home of our banana—another stop on the fruit's ever-more-sprawling ten thousand–year journey, and the place where the original ancestor of our lunchbox staple was likely first tasted by people living in the cooler climates of the north—isn't acknowledged at all.

THE CAVENDISH TRAVERSED THE INDIAN AND PACIFIC oceans, but it had yet to make it across the Atlantic. It would ultimately arrive in our hemisphere by several routes, all of them starting from

Mauritius, via Surrey and Chatsworth. As it traveled, it was joined by other varieties of the Cavendish. As the original Cavendish gained popularity, several other cultivars—all genetically identical but differing mostly in size—were imported from the collections of other plant enthusiasts (all are still grown today). The Grande Naine (Big Dwarf) is most widely grown and the one that usually reaches American tables; it is well suited for Caribbean plantations since it yields relatively large fruit from relatively low trees—a desirable attribute in places susceptible to hurricanes. (If banana diseases are insidious, bringing total destruction at a progressive crawl, high winds are like a sudden explosion. In 1998, the Honduran banana industry was almost completely wiped out by Hurricane Mitch. Eighty percent of the country's plantations were destroyed.) A second Cavendish cultivar, called Williams, is popular in Australia, with direct lineage to the Chatsworth greenhouses—it is named after John Williams, a missionary who carried Chatsworth suckers from Britain to Samoa. (Easily transported, bananas ensured that no matter what other tribulations a conversion-minded proselytizer might encounter, starvation would not likely be one of them.) A Williams colleague carried descendants of the Samoa plant to Fiji and then to what were then known as the Friendly Islands (today's Tonga). These South Pacific locals were already growing bananas, the *fe'i* variety, and they took to the Cavendish instantly. By 1855 the Telfair line had crossed hemispheres again, becoming a local favorite in Tahiti, Hawaii, and New Guinea. Other Cavendish types had reached Egypt and South Africa.

The Cavendish circled the globe. But it skipped the Americas. In the United States, the fruit was unheard of. Even the plantain, consumed in Mexico since the days of the conquistadores, was unknown in the chillier locales above the Rio Grande. While samples were occasionally received by horticultural dilettantes and wealthy collectors, the banana wasn't—and couldn't be—exported in large quantities. There was no need for the starchy green banana in parts of the world that had potatoes. And the Cavendish fruit wasn't tough enough to be carried, in any significant quantity, over great distances. People like Telfair, Barclay, and Cavendish would have been amazed—if not completely unbelieving—if they'd been told that in less than five decades the fruit would spread far beyond its natural range, and not just by ones and twos but by millions.

CHAPTER 25

Falling Apart

B Y THE MID-TWENTIETH CENTURY, United Fruit was buckling under its own weight. It was looking less like a business concern and more like a staggering colonial power. The Guatemala escapade seemed especially ill-conceived, even if the banana giant felt it needed the land Arbenz had attempted to take over, as a hedge against spreading disease. For the most part, what United Fruit had accomplished was more about foreign policy than commerce, and changing times had made the supply-and-demand controls of international politics less important to what Americans ate than cultural forces within our own country. Tastes were changing. For the first time, banana consumption was declining, from a postwar high of just over 6 million bunches in 1947 to a low of 4.5 million nine years later, according to a Harvard Business School study. Potato chips and canned fruit cocktail were taking over.

Yet United Fruit's hunger for territory was unabated. The company's Panama disease "strategy" of flooding, replanting, and breaking new ground was failing to even maintain level output: By the mid-1950s, according to historian Marcelo Bucheli, the number of tons of bananas each acre yielded had dropped by more than half in some banana-producing nations.

There was a domino effect associated with Guatemala, but it wasn't what the banana giant intended. The fruit company's favored status had been restored, but the operation caused fear and outrage in neighboring countries. They began to chafe at United Fruit's dominance. They'd also learned the lessons of the Arbenz episode. United Fruit would still exert significant control over many of these countries, especially Honduras, but as the McCarthy era ended and the hottest spots of the cold war moved to Southeast Asia, small signs of independence—legislation that increased workers' rights and even the creation of some independent banana producers—emerged. (None of this meant peace for Central America, however, where civil wars, dictatorships, and right-wing governments, propped up by the U.S., were the norm through the 1980s.)

Even our own government seemed to be having mixed feelings about the banana giant. Less than two years after Arbenz was deposed, the U.S. Department of Justice filed an antitrust suit against United Fruit. The reason for the action seems especially odd: "The Federal government had charged that United Fruit had obtained control of almost all land in Central and South America used for banana growing," Bucheli writes. United Fruit didn't deny the claim; it argued that the U.S. government had no authority over foreign operations—that these land-ownership issues were the responsibility of local governments. Attempts to break up the world's largest banana grower continued through the early 1960s, when it was forced to divest itself of its railroad holdings in banana-growing countries and its supermarket distribution network in the United States. The final settlement also forced the company to sell some of the land it owned. Its first choice for offloading was Guatemala. The government's newly mixed attitude toward United Fruit, which it had previously promoted with as much fervor as it advanced (and continues to advance, to the present day) the interests of U.S. oil companies, was a huge policy change, though there was no clear reason or consistency to the levels of support and opposition in those shifting foreign, trade, and economic policies.

AT TIMES, THE COMPANY'S BEHAVIOR, too, was especially irrational. In 1957 it claimed to have beaten Panama disease in Costa Rica for a second time, reopening a plantation near Golfito on the Pacific coast. The *New York Times* reported that all of the company's "acreage has now been rehabilitated." It wasn't the case. Golfito was reinfected within months. Top-heavy and distracted by its own size, in a state of both amnesia—it seemed to forget that its mission was to sell bananas—and denial, United Fruit clung to the Gros Michel despite failure after failure of the attempts to protect it from the blight. United Fruit was no longer invincible. It had been beaten by itself, through greed and ego—but mostly it had been defeated by nature. The disease it sowed had overtaken it.

It didn't have to be that way. And there was another banana company that knew it.

STANDARD FRUIT WAS SMALLER THAN UNITED FRUIT—it never controlled more than 20 percent of the U.S. banana market—but it had a similar history. The company was started in 1899 by a pair of Sicilian immigrants. Salvador D'Antoni was a sometime smuggler and gun runner who operated mostly off the northern coast of Honduras. Joseph Vaccaro, who'd later corner the Southern ice market, was a New Orleans–based fruit distributor. When D'Antoni's first shipment of bananas—grown on the island of Roatan, near the coast of current-day Belize, then known as British Honduras—was snapped up by eager consumers, Vaccaro, like his northern counterpart Andrew Preston and future rival Samuel Zemurray, jumped at the opportunity. After partnering with D'Antoni, Vaccaro Brothers and Company became the largest banana grower in northern Honduras, centered around the port city of La Ceiba.

Vaccaro's enterprise quickly became a scaled-down version of United Fruit, building seaports, railroads, and communications facilities. Vaccaro copied another United Fruit tactic as well: using tough, intimidating, and sometimes bloody methods to maintain control over growing areas. In order to gain working capital for railroad building, Vaccaro enlisted the help of local merchants, who— excited by the banana gold rush—put up both cash and their land in return for shares of the newly formed Vaccaro Brothers and Company. By 1903 the company was earning huge profits, and the investors began to demand their rightful portion. Instead, according to Honduran author Antonio Canelas, writing in *La Ceiba, sus raíces y su historia* (La Ceiba, its Roots and its History), Vaccaro ordered the town's city hall to be burned down, along with any records of land ownership and business agreements contained inside. With the support of the Honduran government, the banana importer was able to make a blank slate of the region—over which he took control. By 1925 the company had become United Fruit's most formidable competitor, with a new name—the Standard Fruit and Steamship Company—and an operational distribution network in the United States. United Fruit was an early investor in the company but was forced to divest itself after regulators objected. Standard became the larger banana grower's "powerful and alert rival," according to Frederick Upham Adams, ensuring that the company had "absolutely no control over retail prices." (Adams, whose writing was generally slanted in favor of the banana giant, was correct in his description of the smaller company but not in his claim that the monetary value of bananas was beyond the ability of the Octopus to sway. The competition tended to be over markets rather than cost.)

Until the 1950s, Standard Fruit remained an operational clone of the larger grower. Panama disease hit its plantations in 1910. Abandonment began four years later, and the company also began acquiring territory, moving growing areas farther and farther inland.

But Standard Fruit's smaller size amplified the crisis. It didn't have a half-dozen countries and tens of thousands of acres of untouched land to clear and transform into banana farms. The cost of managing remote plantations on substandard land threatened to price the company, today known as Dole, out of business.

In the end, that hardship turned out to be the smaller banana company's biggest advantage. It knew that it soon would run out of places to grow Gros Michel. That would mean an end to the enterprise—unless it found a replacement banana. In 1927 it began searching for a new, Panama disease–resistant fruit. The candidates it tested were no different from the ones United Fruit had been rejecting. But because Vaccaro's company had more to lose, it looked further into each breed. In January 1927, 108 Lacatan banana plants—related to the Philippine favorite—were planted. By September they were ready for harvest. The Lacatan that were good were great, just as they are today, but there were numerous problems: The darker-colored bananas required rigidly regulated ripening, using ethylene gas, the natural vapor that fruits give off as they ripen. The presence of the gas is a trigger for the ripening process, which is why, if you want green bananas to turn yellow quickly, you can put them in a brown paper bag with an overripe apple. The apple gives off ethylene, and the bananas mature. But banana distributors in the United States were unwilling to implement such methods: With United Fruit delivering thousands of healthy Gros Michel bunches to U.S. ports, it didn't seem necessary. Lacatan had other problems, according to Standard Fruit researcher H. H. V. Hord. It was very sensitive to temperature and humidity, and small variations could cause individual fruit to drop off the bunches during transport. Despite this, Standard began shipping small quantities of Lacatan to the United States. There was nothing else to do with the land it owned.

THE NEXT BANANA the company tried was the Dwarf Cavendish, a smaller relative of the breed that would ultimately replace the Gros

Michel. This pint-sized fruit had better ripening characteristics than Lacatan, though it had what Hord described as an "ashy" color. The fruit also bruised easily. But it grew even better than Lacatan, and like that variety, became part of Standard Fruit's product line.

The company even attempted to market a man-made banana, shipping the IC2 developed in Trinidad to the United States in 1944. By 1950 nearly half a million bunches were exported from Honduras to New Orleans. The fruit resisted both Panama disease and Sigatoka, and possessed the hardiness needed for the long journeys from the tropics to supermarkets. But IC2 was hard to grow—it stumbled in anything less than top-quality soil—and when later generations of the bred banana began succumbing to Panama disease, Standard Fruit halted shipments.

Two more candidates remained, and both were promising. The Bout Rond banana, first grown in Puerto Rico, was tasty, ripened well, and looked like Gros Michel. Bout Rond had one characteristic that made it an especially good choice as the Gros Michel plantations thinned: It could be planted in the same fields, gradually replacing the older variety, requiring no changes in infrastructure. But, like every other potential Gros Michel successor, other qualities were lacking. The fruit withstood Sigatoka poorly, it could bruise and rot easily in cargo holds, and it didn't like cool temperatures. In the field, Bout Rond banana plants blew down easily in high winds. Because of these problems, the Bout Rond stood little chance of replacing the entire Latin American banana crop.

But the Bout Rond, Lacatan, and other small-scale bananas Standard Fruit experimented with weren't just abandoned because they were inadequate. By 1958 they were no longer needed. That second candidate—the one that eventually won the race—was Cavendish.

CHAPTER 26

Embracing the New

UNITED FRUIT KNEW WHAT THE CAVENDISH WAS. They hated it. Thomas McCann, who'd spent over twenty years working as an image-maker for the banana giant—he was the one who allegedly helped distribute phony photographs of dead bodies to the press during the Guatemalan war—wrote in his 1976 memoir that the company believed the Cavendish, along with any company that sold them, would be "thrown out" of supermarkets across the nation. The company that invented banana innovation—and had therefore invented the modern banana—had become hidebound, lumbering, and unable to change.

Instead of seriously considering a replacement banana, the largest banana company cracked the whip on its workers—enforcing strict quotas on productions, trying to squeeze every last Gros Michel out of every last acre of plantation.

Standard Fruit couldn't afford to do that. In 1939 sample Cavendish plants were imported to Honduras from Santos, Brazil, where they'd been grown for local consumption. Wartime interrupted the test, but by 1947 the company began exports of the Giant Cavendish banana.

Turning the Cavendish into a Gros Michel replacement was not a sure thing. The Cavendish had advantages over the original commercial banana: It was entirely resistant to Panama disease and, unlike the Bout Rond, held up fairly well in hurricanes. The Cavendish was susceptible to a host of maladies—everything from the Sigatoka fungus to bacterial infections, along with caterpillars, aphids, and beetles—but these were mostly controllable. And because the Cavendish plant wasn't as tall as the banana it would ultimately replace, it was easier to saturate with Bordeaux mixture.

THE CAVENDISH ALSO LOOKED and tasted right. A ripe Cavendish wasn't exactly the same, either in the hand or on the palate, as Gros Michel. But it was close—close enough.

With the Sigatoka fungus, bacterial infections, and pests under control, there was only one—huge—problem. The Cavendish that resisted the most virulent enemy its species had was, in another way, a fragile thing. Gros Michel bunches could be thrown in cargo holds and shipped on rough seas without bruising or breaking, as long as they were kept cool. As we know from the mushy spots that appear after a mild jostling in our grocery bags, the Cavendish is nowhere near as hardy.

Without another option, Standard Fruit's engineers tried to find a way to make the Cavendish travel better. What they accomplished, in the decade following World War II, was a revolution. They reinvented the banana industry.

TODAY, THAT SOLUTION appears so simple that it almost seems laughable: Ship the Cavendish not on stems but in boxes. Doing so, however, required a complete overhaul of an infrastructure that had been built up for over half a century. While United Fruit's CEO was busy attending mass at New York's Saint Patrick's Cathedral with Guatemalan president Carlos Castillo Armas, and the company's official policy was still to drench plantations across Central America, Standard Fruit was making the Cavendish work. Historian John Soluri points out that the smaller grower, despite calling boxed fruit "the greatest innovation in the history of the banana industry," didn't invent the process. It had previously been used in the Canary Islands. Nevertheless, Soluri writes, "boxed fruit marked the beginning of a new phase in export banana production and marketing."

After numerous tests, Standard determined that an ideally sized banana box would be a little larger than a milk crate, capable of holding forty pounds of fruit. In order to get the fruit into the cartons, it now had to be processed in the field, at packing houses built for that purpose. This decentralized preparatory step meant that fruit was better shipped in trucks, by road. That development would ultimately spell the end of the Central American railroads that had put United Fruit in business in the first place. Boxed fruit was also easier to deliver. In orderly stacks, ripening and cooling became more efficient. Codes on the banana boxes meant that the journey of a particular load of fruit could be tracked from plantation to grocery shelf.

Boxing yielded another hidden advantage: Since bunches were broken up and handled individually, they could also be branded more efficiently as consumer products. Grocers had previously sold Gros Michel by hanging entire bunches of the fruit, straight from distributors, in their stores. Now they could arrange individual hands into attractive, modern supermarket displays. Standard Fruit launched its newly boxed fruit under the brand name "Cabana Banana" and began applying stickers to individual fingers as they were placed into boxes at the packing house.

The empire built by Andrew Preston, Minor Keith, and Sam Zemurray was falling apart. United Fruit's profit dropped from $66 million in 1950 to $33.5 million in 1955 and to just $2.1 million in 1960. By then, Sam the Banana Man's power had diminished. The former mogul died from Parkinson's disease a year later. A new chief executive, Thomas Sunderland, took power. His first order: adopt the Cavendish.

THOUGH IT ARRIVED LATE, United Fruit was a quick study, copying every technique its smaller rival had developed. It began testing Cavendish varieties in 1960, initially settling on a type known as Valery. By the mid-1960s, the changeover was complete. The switch remade United Fruit. In an effort to "reintroduce" itself to American consumers, the company launched one of the most successful marketing campaigns in American history. It changed its mascot from a female-like singing fruit into a musical, wiggling, and busty señorita. Like Standard Fruit, it began putting stickers on individual bananas.

The final Gros Michel bananas to reach the United States were sold in 1965. By then, the entire industry had transformed. Working conditions improved (though they still were far from perfect). United Fruit began to sell much of the land it had taken over during the previous seventy years: The policy of direct control that had driven the company for decades had ultimately failed to either stop disease or please governments. Today's banana industry, with U.S. companies purchasing fruit from local subcontractors, who actually own and operate the plantations, emerged. That market diversification allowed Standard Fruit to compete on a more equal footing. Energized by its success with the Cavendish, it began to catch up to its rival.

CHAPTER 27

Chronic Injury

THE DAMAGE UNITED FRUIT had done to Latin America was beyond imaginable and, even as the Cavendish shift occurred, beyond healing. The dictatorial governments the company installed in Guatemala and Honduras ruled their respective countries for decades, releasing wave after wave of abuse, assassination, and even genocide. In Guatemala, death squads sponsored by the successors to banana-installed governments roamed the countryside, killing anyone suspected of being—or even becoming—a left-wing sympathizer. That meant just about anyone who labored on a banana plantation, and their families. It was the obscene, logical extension to the sentiment that had crushed Jacobo Arbenz and his efforts to bring justice to the country's banana lands. Over 100,000 native Mayas died at the hands of the Guatemalan military; tens of thousands more fled the country (most now live in the United States).

Jacobo Arbenz never recovered from his defeat. In his years of exile, he'd become a stateless vagabond. Half-naked and humiliated, he'd first flown to Mexico City, where the leader he'd deposed, Jorge

Ubico, was also exiled. Mexico was a U.S. ally, and Arbenz—along with his wife and daughter—was soon asked to leave. Arbenz's father was Swiss, and that country was the next to shelter him, but said that he could stay only if he renounced his Guatemalan citizenship. Arbenz refused to deny his allegiance to the country he'd worked to free.

Eastern Europe seemed promising, but the only country that would take him was Czechoslovakia. Even though it was behind the iron curtain, Prague felt cosmopolitan, accessible. But the government there was unable to provide Arbenz with housing or the money he needed to take care of his family; unlike other fleeing dictators, the Guatemalan had not escaped with briefcases or foreign bank accounts filled with looted cash. There seemed to be just one place left to go: the Soviet Union, the country he'd been accused of conspiring with. His arrival in Moscow confirmed, for much of the world, that the U.S. action in Guatemala had been correct. But Soviet officials were less than welcoming. They refused to allow Arbenz to see his family.

What Arbenz really wanted was to go home—or at least to get closer. His native country was out of the question, but as time passed, he believed some other Latin American nation might agree to host him. The conditions offered by Uruguay were less than attractive—he couldn't hold a job or speak out politically, and was required to report into the national police weekly—but it was the only offer he received. It was three years after the coup. Nothing was going right. His daughter, Arabella, became moody and depressed. His wife, Maria Cristina Vilanova—who was so passionately committed to the reforms her husband had advocated that she'd allowed her family's own estate to be returned to the peasants—felt helpless and tired.

In 1960, finally, there was hope. Revolution in Cuba had brought Fidel Castro to power. Though Arbenz's decision would again be seen as confirmation of his Communist leanings, and he knew there was a huge difference between himself and the dictator, Arbenz accepted Castro's offer of permanent, unrestricted asylum.

Finally, Arbenz might have peace, if not happiness.

Arabella, just fifteen years old, refused to go. She protested when her parents tried to send her to what she saw as elitist private schools but also refused to join any Communist youth groups. As her mother and father settled in Cuba, she left for Paris, proclaiming that she'd become an actress.

Arbenz still dreamed of returning to Guatemala. He'd promised, in his last radio address, that "obscured forces which today oppress the backward and colonial world will be defeated." Instead, his defeat was made complete. His daughter was far away, figuratively lost. Soon, she'd be gone entirely. She'd fallen in love with Jaime Bravo, who was, at the time—1965—possibly the world's most famous matador. Bravo was also a notorious playboy, and as the two argued in a Bolivian hotel room, Arabella turned a gun (where it came from was never fully determined) on herself.

Arabella's loss dwarfed Arbenz's defeat in Guatemala. The drinking habit he'd fallen into during the last days of his regime turned staggering during his time in Cuba. Was he still Jacobo Arbenz, the symbol of freedom? Or was he an object of disdain, representing weakness, as Fidel Castro implied when, with the exiled president watching on, he vowed that his country had learned a lesson: "Cuba," he said, "is not Guatemala."

Arbenz knew what had happened to him, but he never understood why. He'd only wanted land the banana companies weren't using. Why had they objected so violently? He'd been willing to negotiate. What he didn't know was how badly the desperate fruit company believed it needed that land. He didn't know that every square foot of fallow plantation was being held, just in case a cure was found for a rampaging disease. Panicked by an opponent that was out of its control, United Fruit wouldn't budge and unleashed terrible vengeance on anyone who tried to force it to yield.

BUT ARBENZ WASN'T AWARE OF THIS. In 1971, he returned to Mexico City. By then, almost thirty years after he'd been deposed, he had fallen into obscurity. If he was thinking of lost opportunities or of new strategies or of the civil war that was killing tens of thousands of his countrymen back home, there's no record of it. There are those who believe that his last moments were filled with terror, at intruders who were looming over him as he lay in a hotel bathtub with a bottle of whiskey by his side. Maybe, at that moment, he was thinking of Arabella.

Arbenz sank into the water. The man who dared to mount the boldest action ever attempted against the big banana company, before or since, wouldn't open his eyes again.

IN OCTOBER 1995, Jacobo Arbenz finally returned to Guatemala. One hundred thousand onlookers wept as the former president's body was drawn down Guatemala City's main avenue in a grandly decorated funeral carriage. The martyred ruler was interred in a white, pyramid-shaped mausoleum that is still visited by pilgrims today. Arbenz, to many Guatemalans, is their country's Lincoln or Kennedy. Carlos Castillo Armas, the man who deposed him, is buried just a few feet away, under a largely ignored gray headstone.

For years a debate raged in the United States over whether Arbenz was in fact a Communist, how much United Fruit was involved in the coup, and whether the entire operation had actually been stage-managed by the CIA. Starting in the late 1970s, Freedom of Information Act requests revealed thousands of pages of U.S. government papers, including budgets for the operation, and cables and correspondence between officials in Washington, intelligence operatives, United Fruit executives, and conspirators in Central America. One document lists over fifty Guatemalan officials targeted for "elimination." A second contains instructions on how to accomplish that goal, in handbook form. The nineteen-page manual, reprinted in *Secret History: The CIA's Classified Account of Its Operations in Guatemala, 1952–1954*, by Nick Cullather, is titled *Study of Assassination*. "The simplest local tools are often the most efficient means of assassination," counsels the booklet. "A hammer, axe, wrench, screw driver, fire poker, kitchen knife, lamp stand, or anything hard, heavy and handy will suffice." The authors do note that murder is not ethically justifiable, and that "persons who are morally squeamish should not attempt it." (I find it almost too grotesque to attempt to contemplate any good reason why a government founded on principles of freedom and democracy could so casually dismiss any debate between right and wrong, especially just nine years after the end of World War II.)

Even as they adopted the Cavendish, and their need for territory diminished, the banana companies didn't change all at once—or even change completely. Political adventures continued, though they'd center around more conventional bribery, graft, and union busting. But for the most part, the banana with stickers became an uncontroversial and beloved consumer product and one the larger world wanted. The fruit gained popularity in Europe and Asia. It was the unique wonder of the Cavendish—portability, convenience, strength, and most of all, consistency—that would make it so ubiquitous. These are, of course, the same things that make it so sick today.

CHAPTER 28

Banana Plus Banana

BANANAS, wrote Australian biotechnology researcher James Dale, are a "plant breeder's nightmare." No seeds means no fertility. Multiple diseases mean that breeding for only a single kind of resistance can yield a new fruit that is promising yet functionally useless if it is still susceptible to another malady. Even if a new banana can fight off most of the organisms that attack it, it still has to meet the other requirements—shipping, ripening, and taste—that make it something more than a locals-only product. Thousands of agricultural experts—scientists and hobbyists, small-scale farmers and huge agribusinesses—spend years developing new species of roses, apples, melons, and citrus fruits. Bananas? Too difficult. Emile Frison, former director of the International Network for the Improvement of Banana and Plantain (INIBAP), estimated that the total number of scientists attempting to grow new bananas in the field was less than the number of fingers on a typical bunch of the fruit they were working on: just five.

To successfully breed bananas, you have to be stubborn; prideful; and, perhaps to the point of danger, obsessed—qualities that carry on, in an academic form, the tradition of the most celebrated and infamous *bananeros*. That was the case with the first scientists who attempted to make modified bananas in the 1920s, and it remains the case today. Most of all, you have to be patient. From the time the Cavendish was adopted until the first sign of the resurgent Panama disease that now threatens to destroy it, the person who best embodied those traits was Phil Rowe.

Rowe didn't invent the painstaking techniques that allowed banana scientists to breed the unbreedable, but he sharpened them, perfected them, and even succeeded with them, through a combination of genius and determination. Rowe arrived in Honduras in 1959, immediately after graduating from college. It was, according to retired Chiquita banana breeder Ivan Buddenhagen, the beginning of "the second flowering of banana research." (The first was the research centered around the Imperial College of Tropical Agriculture in Trinidad, during the 1920s and 1930s, which yielded the first hybrid fruit but failed to find an acceptable replacement for Gros Michel. It also established the fundamental methods banana scientists still use to create new versions of the fruit.)

There were reasons for United Fruit to improve the banana, even after the Cavendish was adopted. Though it wasn't seen as urgent, or even necessary, at the time, to find an alternative to the world's new banana, United Fruit did hope to develop a variety that would be better than the one offered by Standard Fruit and other competitors.

Rowe's lab was in La Lima, at the huge company compound where a community of American employees oversaw the thousands of Honduran workers who grew bananas across most of the country's eastern lowlands. Over the next few decades, the facility would house the world's most successful banana-breeding program (and one that remains in operation today).

The first step in breeding bananas has always been to have good raw material. Because bananas are sterile and generally seedless (the Cavendish is absolutely seedless, which is why it cannot be bred by any conventional method), that means bananas of a kind that *can* be bred. Rowe began with a huge collection of wild and rare bananas gathered by O. A. Reinking, a legendary explorer of tropical fauna, who traveled through Indochina and the Malay Peninsula then island-hopped from the Philippines through Java, Bali, and New Guinea and all the way to Australia between 1921 and 1927. Reinking was one of the early contributors to a greater understanding of Panama disease, helping to pin down the structure of the fungus in 1933. His sample of fusarium, collected in the Philippines, is now housed in the U.S. National Fungus Collections of the Department of Agriculture's Agricultural Research Service (yes, there is such a place).

Reinking returned home with 134 different banana types: 81 that propagated nonsexually, the way cultivated bananas do; 26 that were clones of traditional plantains; and 27 wild, seeded bananas. The collection was initially housed at United Fruit's Panama research labs, not in test tubes and petri dishes like today's preserved bananas, but as living fruit grown in greenhouses. But the company's half-hearted commitment to banana science, motivated by poor results and the land-grab alternative, led to the quick abandonment of the program. In 1930 the entire Reinking collection was moved to Wilson Popenoe's Lancetilla gardens. (Reinking also collected citrus and spent much of his early career attempting to prove the existence of the Rumphius pummelo, initially described in the eighteenth century, which most experts considered to be mythical. He finally found the fruit, which is like a grapefruit with a second grapefruit growing inside, on the Banda Islands in Indonesia.)

The Reinking bananas were mostly forgotten until the mid-1950s, when United Fruit belatedly, and half-heartedly, began searching for a replacement for the Gros Michel. Seventy-two of the

samples were then transferred to La Lima, where Rowe was opening
his research facility, forming the beginnings of a collection that is
still the basis for most Honduran testing today.

A banana breeder needs that kind of variety. It isn't hard to find
seeds in a wild banana: When the fruits—which are generally shaped
like the bananas we eat, though sometimes less curved—are cut in
cross section, they reveal as many as two dozen pea-sized, black
pits. The seeds are the raw material, and researchers will usually set
aside a separate section in a plantation to grow the fertile fruit.
They'll then be exposed to the same maladies that threaten bananas
people eat. Those with desirable strengths are then grown in quantity. Visitors to an experimental plantation will see rows and rows
of them, each marked with a species name and planting date.

The serious manual labor begins in these rows. Since few of the
experimental plants exhibit the necessary combination of traits from
the start, they're often bred with each other. In four decades of research, Rowe and his colleagues created nearly twenty thousand
hybrids, or about four hundred times the number of edible varieties
that emerged over seven thousand years of conventional human
cultivation.

Breeding such a banana is the agricultural version of an arranged
marriage. At dawn, workers head into the fields, sometimes on bicy-
cles, wearing utility belts that hold a dozen or more collecting containers (they resemble, appropriately, baby-food jars). They climb
up ladders to gently scrape finely powdered pollen out of the nine-
month-old male portion of the hermaphroditic plant's flowers, which
hangs upside-down at the top end of the bloom, and brush it into the
jars. Later that morning, the collected pollen is placed into the
stigma, the passageway to the plant's ovary. (In nature this is done
by insects, which aren't choosy enough to conduct decent banana-
breeding experiments.) Four months later, the new plant is harvested.

At the Fundacion Hondureña de Investigación Agricola, or
Honduran Agricultural Research Foundation (FHIA), La Lima's

publicly funded successor to Phil Rowe's United Fruit research station (and the first place I visited when researching this book), Juan Fernando Aguilar, the facility's current director, led me through the fields as we followed the bike-riding pollenators.

This is an experimental plantation, where the fruit grows unprotected, undefended. There is no aerial spraying, no careful bagging to keep fruit unblemished and healthy. Instead, the test plantation invites all comers: beetles, bugs, and burrowing worms; viruses, fungi, and bacteria. The field is a ragtag layout with fruit of different sizes and colors, trees of varying heights, and plants with vastly contrasting levels of healthiness.

We walked over to a large work area, shaded by a tinted, corrugated plastic roof.

"We harvest about one thousand bunches each week," Aguilar told me, as he lit a cigarette and stared down at his white shirt, which was clean when we'd met earlier that day but now had a huge blot of banana sap—unremovable and rubbery, the dark tops of the bananas we peel are made of the same substance—splattered on it. "That's the true banana researcher's logo," he shrugged.

The harvested bananas are first arranged by "cross" (the two parent types) and then by the desired attribute the breeders are hoping for. (So, if a hypothetical Lucy banana is bred with an equally fanciful Ricky fruit, all are put together into one section. They are then further separated according to the various goals of the hybridization: thick skin, resistance to disease, or a specific taste. Generally, a new banana is bred with one attribute in mind; it is then merged with a separate man-made fruit that possesses one of the other desired qualities. The results are then crossed and crossed again until, in theory, the banana that has everything emerges.) Next, the fruit is stored in a ripening room for several days— the room contains a precise mixture of ethylene and carbon dioxide gasses—and then taken into a larger work area to be peeled.

Ordinarily, the only thing a person peeling a banana needs to worry about is where the peel goes. Avoiding a slapstick tumble is not the issue in banana breeding. Instead, the primary objective is finesse. Every single banana from the week's harvest—that can be up to *100,000* bananas—is carefully skinned then segregated (sometimes in separate containers, other times by working on different types at different times) so that one breed doesn't mix with another. The peeling at FHIA is done by women, paid ten dollars a day, about double the typical Honduran wage. Aguilar says they are better at precision work than men. "They handle the fruit more gently," he told me. "And they have better handwriting." Each separate bunch has to be identified and logged, so that its success or failure can be tracked through the entire growing cycle. (The peels are usually composted and fed to pigs.)

The men return in the next step. The logged bunches are transferred to their own barrels, where they're fermented. (The process produces a vinegary smell that's partially sweet, partially overripe. The aroma is a bit sickening—and very much like that of Ugandan banana wine.) The now-oozing bananas are lifted by workers in protective gear—smocks and rubber boots—and poured into an oversized sieve, where they're crushed into a pulp by a heavy, steel mallet with an eight-foot-long handle. The smashing has two primary byproducts: the impossible-to-clean stickum and a gooey banana concentrate. The adhesive waste is discarded, while the fruity muck is transferred to smaller mesh seives—each about the size of a sheet of standard typing paper—where women carefully wash the mixture. The goal is to find a tiny speck of fertility amidst tons of traditional banana barrenness. Aguilar showed me a table with a container that held about two dozen seeds. Since, for the most part, seeded bananas are being crossed with seedless ones, and since seediness is one of the attributes being bred *out* of the bananas, the seed yield is maddeningly low. "Those seeds there," Aguilar said, "came from about a quarter million bananas." That makes the odds of finding a seed ten thousand to one.

That was the end of the process for the banana breeders up until the 1970s. They'd replant the found seeds, crossing and crossing

*Building a banana:
the men pollinate . . .*

*. . . and the women handle
the delicate seeds.*

again until, with luck, a viable commercial fruit was developed. Though a few bred bananas made it to larger plantations, for the most part, the first four decades of banana breeding yielded a success rate of approximately . . . zero.

Rowe helped develop an additional step called "embryo rescue."

In this case, the seed is not the end of the human-assisted banana reproductive process. Every viable seed, when cut open, contains a tiny embryo about one-fiftieth the size of the seed itself. In Honduras I watched as technicians, using Rowe's technique, peered into microscopes and carefully removed the embryos, dropping them into test tubes containing a fertilized growing medium.

Aguilar took me into a brightly lit room and asked me to remove my shoes. "This is a nursery," he said. "No contamination." The space contained row after row of test tubes, with tiny banana plants in various stages of early growth: some just a few filaments snaking down into the liquid, others with fingernail-sized green leaves.

Aguilar narrowed the odds for me again. "Most of these," he said, "will either not grow at all—or they won't grow right." The plants that do will eventually be taken out to a greenhouse and then, when they're big enough, be planted outside. The percentage of plants that make it to the field? Here's the math: one seed for every ten thousand bananas. One percent of those seeds actually produce an embryo that's viable. And the total odds of getting a banana to the greenhouse? *One million to one.*

It isn't over then. That lottery long-shot banana still has work to do: Once that plant is fully grown, it is thrown back into the unprotected field. If it survives, if a needed quality appears, the process repeats, generation after generation, over a period of years, with each new banana begetting another. Many of the varieties Rowe began breeding in the 1960s are still being examined, still being perfected.

Almost fifty years have passed since the time Rowe began the program that is today run by Aguilar. During that time, La Lima's researchers have come up with between twenty and twenty-five viable banana varieties. Some of those are being grown—they're suitable for limited, local consumption—in Cuba, Brazil, and parts of Africa. That's a huge success story, given the odds.

But how many of Rowe's progeny got close enough to be considered as a Cavendish replacement?

Just one.

Phil Rowe's legacy: man-made bananas,
bred over four decades in Honduras.

CHAPTER 29

A Savior?

UNITED FRUIT LAUNCHED THE ATTACK on Jacobo Arbenz from Honduras in 1954. But that country was at the same time embroiled in its own banana conflict. A month after the soon-to-be-deposed Guatemalan leader presented United Fruit with a tax bill, a few dozen Honduran workers walked off the job. By the end of the month, the nation's entire banana industry was frozen in place: Thirty thousand workers refused to enter the plantations, loading docks, and railroad depots.

The Honduran economy—never strong—was on the verge of collapse, and the banana exporters, already in a state of panic over Guatemala, were terrified that the strikers would succeed and that one Central American country after another would then fall. To lose control over their holdings as Panama disease was reaching its coup de grâce was unthinkable.

United Fruit acted first in Guatemala because it was easier to stage an overthrow in a country without strikers than to attack tens of thousands of angry, idled laborers. But the company also knew that success against Arbenz would shift momentum away from the envisioned chain reaction. That's exactly what happened. When the Guatemalan government folded, the morale of the Honduran strikers collapsed, and the country's government was able to arrest labor leaders by accusing them of having ties to Arbenz. The biggest banana strike in history ended four days after the Guatemalan president went into exile.

YET VICTORY TURNED OUT to be a difficult thing to claim—and to hold on to. Honduran workers had accomplished something just by generating such a large number of strikers. That tiny margin of success would resurface a few years later in an even more powerful attempt by banana workers to gain control over their own destinies.

Between 1954 and 1958, Honduras—which since the turn of the century had teetered in what seemed to be a permanent state of instability thanks to constant intervention by banana interests—had one president who never took office; a vice president who became president then quickly attempted to extend his rule into dictatorship; and two military coups, one that failed and one that finally succeeded in 1956. The Honduran army would control the country for decades; the effect on the nation's citizenry, economy, and industries would be to veer between extremes, depending on what particular faction ruled. Honduras would have good times and terrible times, looking sometimes like a sleepy, impoverished republic and other times like a police state. The components of the banana industry's power would change—the way land and workers were used—but those alterations came mostly as tactical responses to maintain the status quo. (Even today, bananas remain Honduras's largest industry, with Chiquita and Dole accounting for nearly 100 percent of the fruit that leaves the loading docks on the country's northeast edge each day.)

In retrospect, the first years following the 1956 coup seem almost like a golden age. The ruling junta allowed elections: The winner was

Ramón Villeda Morales. Villeda Morales had also won the 1954 vote, but he'd been denied office, partly because he'd been seen as too left wing. The Honduran was far less radical than his Guatemalan counterpart, but like Arbenz, Villeda Morales—who'd worked as a rural doctor before going into politics—understood the injustices that Honduran peasants had been subjected to for decades. And like the failed Guatemalan, the new Honduran president understood that the key to change was land reform.

THE HONDURAN PROGRAM was strategically modest compared to what Guatemala had attempted. Small plantations and communities were allowed to form rural cooperatives and labor laws were reformed to allow social security and increased protection for workers. The softer approach didn't result in an immediate disaster, but, by 1963, when it appeared Villeda Morales would be reelected by a large margin, and anticipating even more sweeping reforms, the country's military stepped in again: Elections were canceled, Villeda Morales was exiled, and Colonel Oswaldo López Arellano took power. Many of the earlier land reforms were rolled back, and even the United States—which was beginning to feel uneasy about intervening for the banana companies—officially suspended diplomatic relations with Honduras following the coup. The country's new leader purged perceived leftists, especially those with ties to Cuba's Fidel Castro (this pleased the United States, which restored diplomatic relations, with increased military assistance, a year later).

For those laboring on Honduran plantations, the coup marked the beginning of decades where gains were lost, gained, and lost again. Some unions were banned and others grew. Land was transferred to workers then taken away. The one taboo was strikes: As recently as 1991, the military was killing workers who walked off the job.

Where were the banana companies? They were still exerting influence, though more often by stealth than through armed force.

And they were still hungry for land, still determined to do things their way, opposing every attempt to provide workers with basic benefits. In 1972 a new form of Sigatoka hit Honduras. In a foretelling of today's Panama disease crisis, the new version of the old malady was more virulent. The related diseases are distinguished by the color they turn banana leaves: yellow for the older malady and black for the modern version.

To combat Black Sigatoka, which remains the most widespread banana disease in the world, aerial spraying of the crop was increased, resulting in further damage to the health of workers on the ground. United Fruit needed to gain market share in order to cover the increased expense of fighting the new disease, so it embarked on a price war with Fyffes (the former subsidiary) that ultimately led to the British rival's departure from the country, along with accusations that Chiquita had hired agents to destroy competing banana shipments. In other words, though the actors, techniques, and storyline shifted constantly, Honduras remained the quintessential banana republic.

ELI BLACK WANTED TO CHANGE THAT. Looking at his balance sheets, the entrepreneur who'd made his fortune as a Wall Street takeover king seemed an unlikely reformer. Like Sam Zemurray, Black was a Jewish immigrant who'd arrived in the United States poor, and with a different name, coming from Poland in the mid-1920s as Elihu Menashe Blachowitz. (Black only changed his name as an adult, after he'd entered Columbia Business School.) Black was as ambitious as Zemurray, as well. At age thirty-two, after a successful stint as an investment banker, Black picked a long-shot, troubled company—American Seal-Kap, which manufactured paper cups and drinking straws—and restored it to health; he flipped the profits into a takeover of a meat-packing concern.

Black's next target was United Fruit. The late 1960s were a time when many small U.S. companies merged into huge conglomerates.

In 1967 pineapple importer Castle & Cooke bought Standard Fruit, eventually leading to the use of its Dole brand name for its bananas (sales of the traditionally Hawaiian fruit are now dwarfed by bananas, which are Dole's largest product). Today's third-largest banana importer, Del Monte, which was then a maker of canned fruits and vegetables, entered the business by purchasing the West Indies Fruit Company, which mostly operated in the Caribbean. Over the next two years, United Fruit would become the target of a heated takeover battle. Black's rival was a company called Zapata, which had begun in Texas oil exploration. The owner was the first President George Bush. (Once again, we enter the banana labyrinth: Bush's company was formed in 1953; some of its drilling was on islands on the Gulf of Mexico. These islands were allegedly used as staging areas for U.S.-backed activities against Fidel Castro's Cuba, starting in the late 1950s and continuing through the early 1960s. One of those actions was code-named Operation Zapata. Though the Bush connection has never been confirmed, when the planned operation did go through, two of the boats reportedly used were named *Barbara* (Bush's wife) and *Houston*, the future president's adopted hometown. Some of the other vessels used in the failed 1961 operation, which became known as the Bay of Pigs invasion after the public learned about it, were owned by United Fruit, on loan from the Great White Fleet. The banana giant's motive, allegedly, was anger over Castro's takeover of the island's banana plantations.)

Black won the battle for the banana giant with spectacular fireworks: On September 25, 1969, he bought 733,000 shares of United Fruit in a single day—at the time, the third-largest deal in the history of the New York Stock Exchange. A year later, a weakened United Fruit merged entirely with Black's company; the company that was originally named as a result of the merger between Andrew Preston's import concern and Minor Keith's railroad network was rechristened United Brands.

Black was known as a take-no-prisoners businessman, and his battle with Zapata proved that. But Black was also deeply religious, coming from a long line of Hebrew scholars. Prior to entering the world of finance, he spent three years as a rabbi. Even during his career as a corporate raider, much of the money he earned went to support Jewish philanthropies. He was a member of six different temples and usually spent Saturdays discussing religion with his closest friend, Rabbi Jonathan Levine. It was that background that led Black to feel deeply disturbed about the reputation of the banana company he'd taken over, which he'd almost certainly known about prior to his effort. Changing the company might even have been one of Black's motivations in buying the banana giant: An article in *Newsweek* described the executive as "determined to end United Brands' image as a Yankee exploiter of poor people."

Yet, before he could transform United Brands' personality, Black first had to address a more practical matter—profits. In 1971 the company lost $2 million. Black cut budgets, but the next year, the loss was ten times greater. A Federal antitrust suit forced the company to sell more of its Guatemalan holdings, accounting for about 9 million bunches annually, to Del Monte. Deeply in debt, Black sold additional land in Costa Rica. (The sales set the stage for the structure of the banana industry today, with few plantations actually owned by the fruit companies. Instead, the facilities are owned by local interests, who sell bananas to Chiquita, Dole, and other banana exporters under contract. This has allowed the big banana conglomerates to pick and choose suppliers multinationally, based on who offers the lowest price for their fruit. The arrangement is a softened version of the squeeze technique United Fruit used earlier to pressure client countries that threatened to institute land and labor reforms.)

The next years saw mixed results—and Black under increasing pressure. United Brands earned praise for its efforts in helping Nicaragua recover from a devastating 1972 earthquake; company money was largely responsible for rebuilding the country's capital, Managua. The same year, the spread of Sigatoka increased across the region. The company's response was to use more, and increasingly toxic, chemical sprays. The health of banana workers declined again. The company was profitable in 1973, earning $16 million, but it also suffered an unthinkable embarrassment: It was overtaken by Dole as the number one banana seller in the United States. Even so, Black announced that the company's assets were finally in order and that the following year would see a return to big profits and market leadership.

But 1974 turned out to be a tragic year for Eli Black and United Brands, whose products now included not just bananas but also sausages and sunglasses. For the first time, Central American governments banded together, announcing—in Costa Rica, Panama, and Honduras—a dollar-per-box tax on exported fruit. During the summer, Panamanian banana workers went on strike, leading to the formation of the Organization of Banana Exporting Countries, modeled after OPEC, the Middle Eastern oil-producing alliance that had successfully used a boycott and market pressures to raise gas prices—and precipitate an energy crisis—in the United States the year before. The move hurt the banana company, but were ultimately ineffective because Ecuador, now the world's largest banana-producing nation, refused to join. Nature also seemed to be against the Central American alliance. A day after the organization was founded, a hurricane hit Honduras, destroying three-fourths of that country's banana crop. Once again, Black put company assets into rebuilding Honduras. By the end of the year, the company was on the way to losses nearly three times 1972's record. Black was forced to sell one of the company's few profitable divisions, the Foster Grant eyewear company.

Eli Black was a quiet, almost somber person, not given to revealing his feelings (a former teacher described Black to the *New York Times* as "a boy who always smiled—but never laughed"). Black also hated defeat. Yet the sixteen-hour days he'd been putting in at United Brands' New York headquarters had failed to yield success; instead, they created grumblings on the part of company executives, shareholders, and banks that Black was better as a dealmaker than a day-to-day manager.

On Saturday, February 1, 1975, Black began a typical weekend with his son. The two visited the barber and watched a movie. The next day, Black had Sunday brunch with his family in his Westport, Connecticut, home. Black then drove into Manhattan, where he spent the night at his Park Avenue apartment. Early Monday morning, Black was picked up by his chauffeur-driven company car. It took a little more than five minutes for the executive to arrive at his office, in the Pan Am Building, the fifty-eight-story office tower that rises above Grand Central Station (today, known as the Met-Life Building). Black took the elevator to his small office on the forty-fourth floor, arriving there just before 8:00 a.m. The entrepreneur stepped inside, closed the door, and opened the window blinds. He lifted his heavy briefcase. "Then," wrote the *New York Times*, "the man who never raised his voice swung his attaché case against a quarter-inch thick piece of glass." The window shattered. One final detail: Black meticulously picked up the shards that remained in the window, as if he were neatening the opening he created.

Then, still clutching his briefcase, the man who controlled the world's largest banana empire jumped.

"Mr. Black," the *Times* report continued, "in a blue suit, hurtled down to the northbound Park Avenue ramp, falling on the roadway before horrified motorists."

While Black's body lay in the street, the papers from his briefcase began to blow across the intersection. Neither among them, nor in his office above, was any suicide note.

Eli Black's funeral was attended by over five hundred people; the president of Yeshiva University gave the eulogy. The U.S. senator from Connecticut attended. The overriding emotion was not just sadness: The mourners were bewildered. Yes, things had been bad. But the sunglass division sale, announced the day following Black's death, would have evened the company's balance sheet. Surely, as a successful businessman, Black knew that his situation would eventually turn around. Even the rabbi officiating at the ceremony—he'd

flown all the way from Jerusalem to honor Black—closed his remarks
with an unanswered question: "How many persons," he asked, "pushed
Eli to a desperate option—how many contributed to his untimely
tragedy—and who called on Eli to choose the wrong door?"

The mystery lasted ten weeks.

The police quickly ruled Black's death a suicide. The only investigation remaining to be made was by the Securities and Exchange
Commission, a routine inquiry always performed after such events.
Black was working hard to squeeze every dollar out of United
Brands. What he'd done was absolutely consistent with the company's history—in fact, it seemed comparatively minor—but it
was absolutely contradictory to Black's values: In order to reduce
the company's tax liabilities in Honduras, Black had personally
authorized a $1.25 million bribe to Oswaldo López Arellano. The
bribe had the intended effect—the tax on bananas was reduced to a
quarter per box. But it must have had a huge effect on Black. News
of the bribe would have been humiliating; it would certainly have
led to his resignation—and possibly prosecution.

The answer to Eli Black's suicide may lie in the friction between
two poles: the checkered history of United Fruit, which Black had
vowed to atone for, and the ethos most important in Black's life—
not business, but faith, as exemplified by the Torah, the holiest
Hebrew text, and one that Black, as a rabbi and scholar, had studied
his entire life.

The passage that likely tore Black apart is found in the Old
Testament in Deuteronomy, one of the Bible's opening chapters,
imported directly from the earlier Jewish text. The words, spoken
by Moses, come from God himself, brought to the wandering Israel-
ites from Mount Sinai. This is the same part of the Bible that contains the Ten Commandments and God's promise to reserve Israel
as the Jewish homeland. The pronouncements of Moses also contain
the mitzvah, Hebrew for "commands," strict rules for living a moral
and just life. To pay secret tribute for special favor is considered a

dual sin: "Bribery," says chapter 16, verse 19, "blinds the eyes of the wise, and perverts the words of the just."

The SEC investigation ultimately found that Black had surreptitiously funneled money to Honduran officials. For this, a penalty of $14,000 was imposed.

CHAPTER 30

Golden Child

SINCE 1958 Phil Rowe had slowly, painstakingly been concocting better bananas. In a series of photos—Rowe took snapshots of his progeny, and often displayed them with full parental pride—we see one breed improving year by year. A wild bunch photographed in 1959 has just a few bananas on it, stubby and inedible. By 1969 the fruit, cooking bananas in this case, is robust, with a full-sized, appealing bunch made up of over a hundred individual fingers. The bunches depicted are 2,000 iterations from their original ancestor. By 1979, about 3,500 steps from the start, the bunches are even larger and have yielded several distinct varieties. But despite these successes, the 1970s were a time of decline for banana breeders. Eli Black's cost-cutting measures eliminated much of the funding for the La Lima laboratories. Company managers had concluded there was little need for a better commercial banana after all: Panama disease appeared to be gone, and Sigatoka was controllable with chemicals (which consumers were unaware of and unaffected by, since the fruit, protected by thick skin, carries only trace amounts of residue, and what little remains washes off in processing).

Rowe turned his work toward plantains. But United Brands needed the starchy green bananas far less than it did sweet yellow ones. Every banana dollar the company earned came from the Cavendish. Even when Rowe did concentrate on developing a dessert-type fruit, results were relatively poor since such a fruit needed a wider variety of qualities to be considered acceptable. There was another issue: During that era, the ability of U.S. breeders to patent plants was limited and poorly enforced. Exclusivity was restricted to just seventeen years, and in practice the rules—even if infringement could be detected, which was often an impossible task—didn't necessarily apply internationally. (Today, because much breeding is done on a molecular level by biotechnology countries, the rules on plant patenting have become even more confused; efforts to "correct" the situation have generally not succeeded in making sure that the interests of people who grow food for subsistence are preserved along with the corporate right to market exclusively developed products.) Why would Chiquita develop a better banana, wrote former company researcher Ivan Buddenhagen, who was working with Rowe at the time, "when any new cultivar would be stolen and used by others? Why subsidize anyone else?"

Rowe continued his work. But increasingly, he seemed to be falling behind. New breeders, mostly funded by European institutions and philanthropic organizations, began to spring up in Africa. These pursuits were aimed at subsistence-level bananas, and though they didn't generally move beyond the theoretical stage until the 1990s, according to Buddenhagen they did tally one major success: In 1981 Brazilian researchers developed a fusarium-and-Sigatoka-resistant hybrid. The fruit is considered a sweet, or dessert, banana and is widely grown there, but is not seen as a good candidate for Cavendish replacement. Brazilians prefer bananas that most consumers of yellow bananas would consider odd-tasting: They're just a tad sweet, with a consistency and taste closer to an apple or unripe pear. Not great for cereal. But no Brazil-like progress was being made in Honduras. "The key banana research center and only viable breeding program," Buddenhagen says, "was dying."

Chiquita was simply too distracted, Buddenhagen adds, with "anti-trust, new Latin exporting groups, tariffs, overproduction, hurricanes, buy-outs, and take-overs." In 1983 Chiquita stopped research altogether. It didn't close the facility—instead it left a skeleton staff (Rowe and few others) to find another way. The answer was FHIA. The new program, funded by international institutions, would take over the old United Fruit labs. Rowe and his colleagues would now begin to do what the rest of the world's banana scientists were doing: focusing on the bananas people survived on.

At the start, FHIA was handicapped by its reputation. Most of the world that knew bananas couldn't disassociate it from Chiquita. "Too much negative stigma," Buddenhagen says. Instead, as FHIA scraped by, global banana breeding finally began to take off, with work advancing on nearly every continent. Moreover, though much of the traditional breeding clearly followed in Rowe's footsteps, new ideas about manipulating bananas at the basic DNA level were beginning to take hold. Conventional breeding had seen too many results that were considered, at best, half successes.

To outsiders, it seemed that Phil Rowe had become irrelevant.

Then came Goldfinger.

IT TOOK A QUARTER CENTURY for Phil Rowe to come up with his dream banana. During that time, Honduras had had nine presidents; Guatemala, ten. The company he began with had changed its name, lost money, lost its leadership position in the market, and lost Eli Black. Black Sigatoka had begun to decimate plantations across the region and had spread to Africa and Asia. The La Lima research facility was abandoned and reborn as FHIA. Through all those years, just twenty banana varieties out of the twenty thousand tested by the facility showed any of the desired traits. But even those bananas weren't fully realized. They had some of what they needed, but not all.

Then came the fruit good enough to be designated FHIA-01. Because of its rich color and stubby profile, Rowe nicknamed it Goldfinger.

I TASTED A GOLDFINGER as I walked through FHIA's experimental plantation with Juan Fernando Aguilar. "Try this one," he said, pulling an almost rotund fruit from a towering plant.

The banana is a cross between the applelike Brazilian Prata and a rare Asian variety collected by United Fruit's explorers in the 1960s.

For months I'd been learning what the world's dream banana needs and repeating it like a mantra, because it is the single most important element of finding a way out of the Cavendish crisis: controllable ripening, tough skin, good taste, high yields, resistance to disease, sturdy trees. I'd also come to believe that such a banana could never truly exist.

I was about to be proved wrong.

Phil Rowe's masterpiece does things no other banana can: It *never* turns brown. The fruit remains firm and solid for far longer than the Cavendish does. It is a dual-purpose banana: It can be cooked like a plantain when green or eaten like a Cavendish or Gros Michel once it brightens. Goldfinger bunches are full and even oversized—more robust than the Cavendish, even approaching Gros Michel. The leaves that protect Goldfinger are green and thick.

I stood under the shade of those leaves in the experimental banana farm Rowe founded. For several rows around me, they were the only available respite from the sun. There were other plants as close as three or four feet, but their leaves were rotted and crumbling. They were infected with Black Sigatoka. Goldfinger is virtually immune.

Aguilar told me that the soil has also been infected with Panama disease. Goldfinger resists that malady as well.

There's even more good news about Rowe's creation. Goldfinger can be grown across a wider spectrum of terrain and weather conditions than the Cavendish, making it—in sufficient volume—cheaper to produce. Because it resists so many pests, it can be grown organically on land that has already been cleared. Other organic bananas need to be grown on relatively freshly cleared land and at higher altitudes, where diseases spread more slowly. There just isn't enough terrain like that to make naturally grown Cavendish an answer to the Panama disease resurgence, even if the environmental costs of clearing forest for plantations could somehow be mitigated.

But, even as Aguilar tells me about Goldfinger's very real virtues, he and I both know that there is one attribute that can't be described in words or pointed out on the vine.

How does Goldfinger taste?

Aguilar pulls one down—a thick, bright yellow fruit—and hands it to me.

It peels easily enough, and I'm impressed that the skin is thick: I know enough to recognize a strong banana when I see one.

I bite into it.

This is what's good about Goldfinger. And it is the same thing that isn't good about Goldfinger. I like this banana. I like it a lot.

But it doesn't taste, or feel, like a Cavendish. The flesh is heavier, less creamy. It is tart, with a taste at least as sharp as a Brazilian Prata. You can occasionally find a Goldfinger in a specialty market. Some refer to the fruit as an "apple banana." The more proper term, when experts characterize the fruit's taste, is an "acid banana."

The question is simple: If it doesn't taste like the Cavendish, does that mean it also doesn't taste like a banana? "What happens when Cavendish goes against an acid banana," says Aguilar, "is that people pick Cavendish."

SO DO THE BIG BANANA COMPANIES, who also know the complications that would arise if Goldfinger, which requires different shipping, storage, and ripening techniques, were mixed in with Cavendish.

Could Goldfinger replace the more common fruit if the Cavendish were to disappear, if buyers and growers had no choice? It is impossible to say, but it is certain that making the changeover would be a gamble. Rowe's greatest banana tastes so different from what we're now accustomed to that the transition could be much more jarring to the consumer than the Gros Michel changeover.

It's difficult, Aguilar told me, to see Goldfinger as the grail banana.

Could it provide the genetic material for that banana, though? Could Goldfinger, through more breeding, more experimentation, be turned into something better, something more acceptable?

Phil Rowe believed it could. The breeder, wrote Franklin Rosales, a close colleague and codeveloper of many FHIA varieties, "tried in all possible arenas to convince people that 'traditional breeding' was the best alternative for the banana and plantain industry." Rowe was an enigmatic genius; he was an accomplished scientist; he was also an evangelical Christian. His understanding of how important bananas were made him a beloved character in impoverished Honduras. On many mornings, a half dozen or more locals would queue up at the La Lima research station. Rowe would give them fruit, or jobs, and sometimes even pay for their schooling. It was as if he was trying, all on his own, to right the wrongs of United Fruit—both social and biological. It would be hard to say whether or not Rowe succeeded. His banana varieties are now growing across the world and have been productive as subsistence bananas, which have far fewer requirements for success than their commercial counterparts. There are now over twenty fruits with the FHIA designation.

FHIA director Adolfo Martinez grimaced when I asked him for Rowe's contact information. The pioneering banana researcher, he told me, passed away in 2001. He was sixty-two years old. His dream of a perfect banana had gone unfulfilled. One of his colleagues told me that Rowe was reserved and revealed little of his own deepest thoughts, other than to express unbridled optimism, so it is hard to say how much of a toll this took on him or whether he felt that the mission he'd set for himself was too large, too frustrating, too impossible. Rowe's biggest influence was in Cuba—a country so poor that it couldn't afford to spray existing crops against Black Sigatoka, forcing it to convert, wholesale, to a FHIA variety that resisted the disease.

"We will always remember him with admiration, love, and respect," wrote Cuban banana researcher Jose Manuel Alvarez. "All of those feelings will be materialized in the farms around the island where today the fruits of his work are flowering."

Cuba proved that a human-modified banana could be grown successfully. But it was a small victory when viewed against the backdrop of decades of frustrating results.

On Sunday, March 25, 2001, near the La Lima research facility, Phil Rowe committed suicide. His body was found hanging from a tree, surrounded by the banana plants at FHIA's Guarama Uno plantation. A note he left to his wife and two children said, "Please forgive me."

Rowe's impact wasn't just on banana science—he'd also, in a way, helped rehabilitate the reputation of the United States in Honduras. It wasn't possible for Rowe to erase nearly a hundred years of history, but he accomplished as much as any one person could: "We have lost the best American who ever came to Honduras," wrote Billy Peña, a columnist for the *Tiempo* newspaper.

It is impossible to know why Rowe took his own life. What is certain is that his death cost the world of traditional banana husbandry the most important and experienced mind it had. And if breeding a Cavendish replacement with Rowe alive was difficult, his departure set back the effort even further.

PART VI

A NEW
BANANA

CHAPTER 31

A Long Way
from Panama

I N ONE SENSE, it was business as usual for the banana giants as
they moved into the 1980s. Many of the downsides to the way
they conducted their affairs in Latin America—interference
with governments and ignoring the complaints of workers—
continued. But more and more, their actions resembled the norm
for a multinational corporation, for better or worse. Chiquita was
not that different in the way it behaved than Exxon, General Motors,
or Burger King.

If the echoes of the past became more muffled, one distant sound
became quietest of all: Panama disease.

The issue was thought to be solved, and the banana companies
hadn't just put it behind them—they'd almost completely forgotten
it. But the fundamental characteristic that made the malady so devastating to the Gros Michel remained: If one Cavendish happened to
get sick, every other Cavendish would. When this problem was considered, if it ever was, it was seen as alarmist—an assertion that the
sky above the plantations was falling—or at best hypothetical.

It wasn't.

And in labs and research facilities across the globe, a new set of banana men, more interested in science than empire, began working toward a solution that could finally help the people, throughout the world, who depended most on the fruit.

IT ISN'T UNUSUAL for packages filled with dirt to appear at Randy Ploetz's Florida doorstep. At any given time, visitors to Ploetz's laboratory at the University of Florida's Institute of Food and Agricultural Sciences will find busy graduate students staring through microscopes at clumps of soil, tending to tiny newborn plants, not much more than a speck of green, or handling larger banana trees grown under tightly controlled conditions in a humid greenhouse.

One box arrived in 1992, from Sumatra, part of the Indonesian island chain. Banana plantations were new to the island (which is a bit larger than Sweden) in the 1980s, but they'd quickly become big business. The burgeoning urban markets of the Far East were demanding more of the fruit, and thousands of acres of rainforest and former oil palm plantations were being shifted to Cavendish bananas. But within a few years of breaking ground, the new farms began to die. An unknown pathogen seemed to be working into the roots of each plant, discoloring leaves, choking off water supplies.

Ploetz is, and has been since the mid-1980s, the botanic equivalent of a crime scene investigator. He is also the world's leading authority on Panama disease. He's authored dozens of papers on the disorder, frequently traveling to remote areas to conduct on-the-ground forensics. Ploetz had heard about the blight that was devastating plantations in Sumatra and other areas halfway around the globe. The symptoms were familiar. It sounded like Panama disease, but that made no sense. These were Cavendish bananas, specifically resistant to that fungal malady. That trait was the very reason the Cavendish was introduced to commercial growers and how it became humanity's most consumed fruit. Ploetz examined the soil samples. His suspicions were confirmed. It seemed impossible, he thought, but there was no denying the reality. "The Cavendish," he said, "was getting hammered by Panama disease."

As the banana world remained in a holding pattern of corporate normalcy, as Chiquita and Dole began to diversify, selling other fruits and snack products, Ploetz understood what few others, and certainly not the big banana companies, comprehended: History was beginning to repeat itself.

RANDY PLOETZ DOESN'T JUST STUDY BANANAS. He loves them. His academic papers are illustrated with archival images of the great explorers, entrepreneurs, and robber barons who established the banana industry over a century ago. One of Ploetz's main interests is discovering how maladies like Panama disease evolve. Among the biggest questions to emerge during the first outbreaks of the disease in the 1990s was how, exactly, Cavendish suddenly became susceptible to something it had resisted for decades.

Ploetz's answer reaches back to the very beginnings of the idea that plants and animals evolved in an orderly way instead of appearing fully formed and created by a divine hand.

Like Charles Telfair, Alfred Russel Wallace was a British explorer who spent most of his life searching for exotic animal and plant specimens that he could sell to wealthy collectors in his native England. Wallace was a grittier, less well-heeled contemporary of Darwin. The two men came to their conclusions about how life on earth emerged, and moved forward, at about the same time. They share credit for the theory of evolution.

One of Wallace's most important concepts was a hypothetical barrier that has come to be known as Wallace's line. The line serves as a nearly impenetrable wall differentiating biological groupings; it is a physical rift, where the large landmasses that once covered our planet were torn apart by geologic forces, separating like species by oceans and setting them on divergent evolutionary courses. If you look at a diagram of the line, it seems rather modest: It runs along the string of islands that separate Borneo and New Guinea. In some cases, the landmasses on either side of the barrier are less than twenty-five miles apart. But the kinds of flora and fauna found on either side of the line are vastly different. During Wallace's time, kangaroos, koalas, and eucalyptuses were found only on the Australian side. Tigers, squirrels, and rhinos were only endemic north of the divide. Those separations can be seen far beyond the line itself: In birds found only in South America, trees that are seen only in India, and wild bananas that never appeared on our side of the evolutionary frontier.

How did this narrow line turn into an *our side* and *their side*? A brief natural history lesson: Five hundred million or so years ago, the planet was made up of just a few megacontinents. The giant mass that included today's Africa, Australia, New Zealand, South America, and Antarctica has been named Gondwanaland by present-day geologists. Over millions of years, the continents now familiar to us broke off and moved apart from each other. What were on contiguous land single species eventually became widely separated and often only distantly related organisms. Evidence of that movement can be found by examining even the most tiny and seemingly insignificant fauna of today. For example, a midge is a species of fly. They live near swampy water nearly everywhere on earth. The remains of ancient midges are often found preserved in amber, fossilized tree sap. Comparing the ancient midges to those living today yields surprising results. "South American and Australian midges are more closely related to each other than they are to New Zealand species," explains *Understanding Evolution*, an online primer published by the University of California. "And the midges of all three land masses are more closely related to one another than they are to African species. In other words, an insect that may live only a few weeks can tell biogeographers about the wanderings of continents tens of millions of years ago."

Wallace's line represents not a present barrier, but one of the past: the place where continents were ripped apart by plate tectonics.

(The line was a source of great controversy until the 1960s. Until then, geographers thought the idea that continents could actually move was nonsense. It took intensive studies of variations of the sea floor to prove what seems obvious after a look at a map of the Atlantic Ocean, with the east coast of South America locking like a jigsaw puzzle piece into Africa's western shoreline.)

As with Darwin's basic theories, the particulars of the single divide proposed by Wallace have expanded. There are now believed to be six distinct regions where tectonics created major, permanent species separation, at least until humans started carrying plants and animals across the borders.

This distinguishability of both unique species and ones that have evolved into distantly related and removed cousins even extends to humans. "The lines . . . seem to divide us into races," wrote Jared Diamond in a 1997 issue of *Discover* magazine. "The Atlantic Ocean, which separated Europeans from Native Americans; the Sahara, which lay between black sub-Saharan Africans and white North Africans; and the Indian subcontinent, between East Asians and the whites of West Asia and Europe."

But one thing that was never truly recognized as having undergone the split-and-separate process—and this is key—were pathogens. The idea that bacteria, fungi, and viruses could also have moved apart in the same way was something many scientists hadn't considered—until Randy Ploetz began thinking about his box of dirt.

The first epidemic of Panama disease took place during the early days of international trade. Jungles were cleared by hand. Banana farms were grown one plant at a time. Under those conditions, it took a meandering seventy-five years for the Gros Michel to vanish. What Ploetz and the rest of the banana world are seeing is far more rapid. That the Cavendish fell ill when it arrived in Asia seemed, on one level, easy to understand. It was a newcomer. Then again, this didn't explain how, or why, it was happening to the *Cavendish*. After all, this wasn't something *new* killing the imported bananas. It was the disease that the banana had been chosen to withstand—and *had* withstood, in dozens of other countries.

The answer lay in Wallace's line, and Ploetz's epiphany.

ONE OF THE FIRST SIGNS of trouble appeared in 1991 at a Malaysian factory farm—known as "estates" in that part of the world—called Nam Heng. The plantation, which had grown mostly palm trees, seemed to be a perfect place to raise bananas. It had plenty of water, a stable workforce, and an existing agricultural infrastructure. Nam Heng's initial efforts were modest by banana standards: forty-two acres—about the same size as California's Disneyland. At first, the tiny plot of bananas seemed healthy. But within six months, something curious began to appear: brown flecks. Leaves brightening with yellow, then wilting. The blight quickly spread, first appearing at nearby farms, then distant ones. It was clear that whatever was affecting the bananas was not something that had come along for the ride from Central America. It was moving too fast for that. Reports began pouring in. A Del Monte plantation covering five thousand acres was among the largest to be afflicted—though it wasn't the size of the operation that surprised growers, it was the plantation's distance from Nam Heng. Del Monte's operation was one thousand miles away, in Sumatra, across a body of water.

By the mid-1990s, even more distant banana farms began to fall, in Halmahera, Papua New Guinea. News accounts of the Malaysian venture occasionally mentioned the growing crisis, usually couching it in wishfully positive terms. A 1995 story in the *New Straits Times* portrayed the issue more as a challenge than a calamity, something the country's respected scientific community could easily brush aside. (There was precedent for this: A few years earlier, Malaysia successfully strengthened rubber trees from Brazil, and the hardier plants allowed the country to quickly surpass its Latin

American rivals.) "We *can* breed disease-resistant bananas," the article quoted one researcher as saying.

Wishful thinking. The reality was a total—and precipitous—wipeout. Statistics released by one grower show a nearly unbelievable fall. In 1991, 1,650 acres of land were cultivated; the next year, the number rises to 1,892. Then it drops to 1,378, rises a bit to 1,440 in 1994 (following an attempt to plant new bananas in recently cleared land), and crashes: just 256 acres in 1995, and zero, zero, zero, zero for the rest of the decade.

PLOETZ FOLLOWED THE PATH OF EVOLUTION backward, across Wallace's line, retracing the banana's journey to its modern home. Malaysia is a place—possibly the world's best place—for biological superlatives. The nation is warm, wet, and hilly. Mangrove woodlands hug the coasts. The interior is covered in tropical rain forests, which yield to mossy stands of oak as mountains soar as high as 13,000 feet. Rivers flow, sometimes in steep, thundering waterfalls, down from these upper reaches into the forests, homesteads, and pasturelands. This terrain hosts a giddy trove of biological riches: eight thousand species of flowering plants, thousands of kinds of trees, and a spectacular assortment of fauna, including tigers, bears, and rhinos; scores of bird species; and one hundred types of snake.

But as in most of the world, Malaysia's biological diversity is on the decline. Over two thousand of Malaysia's life-forms are found nowhere else. Many face extinction. The region's oversize mahogany trees are among the most threatened on earth; no country exports more of the coveted hardwood.

Farms are replacing Malaysia's fallen forests. About one-quarter of the country's area is now dedicated to agriculture. Millions of Malaysians—ethnic Chinese and Indians along with native Bumiputras (the name means "children of the soil")—work on factory estates. Malaysia is the world's leading exporter of palm oil and a major producer of sugarcane, pineapples, cacao, and coconuts.

All that land, all those workers, and all that infrastructure made the nation look wide open to growers of commercial bananas. They needed someplace in Asia that had ready shipping facilities, so the delicate fruit could be quickly and efficiently brought to city markets in time for it to spend the banana industry's magic number—seven days, from green to brown-flecked yellow—on store shelves. Even Malaysia's soil seemed right for bananas—after all, they'd evolved there.

It turned out that Malaysia was a terrible place—maybe the worst place on earth—to grow the Cavendish. Evolution was what had *attacked* the Cavendish. Malaysia's wild banana population is hugely varied for a reason: The fruit has been developing there longer than just about anywhere else in the world. Since the diseases and the organisms they strike tend to evolve with each other—creating an alternating equilibrium of virulence and resistance—Ploetz quickly guessed that the types of Panama disease found in Malaysia, having had tens of thousands of years to develop, would likely be "as diverse as the bananas."

Malaysia's native bananas developed resistance to the diseases that grew along with them. Newcomer fruit had no such inherited advantage.

The answer was suddenly obvious. This wasn't a recently emerged mutation of the blight that destroyed the Gros Michel. This "new" race of Panama disease had been in the Asian soil all the time, living in balance amidst mostly immune plants. The earlier incarnation of Panama disease had probably been brought to the Americas, where it did the most damage, from Asia. The same process was now happening in reverse: Bananas were being brought to the disease.

History is filled with examples of how destructive a disease one population has already been proven to withstand can be when introduced to nonresistant groups. In the United States, chestnut trees were nearly wiped out by an imported blight in the early 1900s. Today, a malady called Sudden Oak Death, which initially appeared in the Pacific Northwest, is arriving along the eastern seaboard, possibly through shrubs and soil sold by commercial nurseries. In human history, such incursions are often tragic and calamitous: Smallpox killed up to 90 percent of the Native American population within a few decades of initial European contact.

This wasn't a new kind of Panama disease at all. What was destroying bananas in Asia was a long-lost progenitor of the strain that appeared in the Americas a century earlier. It had never crossed Wallace's line. This version of Panama disease, which Ploetz dubbed Race 4, had long since reached a biological truce with the other organisms it shared the forest with. Our Cavendish had no such evolutionary defenses. It returned to a home it no longer knew— and that no longer knew it.

The Asian banana rush was over. Panama disease was back. Randy Ploetz knew what that meant. Race 4 would spread. Maybe it would take twenty years. Maybe more. Maybe less. One thing was certain: "The moment it hits a new continent," Ploetz said, "it will be game over."

CHAPTER 32

Know Your Enemies

E VER SINCE CLAUDE WARDLAW, the pioneering banana breeder who worked in Trinidad in the 1920s, became the first to suspect that Panama disease was being spread by plantation building, those researching the fruit have maintained that humans could stop the malady by adopting some relatively simple practices: learning to farm better, enforcing quarantines, and making sure contaminated water and soil aren't transported between plantations.

The idea is a good one. But in practice it has almost never worked. Hadi Bux Leghari, a technical manager at a Pakistani plantation called Asim Agriculture Farm, learned this frustrating lesson when he attempted to fight another banana malady.

Bunchy Top is almost as scary as Panama disease. The virus is transmitted by aphids, tiny insects that feed on plant sap. Aphids carry disease-causing microbes to many plants, causing diseases with exotic names—cucumber mosaic virus, plum pox—much in the way mosquitoes cause malaria and yellow fever in humans. The aphid's fecundity is legendary. Millions of the insects can be born in a matter of hours.

Bunchy Top appeared in Pakistan in 1989, hitting plantations along the country's southern coast, near a village called Thatta. (It arrived in that country after having followed a century-long path from its first recorded outbreak, on Fiji, in 1889, through Australia then Sri Lanka, India, Bangladesh, and Burma. It is now present in Hawaii, where it has caused a 30 percent decline in local banana production over the past decade.) Growers and the agricultural technicians called in to investigate couldn't initially identify the malady that would soon spread through Pakistan's Cavendish crop. Plants afflicted with the unknown blight were easy to recognize, though, with leaves bunching together then descending in ever-more-compact spirals until the plant's shape resembled the multilayered petals of a rose. Infected plants rarely produced fruit or grew beyond three feet high.

As the plague spread across Pakistan, losses averaged between 25 percent and 75 percent per plantation. Many experienced total destruction: Not a single plant survived. Without knowing what they were attempting to fight, growers doused their crops with every chemical they had available. Nothing worked. Samples of diseased banana tissue were sent to scientists across the world. Finally, in 1991, the diagnosis was made.

Knowing his opponent's name did little to help Leghari. He'd surveyed dozens of plantations across the country, and the results were discouraging. "There are so many areas affected by BBTVD [Banana Bunchy Top Virus Disease]," Leghari noted in a 2006 report for the United Nations Food and Agriculture Organization. The situation in some regions was apocalyptic: "The whole area is devastated," the investigator wrote of a growing region called Khairpur. "The district is supposed to have more than 20,000 acres of banana. It is ruined." The area of land turned fallow by Bunchy Top represents more than one-third of Pakistan's predisease plantation holdings. That's a loss of about 140 million pounds of bananas annually, or about 10 percent of total production for a major banana-exporting country like Costa Rica. (Pakistan's bananas are mostly consumed domestically.)

With no conventional treatments available to completely inoculate the fruit against the virus or prevent the aphids from arriving in the first place, Leghari attempted to institute complex control measures as a way of containing the malady. He developed an eleven-step plan that, if implemented, could at least contain the spread of Bunchy Top. The program included ensuring that initial planting materials were free of disease; that a cocktail of pesticides and biological control agents be applied to the plants; that manual thinning—the aphids live on weeds interspersed beneath the banana plants—be done regularly; that planting areas be kept free of debris like the fallen leaves and stems that form a plantation's underlying mat; and that individual plants be isolated by growing them at greater distances from one another. Each plantation also needed to have a natural barrier—rows of high trees—on its perimeter.

When Leghari tested the plan at his own plantation, it succeeded. The variety of measures, none of which would have been terribly effective if used alone, combined to slow the disease to a near stop. Yields increased, and infection dropped to less than 1 percent.

Rigorous discipline can be effective. Australia has managed to keep Panama disease in check by erecting physical barriers between plantations and enforcing strict quarantine procedures. But Australia is a rich country with plenty of technical resources, and as Houbin Chen—the Chinese scientist who removes his shoes when he travels between plantations in Guangdong, only to watch as dozens of people on foot, animal, and bicycle track infected dirt alongside him—learned, the problem with this seeming panacea is that it requires a kind of discipline that appears to be impossible in the patchwork plantations where most bananas are grown.

Parts of Leghari's report bristle with anger and dismay. Sixty students were trained in his technique at the Asim plantation, with the hope that they'd spread out to the countryside and transfer their knowledge to local growers. It didn't work. In 2003 Leghari made a two-day presentation to farmers in the hard-hit Khairpur district: "I explained to them how [their bananas are] getting infected with BBTVD," he recalled. "This is the time you should start to manage your bananas by controlling the vector [the aphids] and removing diseased plants." But the measures seemed too complex, too time-consuming, too expensive: Not only would additional labor have to be hired and new materials have to be bought, but the number of plants actually produced would be severely decreased. (These same issues have become a problem at large-scale banana operations around the world, where growers play chemical leapfrog with a growing array of banana maladies. In a tight-margin business, such activity can quickly lead to unprofitability.) In Khairpur, Leghari left the plantations knowing he'd failed in his mission: "They refused to accept my open offer [for assistance in fighting Bunchy Top]," he recalled. "They have now lost 100 percent of their crop."

BUNCHY TOP HAS SPREAD IN ASIA AND THE PACIFIC, but like Panama disease, it has yet to reach the Americas. Black Sigatoka, which was first noted in the early 1970s, has. As I walked through the Honduran plantation with Juan Fernando Aguilar, viewing row after row of numbered plants—each representing a different generation of hybrid—I asked the scientist which plants were being bred for resistance to Panama disease.

"A few," he laughed, "but we've got a bigger problem right now."

We stepped toward a smallish banana plant. It looked skeletal, nearly bare. The few remaining leaves were yellow and mottled with expanding spots of black. If Panama disease is the uncontrollable natural disaster, then Sigatoka is today's most dangerous, immediate attacker and, like Pakistan's Bunchy Top, a worrying portent. "In spite of other diseases and pests, none has jeopardized the production of bananas as severely as Sigatoka," wrote Del Monte researcher Douglas Marín in a 2003 issue of *Plant Disease*.

The rapid spread of, and difficulty in treating, Sigatoka is a worrying sign in the upcoming fight against Panama disease. As with Panama disease, Sigatoka infects many different banana types, ranging from subsistence bananas in Africa to our Cavendish. Also, like the malady that wiped out the Gros Michel as a commercial crop, it is a fungus that appears in multiple strains, each with different distribution and virulence. Compared to the yellow Sigatoka, which began to become widespread in the 1920s and was easier to control (with the help of Bordeaux mixture), Black Sigatoka is speedier and more calamitous. The disease arrives in wind and water and on dirt. Different regions suffer from different manifestations of the bug, each of which requires unique treatment procedures. Sigatoka kills quickly. Symptoms appear as soon as two weeks after infection, and the plant is destroyed not long after. The disease can be worse when symptoms don't readily appear, taking hold only after the fruit is harvested, so your local grocer might open a banana box and, instead of a dozen nicely green bunches, find a rotted mess.

Sigatoka can be treated, but the development of a "cure" isn't necessarily a good tiding for the future. The pesticides and fungicides in the banana grower's arsenal have widely varying levels of effectiveness on the disease. (Bordeaux mixture is no longer among them; it was banned in the 1960s.) And besides being costly, the spraying of heavy, oil-based products can damage plants. Waste materials leach into watersheds. Most of all, the health of banana workers is severely compromised. A 1999 study of women in banana-packing facilities, conducted by the National University of Costa Rica, found that their rate of leukemia and birth defects was twice the national average. Twenty percent of male Costa Rican banana workers have been left sterile, according to Jeremy Smith, writing in the April 2002 issue of the *Ecologist*. (In 2005 Chiquita, the largest banana company operating in Costa Rica, began adhering to SA8000, a comprehensive series of workplace standards developed by Social Accountability International. Local workers hailed the move—it ended a strike—but banana companies, even after they began expressing an environmental awareness in the 1990s, in general get a mixed grade in worker and environmental protection. Over the past five years, Chiquita has become the banana company with the highest levels of compliance, up and down its supply chain. Other banana growers have good programs in some countries and nonexistent ones in others, usually claiming that they're simply middlemen, buying from contract growers who bear true responsibility for obeying local, and usually poorly enforced, regulations.)

Conventional hybrid breeding has not fared well against Sigatoka. Scientists have created plants that are resistant, but often not by much. The standard Cavendish develops symptoms of Sigatoka in about 222 days. A typical lab-bred variety might last just ninety-six hours more. Even worse, nearly every treatment for the disease is ultimately foiled by the fungi's rapid mutation cycle. Within as little as two or three years, immunity is developed—and the malady returns, ferociously. Quarantine and clean-farming measures can help large-scale plantations but are difficult to maintain in the tiny, randomly distributed plots of African villages or even in places like Ecuador, where hundreds of smaller farmers form the first link in a chain that leads to the global banana packers and our supermarkets. The current approach, a chemical blitzkrieg, means that Sigatoka so far hasn't affected the supply of Cavendish bananas to the United States and Europe, but the sickness has had far-reaching effects in Africa, where even the loss of a few plants per village can have disastrous nutritional consequences.

The real lesson of Sigatoka isn't necessarily in how bananas react to the disease: it is in how the disease reacts to the banana. The cost of the fight against Sigatoka is rapidly pushing against the borderline of benefits, says Adolfo Martinez, the agricultural economist who directs FHIA. "Ten years ago," he told me, as we walked to the Honduran research facility's library, which is situated where there used to be a bowling alley for banana company executives, "we sprayed once or twice a month. Now, we're up to weekly treatments or even more." Those extra applications of Sigatoka-fighting chemicals aren't just bad for the environment and workers. They're also expensive, costing up to an extra $500 per acre every time they're needed. Bananas have to be cheap, and treating them continuously isn't. Something, Martinez says, has to give.

No solution developed in over a century of studying and treating the blight has resulted in anything more than a fruit that is just mildly stronger. Sigatoka's rate of "improvement" is far greater than anything anyone has come up with to fight it. Every remedy results in a more powerful malady. That's a common problem in nearly every aspect of fighting disease, whether in people or plants, and the only reason it hasn't appeared in Panama disease is that there's nothing yet forcing that malady to evolve into stronger and more virulent forms.

If there is an answer—to *all* of these maladies—it lies in the natural pace of evolution and resistance. In order to save the banana, the fruit has to jump a few steps ahead—and there's only one way to do that.

CHAPTER 33

A Banana Crossroads

RONY SWENNEN, the banana scientist who heads the Belgian lab, started out as a conventional banana breeder. He'd just graduated from the Catholic University at Leuven—the same place where he'd later open his banana genetics lab—and he was searching for adventure. "I'd always dreamed of being somewhere very remote," he says. In 1978 the United Nations Food and Agriculture Organization offered him a job in Africa. He'd be attached to one of the continent's most active research organizations, the International Institute of Tropical Agriculture; he'd be traveling through the heart of the continent, collecting banana specimens to send back to Leuven, where they'd be stored for future research. (Belgium has been involved in Africa since the late nineteenth century, when King Leopold II sent explorer Henry Morton Stanley—the rescuer of Dr. David Livingstone—to help set up the colony of the Congo.)

Swennen saw firsthand the devastation Black Sigatoka wrought when it arrived in Africa: Many villages seemed to be on the verge of the doomsday scenario, with their sole source of food in danger of being wiped out. Suddenly, his research developed a very sharp focus. "We had to learn to breed new bananas faster than ever before," Swennen says. He was sent to Nigeria to build a research station. It was there that Swennen made one of the first breakthroughs that shifted the momentum in banana breeding from Honduras to newer research organizations around the world: He determined a way to get more seeds from bananas (at least, those that produce seeds). It turns out that the fruit produces that basic reproductive material in cycles. "If you really observe the plant," Swennen says, "you learn when to look for the seeds—the right days of the year, the right hours of the day." Like most other plants and animals, bananas have a specific fertility rhythm, but it is subtle enough that nobody had detected it. Swennen's techniques—careful, numeric tracking of banana plants and analyzing those numbers to find patterns—resulted in a quantum improvement: Plants that yielded just one or two seeds across a hundred-acre plantation were suddenly producing up to two hundred per bunch.

That led to a revolution in the way bananas were bred. The older method was to mate a wild, seeded fruit with an edible one. That produced plenty of new and interesting hybrids but none that were truly satisfactory, because one half of the happy couple was, by definition, not edible. "It wasn't our intention," Swennen says, "but our results showed that the old way of breeding wasn't entirely sound. The crosses were getting resistance from their 'mothers,' but the [seeded] 'father' gave them very poor fruit."

Swennen's approach was to use fertile plantain varieties—there are about forty in the world—and cross them with the more common sterile fruit. The results were hardier bananas that tasted good. But that still wasn't enough: Swennen's bananas needed further improvement to resist Black Sigatoka, which was the only way they could function either as a hedge against hunger or as the raw material for a commercial fruit. Over the next dozen years, Swennen became one of the most successful—if not *the* most successful—breeders in banana history.

African banana market.

Enough of his bananas were grown in enough places that Swennen was made an honorary chief, complete with ceremonial walking stick. On a shelf in his office in Leuven there's a photo of the young scientist in the full red garb of an African tribal leader. Somewhere in Nigeria, perhaps eating a bred banana, is a young man named Swennen Akauque: when the child was born, a grateful family endowed him with the Belgian researcher's first name.

SUCCESS AT LAST? Honors and tributes aside, and as strong and tasty as Swennen's bananas were, it wasn't enough. In Africa, Swennen noted, "We couldn't just look at resistance." He'd come up with bananas that the disease completely passed over; the fruit would have gorgeous, eighteen-hand bunches—a feast growing on a single tree—but they were twenty-five feet high. That was an unexpect-edly negative attribute, not because tall banana trees are susceptible to high winds—which is more of a problem in Central America—but because they were nearly impossible, in a primitive village, to pick. Another quality his bananas had to have was stiff, erect leaves, since bananas are part of a growing system that also includes cas-sava, cocoa, tobacco, and dozens of other crops and the canopy they provide helps to protect the entire garden plot from the sun. That was something else Swennen hadn't originally thought to breed for. Village fruit is part of a complex agricultural routine that may look haphazard to the average observer but which is in fact the result of generations of local trial and error. "When you're talking about a thousand years of tradition," Swennen says, "anything you intro-duce had better work within that structure."

It wasn't that Swennen didn't believe his bananas could, eventu-ally, have these qualities. But, as with all conventional banana breed-ing before and after, it was taking too long to get results. "That's the banana's drawback—to get a real, wide-scale evaluation, it takes years." With Black Sigatoka and other banana diseases advancing, time was something these tiny villages, and the rest of the world, was running out of.

In 1993 Swennen returned to Belgium. He still misses the adven-ture of the field, but he now believes that conventional breeding methods just won't cut it—that saving the banana is something that can only be accomplished in the lab.

CROSSBREEDING AND BIOTECHNOLOGY are both forms of ge-netic manipulation. The first has been effective and widespread for thousands and thousands of years. Changing life-forms by directly manipulating their DNA, however, is such a new technology that most scientists believe only a tiny fraction of what needs to be un-derstood about it has so far been discovered. Even so, industrial agri-culture is exposing the public to such technologies (often without disclosure) with daily frequency. In 2000, 90 percent of the corn Americans ate was bioengineered, as were more than half the soybeans, according to the U.S. Department of Agriculture. Both numbers have increased since then.

The acronym GMO (genetically modified organism) is used as a blanket term for nearly all forms of food biotech, though it is technically less than accurate since genetic modification is also the basis of conventional breeding methods. Nevertheless, the term has stuck, and I will use it here instead of proposed but less familiar substitutes like transgenics, *GM foods*, or *GM crops*. Creating a GMO is a complex process. But the basics can be explained fairly simply: Genes from one organism that carry specific traits—resistance to a disease, increased size, or more rapid maturation—are added to the genetic material of another. The organisms can be vastly different, such as DNA from a bacterium added to tomatoes, or relatively similar, like crossing radishes with bananas (such a mixture is currently being studied for providing resistance to fusarium fungus).

The techniques are precise—microscopic tools make researchers in the field the modern equivalent of Swiss watchmakers—but the basics you learned in high school biology are the same. You'll recall that chromosomes are sort of a package for DNA; every living thing has a specific number of chromosome pairs—in nature, for the most part, one from each parent. Human-influenced crops can be different: A and B sequenced bananas can contain two or three sets of chromosomes. Cavendish contains three.

The DNA is arranged in the chromosome in wrapped strands. The commonly used analogy is a spool of thread; if a strand of human DNA was pulled straight, it would be about the height of Yao Ming, currently the tallest player in the NBA. If DNA is one of the "building blocks" of life—containing a blueprint for an organism's specific traits (like the ability to hear or see, or thickness of skin)—then the genes it is made up of are the workers that execute the blueprint by creating specific proteins that assemble to form the structure that supports the trait, whether on an individual level, to make hemoglobin, the protein that allows blood to carry oxygen through the body, or in concert, as multiple proteins gather to form an eye or an elephant or a banana plant. Sometimes genes mutate. A hemoglobin mutation causes sickle cell trait, and it was probably a mutation that initially yielded a seedless banana thousands of years ago.

Understanding genetic modification requires shifting the metaphor. Instead of a spool of thread, imagine that chromosomes are an old-fashioned film reel—the kind that used to jam up the projectors in that same biology class. The film wrapped around the reel is made up of individual frames. If the frames are genes, then creating a GMO involves splicing the genes from one movie, perhaps *Gone with the Wind*, into another—let's say *Star Wars*. The result is something that should contain the best qualities of both: Rhett Butler played by Harrison Ford and Scarlet O'Hara with a cinnamon-bun hairstyle.

If you're using handy, expensive lab toys, the cut-and-paste job isn't all that difficult. The hard part is determining which gene performs what function. That was the purpose of the human genome project—launched in 1990 and completed in 2003—that mapped the approximately 25,000 genes contained within the human body (the function of each and every gene is far from known, but having the map has allowed thousands of scientists around the world to begin individual and highly specialized efforts to determine and take advantage of that information).

Mapping of the banana genome was begun in 2001 by a consortium of twenty-seven publicly funded organizations in thirteen countries. The goal was to have the entire banana genetic sequence—using a wild Asian banana as the base material—decoded within five to ten years. The banana is only the third major crop to undergo gene sequencing. The first was rice—though rice lags behind wheat and corn in global consumption, there are more people absolutely dependent on it, as with the banana in Africa—completed in 2005. (Rice contains about 37,000 genes. The 25,000 found in Homo sapiens is double that in a fruit fly and about the same as in the Japanese *fugu* puffer fish; the seaborne creature's genes contain the recipe for a deadly toxin, which kills several hundred Japanese diners a year as they eat the fish, which has to be precisely sliced in order to avoid the poison in its liver and skin.)

The first concrete results of the banana genome project came in 2005, when researchers announced they'd mapped more than half of the banana's genes (the project is on track to be completed by the end of 2008). About five thousand of those genes were decoded by Brazilian scientists, who said they'd found twenty that could potentially be used to bestow disease resistance on cultivated bananas. That may sound like a small number, but that total has already made the process forty thousand times more efficient than the million-to-one success rate yielded by the manual search for seeds required in traditional breeding.

IN THE DOCTOR'S OFFICE-LIKE BASEMENT of the Leuven lab, I am looking directly at some of those genes—though without a microscope, they look like little more than a flask of water. Serge Remy, one of the Leuven researchers, is taking me on a step-by-step walk-through of the banana-manipulation process. The flask contains thousands of banana cells, derived from one of the 1,200 varieties cryogenically preserved at the Belgian facility; each cell can mature into a plant, using a process similar to the one that yields banana embryos at FHIA. But rather than simply growing these cells into baby bananas, Remy is using them as base material for what geneticists term *transformation*.

Though cut-and-paste is a good metaphor for the process, the actual procedure isn't done with an X-Acto knife and glue. Most modern transformation of plants, including bananas, is accomplished two ways. The first technique involves brute force: In a process called "particle bombardment," tiny pieces of gold or tungsten are coated with DNA and blasted at high velocity into living plant cells or embryos. The shooting can be done with miniature air guns, mechanical devices (think of toy cannons), or via magnetic or electrical discharge. The most subtle and ingenious way to carry transforming material into a test organism is by using bacteria. Remy holds up the flask and taps on it, as if I could see what he's about to explain: "We use bacteria that are naturally found in soil," he says. The bacteria carries the material with the desired trait into the host's DNA. The bacteria attaches itself to the cells and will (if it works; success isn't guaranteed) ultimately turn up—the formal term is *express*—in the growing plants. "It really is pretty neat," Remy adds, pointing at the flask again. All I see is water, but I nod my head in agreement.

The part that I thought was coolest came next. The biggest problem with a conventional hybrid banana, as I learned both from Swennen and during my visit to Honduras, is time. With a conventional hybrid, you've got to wait weeks or even years for a growing plant to emerge. Even then, you'll need several generations to determine if the qualities you've tried to breed into the new banana actually exist. With genetic transformation, that information can be obtained in just days or hours. The trick is to create flags, or markers, that indicate whether a change has occurred. These markers are supplementary genes that impart an additional, easy-to-see quality to the transformed organism. A common marker gene is one that confers resistance to antibiotics. Scientists insert the marker, and then dose the transformed organism with the antibiotic. Only the ones that have picked up resistance will survive; the marker gene acts as an indicator that the real-deal genes have actually come along for the ride. Other marker genes are called "reporter" genes. They provide a visual cue that the transformation has taken place. Some reporters genes actually emit light—like a firefly—when activated. You can see them glowing in the dark.

REMY AND I MOVE AWAY FROM THE TEST TUBES, toward a container filled with petri dishes. These microbananas are a week old, and many are turning black, succumbing to the bacteria. They'll soon be discarded. For the next four months, the winnowing process will continue; after six months, the cells will have become plantlets and are transferred to test tubes.

After a year in vitro, the infant bananas head out to the field. At this point, the process becomes more traditional. Genetic transformation of bananas is efficient in the early stages because you can produce thousands of transformed organisms very quickly. Once the plants start to look like plants, the growth pattern is the same as with any other banana. "You need to see the plant go through several cycles, probably five years," Remy says, "in order to find out if what you've been trying to obtain is actually there and functional."

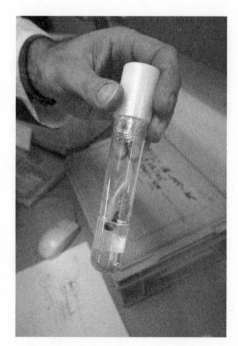

A test-tube banana, at the Belgian banana genetics lab.

Or that's the way it should work. I ask Remy if there's any place I can go to see those test-tube fruits actually growing on a plantation. He frowns. He's bombarded and vectored tens of thousands of genes into a never-ending parade of test tubes and petri dishes. "I'm talking about the ideal timeline," he says. "But that's not the way it works at the moment."

I ask him why. His frown deepens. "It has nothing to do with science," he says.

CHAPTER 34

Frankenbanana

THE WORD PHIL ROWE USED to describe the banana's receptivity to conventional breeding was "intractable." He meant "stubborn." When time is short, it would be more accurate to say: *impossible*. The first epidemic of Panama disease appeared in a less-connected world and took most of a century to run its course—and even then conventional banana-breeding methods crawled along, unable to keep pace. Black Sigatoka spread across Africa in less than a decade, reducing crop efficiency by more than two-thirds by the 1980s. Panama disease has been on the move for about twenty years now. That malady's boundaries—China to the east, India to the west, and all the way through Australia to the south—cover a much larger range than Africa's. Its speed is especially disconcerting given the bodies of water separating the afflicted areas.

Since the traditional method of creating hybrids—hand pollinating, hunting for seeds in thousands of bananas, and then searching for the right qualities in millions of fruit—takes so long, today's banana producers must rely on external techniques to build resistance to ailments. That means practices that look much like those used in the past by United Fruit and the rest of the early banana industry: New plantations in virgin forest; applications of chemicals; environmental damage—the cycle that began a century ago continues. When an airborne blight strikes, the malady must be fought with expensive applications of chemicals, dumped from the sky.

The banana has changed the world, but for all practical purposes, it can't change itself, and it has so far not cooperated with human efforts to make it turn a new leaf. The techniques being developed by the scientists in Leuven and at similar labs around the world—in Australia, Canada, Brazil, India, and a dozen other countries—may be the banana's only hope.

But something strange happens when the mechanics of banana biotechnology are explained. Scientists like Swennen and Remy see it all the time. So did I as I was researching this book.

People become uncomfortable. Even scared. When they learn about modifying a Polynesian banana to contain extra quantities of vitamin A, they seem to approve. When they learn that the marker genes come from fishes (it's true), they're horrified. It doesn't matter that none of this foreign genetic material would actually get into a growing banana plant (no more than a socket wrench would get into your car's oil supply after you've visited a Jiffy Lube). People cringe. They don't like the idea of marine life, or any member of the animal kingdom, having anything to do with a banana. "Don't mix anything that has eyes with my fruit," one friend told me when I described the process to her.

Even straightforward banana-improvement projects—only affecting taste or ripening or the ability to fight in-the-field maladies—unnerve a large number of consumers. Crosses with radishes and, of all things, azaleas may help bananas resist Panama disease, since varieties of both of the added plants fight fungus fairly well. Other lab-bred bananas have successfully overcome Sigatoka or gained more controllable ripening and nearly bruise-proof flesh.

Yet, the truth is that it *is* unnatural to mix fish with fruit, no matter how harmless; the idea of a vegetable meeting a banana is less discomforting, but it still *feels* like something beyond the normal.

"Genetic transformation," Rony Swennen says, "is revolution, not evolution."

For Swennen and his colleagues, that's a good thing. But for groups against the genetic modification of food—including well-known environmental organizations like Greenpeace and Friends of the Earth—the idea of speeding up, or even replacing, natural processes that have evolved over thousands of years seems like a very bad idea. Lab-made products are often referred to in the media, and by these groups, as "Frankenfoods." Those using the term typically accompany it with a curdling litany of what sound like edible monstrosities: "Potatoes with bacteria genes, 'super' pigs with human growth genes, fish with cattle growth genes, tomatoes with flounder genes, and thousands of other plants, animals and insects," according to a report from the Center for Food Safety, a Washington DC–based advocacy group. The risks of those products, the group argues, extend to "humans, domesticated animals, wildlife and the environment. Human health effects can include higher risks of toxicity, allergenicity, antibiotic resistance, immune-suppression and cancer. As for environmental impacts, the use of genetic engineering in agriculture will lead to uncontrolled biological pollution, threatening numerous microbial, plant and animal species with extinction, and the potential contamination of all non–genetically engineered life forms with novel and possibly hazardous genetic material."

That's scary. But it is also overblown, according to James K. M. Brown of Britain's John Innes Centre, an independent research center specializing in plant science and microbiology. "There is no good evidence that, in itself, GM technology harms the safety of food," Brown says. Some of the issues cited by anti-GM forces are clearly bogus: The use of bacteria, for example, is not inherently dangerous—bacteria are found everywhere; they're a natural and desired part of yogurt, for example, and adding them to products ranging from soft drinks to candy bars is currently a trendy way to get consumers to spend more money in the supermarket (those products are usually described as "probiotic"). The claim that more people might be allergic to genetically modified foods comes from a study of soybeans crossed with Brazil nuts. The resulting soybeans did exhibit signs of allergenicity, but that wasn't a surprise, since many people already have an allergic reaction to Brazil nuts (in fact, says Brown, this is a *good* result, because it "implies that other proteins . . . such as oral vaccines, should also retain their useful properties when expressed in different plants").

The current distribution—and regulation—of biotech crops around the world is mixed. The United States is the world's most GMO-loaded country. The 123 million acres of transformed crops we grow each year is more than the quantity produced by every other country on earth combined. We also eat more biotech food than anywhere else. Some estimates claim that more than half of the processed foods we consume contain GMO ingredients. One of the reasons our food supply is so laden with such products is that development of them is encouraged by the government, and food labels here, unlike in most of the industrialized world, aren't required to reveal whether, or what, GMO ingredients the product contains (food manufacturers are, however, required to disclose whether or not allergens are contained in their products, which is why you see peanut warnings on everything from loaves of bread to ice cream).

In Europe the situation is reversed. Though limited development of biotech crops is allowed—researchers have to follow a rigorous permitting and monitoring process—the sale of such foods is almost completely banned. If a GM product is sold, it has to be labeled as such, which tends to make shoppers run away. That bodes poorly for engineered bananas. In 2000, Fyffes—the former United Fruit subsidiary that is one of Europe's biggest banana importers—surveyed British shoppers, asking if they'd be willing to purchase GM bananas: 82 percent of the respondents said they absolutely wouldn't. Del Monte has said it will never market transformed bananas; Chiquita and Dole have been less committal, but so far they've pledged that nothing on the market is currently modified. It is unlikely that a major banana company would undertake production of a GM fruit if most of the world's consumers would refuse, or even be unable, to accept them (yet another criteria added to the long list of things that *don't* make a commercial banana viable).

That's why researchers like Swennen and Remy also find it nearly impossible to conduct field tests on their experimental plants. Many countries ban them completely. "For a scientist," says Remy, "that's hell." Until recently, there was no place on earth to test engineered bananas outside of greenhouses and laboratories. Halfway through 2007, Ugandan researchers announced that they'd accepted engineered Belgian bananas and were allowing a small test plantation—just a few acres—to be established outside Kampala. There were different opinions on how Ugandans might react to the project. "People have more pressing concerns, like the rebellion in the north, AIDS, droughts and poverty," Richard Markham, director of the Commodities for Livelihoods program at Bioversity International (formerly INIBAP), told *Nature* magazine. But Godber Tumushabe, of Uganda's Advocates Coalition for Development and Environment, was quoted in the same article as saying that there is debate over biotech in his country. Though it has "died down in recent years," he says, "when field trials begin, it could start again." (Swennen, for his part, couldn't have been happier; he sent me an excited e-mail immediately after his permissions came through: "YESTERDAY!!!" he wrote, "we shipped the first transgenic plants to Uganda!")

Despite skepticism, the use of biotech crops has been growing steadily, more than tripling in both developing and industrialized nations since 2000. That increase has led to the development of an international standard that regulates the use and production of genetically modified foods. The Cartagena Protocol on Biosafety requires producers of genetically modified foods to accurately label their output while adopting "precautionary" measures in research, growing, and transport. Every crop-growing European nation has

signed or ratified the agreement. In the Americas, the only countries that are not protocol signatories are Bolivia—and the United
States.

Those opposed to biotechnology point out that the U.S. Congress
has never adopted any form of legislation related to GM foods, argu-
ing that, in fact, they're beholden to special interests, much as parts
of the U.S. government were linked to banana companies through the
1950s. The lack of any sort of labeling requirements seems—even to
those in favor of biotech—like good evidence for that charge.

Yet the villains opponents usually point to, like companies that
develop proprietary seeds, which lock farms into a sort of agribusi-
ness indenture (the seeds are designed to produce plants with limited reproductive cycles, forcing farmers to repurchase growing
materials each season) don't exist in the banana world, where research is mostly conducted by publicly funded institutions and is
aimed at hunger relief rather than commercial interests. Scientists
working on the banana genome have signed agreements that any
transformed fruit derived from their work must remain in the public domain, which would eliminate the "lock-in" effect of proprietary crops.

Bananas are also likely not subject to the "genie from the bottle"
issue that biotech opponents cite—the idea that releasing modified
foods into the environment will allow bizarre mutations to escape
into the wild, having potentially devastating effects on health and
the environment. That's virtually impossible with bananas, for the
same reason reengineering the fruit is so difficult: Bananas are sterile. A banana engineered for human consumption would, by definition, contain no seeds or pollen. The means by which a stray crop
could escape into the wild and contaminate traditional crops (this
has happened with corn in many parts of the world, with the local
crops becoming so hybridized that it becomes impossible to determine their true provenance) don't exist in bananas. It is difficult to
see how the returns yielded by modified bananas couldn't far out-
weigh either their real or speculative risks, especially in Africa.

"The bottom line," says Swennen, "is that bananas need bio-technology." That's especially true for the Cavendish. "I don't see any other way to save it."

Far from any point at which the results of these breeding experiments could be determined—and absent all but the most limited trials to hasten those findings—the banana, this weak, essential food, is in danger of fading away. Already, banana production in some parts of Africa is down by more than 60 percent, thanks to Black Sigatoka, Panama disease, and a dozen other major banana maladies. Swennen is not reserved in his opinions. He explains that it was the spread of Sigatoka in Nigeria, and the frustration he faced as a conventional breeder, that finally convinced him that his best chance was in the lab. Those who oppose the attempt to engineer a better banana, he says, are against something that would—that has to—protect millions of people. On a winter day in Belgium, a dozen meters from the greenhouse that is the only place in the world where many of these strengthened bananas are allowed to grow, Swennen spoke two words, forcefully, for the people who didn't understand what was at stake, then repeated them to make sure I'd understood.

"They're wrong," he said. "They're wrong."

CHAPTER 35

Still the Octopus?

I N THE MID 1980s, while Rony Swennen was beginning to grow bananas in Nigeria—laying the groundwork for today's multinational effort to improve the fruit not for commercial purposes but to feed the hungry—United Brands had entered a steep decline. The once-powerful banana company was still selling lots of fruit, but it continued to be unable to manage itself. CEOs came and went. In 1984, a year after the company announced a $200 million loss, *Fortune* magazine offered a bleak assessment: "For more than a decade, United Brands has looked as appealing to investors as a black banana."

There was a certain irony to Chiquita's solution. For most of its history, the company had argued that developing nations *needed* dictatorial regimes. It was the only way the engines of progress could continue to run smoothly. Now, it was the fruit company itself that searched, once again, for a strongman.

It found one in Carl Lindner.

The Ohio native fit with the United Fruit tradition. He was a self-made billionaire whose first business experience was running his family's ice cream parlor and dairy store after the 1952 death of his father. Lindner then expanded the homespun enterprise into a chain of convenience stores—United Dairy Farms still operates throughout the Midwest—and reinvested his profits until his American Financial Group owned several of the country's largest insurance and banking companies (including the Great American Insurance Company and the Provident Financial Group) along with real estate throughout the United States (which today includes the air rights to develop open space above New York's Grand Central Station. Anything built there would stand adjacent to the MetLife tower, the building Eli Black leapt from).

Lindner began purchasing United Brands stock in 1973 and, like Zemurray, watched as his holdings declined in value.

But Lindner didn't see Chiquita's decline as terrible news. As a self-described "bottom feeder," he loved finding companies that were—through mismanagement, bad luck, and competitive pressure—worth far less than he believed they could be. In 1984 Lindner took control of the company.

The ice cream and insurance mogul made the usual changes. He sold subsidiaries that were deemed unimportant to the company's banana business. He cut costs, moving the corporate headquarters from New York (Black had relocated the business from Boston) to his home base of Cincinnati, where it remains today, and further reinforced the company's branding efforts by officially changing the name from United Brands to Chiquita in 1992.

What the Lindner era most brought back was aggression. It wasn't the all-encompassing muscle the company wielded through most of the twentieth century, but there were times when it resembled it: In 1994, near Tela, Honduras, Chiquita closed Tacamiche, a company town for sixty years. The company said it was abandoning the village because of poor soil conditions; opponents argued that the move was

part of the company's strategy of reducing plantation ownership in
Latin America in order to work with contractors, who wouldn't be
subject to the kind of labor oversight a multinational corporation
might draw. When the residents refused to move, bulldozers—
escorted by bayonet-wielding Honduran military police—arrived
and razed the entire town. Six hundred people—138 families—were
made homeless.

Lindner's outward personality was more like Black's than Zemurray's. He didn't swear, drink, or smoke. One account described him as
"mild-mannered and shy." Lindner's trademark was to offer gold-
flecked cards, embossed with slogans, to folks he was meeting for the
first time. One says: "Only in America. Gee, am I lucky." Another reads:
"I like to do my giving while I'm living, so I know where it's going."

But the Lindner era, despite his single-minded leadership, continued the Chiquita seesaw. It was as if the company were caught
between two worlds: the old one, where it wielded absolute power,
and a new one, in which corporations needed to conduct activities
more strategically and even try to do some good. That back-
and-forth was demonstrated in 1998. The company agreed to a Guatemala City meeting with representatives of each Central American
banana workers' union—something that would have been unthinkable a few decades earlier. The union advocates presented the banana giant with a proposal for a region-wide initiative that would
improve labor conditions and raise environmental standards.

The company patted itself on the back for coming to the bar-
gaining table—but refused to make a single concession. Three years
later, the company veered back into contrition. It negotiated an
agreement with the Central American unions and created its part-
nership with the Rainforest Alliance, which agreed to certify environmental practices at the farms Chiquita owned. This was progress,
given the prior three decades of plantation divestment. (Today,
Chiquita has instituted uniform standards throughout the supply
chain; it is the only banana company to do so. Critics say those standards aren't consistently enforced.)

But the biggest battle the company once known as United Fruit had to fight as it moved toward the new millennium had nothing to do with workers on strike, the destruction of rain forest, or even the American breakfast table. It is a conflict that continues today. On the surface, it seems like a pure business matter. But like the industry's earliest expansion, it portends dire consequences for the world's banana crop.

IT BEGAN IN 1993. Europe had unified and in doing so had become an even bigger market for bananas than the United States. (Not by much: Continental consumption averages about 30 million tons of the fruit annually versus 26 million tons in the United States.) Among the lesser-known elements of Europe's consolidation were programs designed to aid former colonies. That included the Caribbean banana plantations Chiquita had mostly abandoned as Panama disease moved from island to island. Now, those small farms, growing Cavendish but no longer owned by Chiquita, were given preferential treatment by European governments—the measures were designed to ensure the economic health of those now-independent countries. The result? Chiquita, which had held 20 percent of the European market, suddenly found itself with less than half that. The company had to do something with all those excess bananas, so it sold them in the United States, creating a banana glut that caused prices to plummet.

Chiquita's lawyers and lobbyists argued that the European regulations were both unfair and illegal under World Trade Organization rules, a case of government policy mandating preferential treatment to specific companies in what was supposed to be an open market. Lindner went directly to U.S. officials—at that time, the Clinton administration—and in 1996 the United States lodged an official protest with the agency. The day after Lindner's meeting with administration officials, the banana mogul donated $500,000 to the Democratic Party.

One of the things that seemed to be forgotten in the fight was *why* the European tariffs were enacted in the first place: to help the banana-growing islands keep jobs and emerge from poverty. In an interview, one Dominican farmer imagined the consequences of an outcome favorable to Chiquita, which would return the banana industry to the grown-where-they're-cheapest status quo: "If they squeeze us out, we will be the ones that will suffer. When you take away a man's daily bread, you take away my livelihood. You send me to common crime. You force me to [traffic in] drugs."

At the height of the battle, Chiquita scored a minor victory at home, with a tactic that was familiarly heavy-handed. In 1998 an article nearly twenty pages long appeared in the *Cincinnati Enquirer*. It painted the company not as one that was merely in turmoil or pursuing policies that resembled those it had embraced in the past. Instead, the story alleged, the system that led to the banana republics still existed: Chiquita ships were being used (without company knowledge) to import cocaine; environmental damage and labor exploitation were as bad as ever; and there was just as much behind-the-scenes interference with government, at home and abroad, as there was in the past.

The story—which can still be found on the Internet—was a direct attack on everything the company had ever been, and, in the estimation of the writers, everything it still was. It was the boldest assault on the United Fruit legacy ever mounted.

It did not turn out well for the press. One of the reporters was found to have gained illegal access to the banana company's voice-mail system. The reporter was fired and criminal charges were brought against him. Another reporter resigned. The paper's top editor was transferred. In a front-page correction, the *Enquirer* disavowed the stories, declaring them "false and misleading," and paid the banana company a settlement that the *Columbia Journalism Review* estimated at $14 million. Later, it was revealed that the agreement included restrictions that amounted to the newspaper promising to *never* write about Lindner or any of his businesses again. *Editor & Publisher*, the print-journalism industry trade journal, said that the *Enquirer* "turned over editorial control of its newsroom to Chiquita." Other media, in analyzing the story, found the apology odd. The *New York Times* noted that nobody "disputed the authenticity of the . . . Chiquita records that formed the basis of the most sensational allegations."

But the fight against negative press, as pitched as it was, amounted to little more than a sideline compared to the battle against Europe. At the company's urging, a tit-for-tat trade war began. Europe raised duties on American steel. The United States imposed charges on European cheeses, wines, and luxury goods. Once again, the interests of a banana company had an effect that reverberated far beyond the fruit aisles.

Did it work?

In 1997 Dole once again surpassed Chiquita in market share. Chiquita would never again solely dominate the world's banana sales. It would, and continues to, swap the title with its longtime rival.

Americans still loved bananas. We showed no sign of making apples our favorite snack (though Pringles were another story). Banana growers continued to face the pressures they always had. There were hurricanes, labor unrest, and taxes—the same things that prompted Sam Zemurray to wrest control of Honduras, the same things that turned United Fruit into a symbol of overreaching, blindness, and cruelty.

In 2002, after more than a century in business, after four different names and billions of bananas sold, Chiquita declared bankruptcy. It would never be an ordinary company. It would never stop being *the* banana company. But it would be a humbled one.

CARL LINDNER WAS THE LAST IN A LINE of strongmen who ran— sometimes for the public good, sometimes simply for profit, but most memorably out of pride and greed—United Fruit. The Lindner era ended, appropriately enough, with a frank—perhaps for the first time ever—admission on the part of the company. While previous corporate histories had omitted or quickly glossed over the company's checkered past, a new document, issued as part of a "corporate responsibility report" alluded, for the first time, to the company's *real* history—to the Octopus. (Such documents are offered by companies wishing to highlight the good they do. The issuance of such a report usually comes with the creation of an in-house oversight position. Whether these efforts are meaningful or just image doctoring varies.)

The 2003 report, 103 pages long, was—by American corporate standards—blisteringly frank. It began with a bold headline that read "Our Complex History," under which the company attempted to summarize a century of adventures in a bit more than one hundred words:

> It is often interesting to look back at a company's history, to understand its roots and how it has evolved. In Chiquita's case, that look back is both inspiring and humbling.
>
> The Company has spurred much economic and social progress in rural communities in Latin America, where it has consistently been a leader and innovator in the development of the banana industry. But its predecessor companies, including the United Fruit Company, also made a number of mistakes—including the use of improper government influence, antagonism toward organized labor, and disregard for the environment. These actions clearly would not live up to the Core Values we hold today or to the expectations of our stakeholders.
>
> Today, we are a different Company. But we acknowledge our complex past as a way to begin an honest dialogue about our present and our future. It is humbling to consider the impacts—both positive and negative—that a corporation can have. At the same time, it is uplifting to note the distance a company can travel.

The report went on to firmly establish, for the first time, a genuine ethics policy—and how it would be enforced—for the banana giant.

When I first read this statement, it struck me as an earnest, yet fitful embrace of more principled behavior. Though some activists argued otherwise, saying that the company's supposed reforms were more show than substance, Chiquita was generally perceived as having come a long way.

But in the past few years, that progress has slowed. The annual responsibility report has gotten smaller and smaller; it is now folded into the company's general annual report. In 2006 it spanned just three pages, with additional material online. What appeared to be an earnest attempt to do good now looks like a press release.

I don't know for sure whether this diminishment was intentional or just emblematic of a recidivist corporate culture, whose ill doings would be fully revealed in March 2007, when the U.S. Department of Justice announced that the banana company had admitted to dealings with groups Washington officially lists as terrorist organizations. From 1997 through 2004, the Justice Department found, Chiquita paid $1.7 million to the United Self-Defense Forces of Colombia, known in that country as the AUC.

The AUC is one of the most violent outlaw groups on the planet. According to *Forbes* magazine, the organization, which controls a private army of 15,000 troops, is involved in "kidnapping, torture, disappearance, rape, murder, beatings, extortion, and drug trafficking."

In 2001 Chiquita's own lawyers determined that the payments were illegal and warned that they had to be stopped. Management ignored the advice, instead converting the remittances from checks to cash. In April 2007, the company's current CEO, Fernando Aguirre, wrote a three-page article that appeared on the U.S. Chamber of Commerce's Web site. The document was an odd combination of what appeared to be both genuine anguish—and ignorance. He wrote about the general environment of extortion and murder in Colombia. If Chiquita wanted to protect its Colombian employees, he said, it had to "make protection payments to safeguard our workforce." When it was discovered that the payments were illegal, he said, it created "a dilemma of more than theoretical proportions for us: The company could stop making the payments, complying with the law but putting the lives of our workers in immediate jeopardy; or we could keep our workers out of harm's way while violating American law."

For three years, Chiquita chose the latter. Finally, in 2004 the company "found a business solution to our dilemma," Aguirre wrote: It sold its Colombia assets. (The company continues to buy Colombian bananas from its former division; you can find them in your supermarket.)

WHAT THE BANANA INDUSTRY NEEDS, and faces, has changed little since the early days. Chiquita still fights Dole; banana consumption is still increasing worldwide; the fruit is still sliced into cereal. Bananas still need to be grown and transported cheaply in order to be sold cheaply. The biggest obstacle in the equation remains disease. More chemicals are being used to fight Sigatoka, and more workers are getting sick. Over the past several years, five lawsuits were filed against Dole on behalf of banana workers in Costa Rica, Nicaragua, Guatemala, Honduras, and Panama. The suits alleged that the former Standard Fruit had, since the 1970s, knowingly used a pesticide called DBCP—mostly to fight Black Sigatoka—that made workers sterile (the chemical is banned in the United States). In August 2007, Dole CEO David DeLorenzo testified in a Los Angeles courtroom that his company safeguarded the health of workers by instituting screening programs and offering free medical care. Company documents uncovered during the case confirmed that the fruit importer did test employees—and also ignored reports that came back positive. At one point, Dow Chemical, the manufacturer of DBCP, told Dole that the chemical was dangerous and that it would no longer sell it to the banana producers. Dole threatened Dow with a breach-of-contract lawsuit, and the spraying continued. The court case is ongoing.

Many banana workers continue to find themselves in desperate straits, especially in Ecuador, the world's largest producer of Cavendish bananas. In that country, plantation conditions remain primitive, and worker protection laws—including those against child labor—are poorly enforced.

Over the past decade, Ecuador seems to have teetered on the edge of returning to the era of old-style banana republics. In 1999 the country defaulted on its foreign debt and was forced to eliminate its own currency, adopting the U.S. dollar. Ecuador has had eight presidents in the past ten years. But for the moment, the country seems to be pulling itself back into shape. The country's 2006 presidential elections saw a former finance minister, Rafael Correa, go up against the nation's richest private citizen, Álvaro Noboa. If you've looked carefully at the bananas you buy at your local grocery, you may have noticed a sticker identifying some with the Bonita brand name. That banana company is owned by Noboa. In the United States, government officials noted that they were watching the election closely, and that the election of Correa—who promised to close a U.S. military base in Ecuador—would be considered troublesome. Those pronouncements contained echoes of the past, but this time they contributed to Noboa's loss. Almost 60 percent of Ecuadorans cast their votes for Correa. In a nationally broadcast radio address in January 2006, the new president outlined his reformist agenda. What he would do, he said, was "end these mafias that have plundered the country."

Once again, it was not hard to hear echoes of the past in the pronouncement, and it was not hard to imagine who he was talking about.

CHAPTER 36

The Way Out

W HAT MAY BE MOST IMPORTANT about bananas isn't that they've started wars but that they can also help end them. The two banana worlds—ours, where we *want* the fruit, and the other, where people *need* it—are merging in many ways. But with the growth of commercial plantations and the concurrent spread of disease, it is important to remember that, no matter how much we love our bananas, the latter world is much more important, and the choices we make reverberate through both of them.

A crisis hit Africa in the late 1990s. Hundreds of thousands of people were killed, and millions were left displaced or homeless. The ethnic bloodshed that spread across Rwanda and Burundi captured the world's attention with accounts of bloody ethnic warfare and large-scale massacres, but in the refugee camps that sprung up in Tanzania following the conflict, the issue was more pragmatic: The survivors were hungry.

They needed bananas.

Foreign food aid was arriving—but too slowly and often in the form of products (wheat flour or rice) that were impossible to prepare easily in the vast, primitive camps. Even if those foods could help solve immediate hunger, they could ultimately make the situation worse. "People can't grow those crops in places like that," Swennen says. Thus, a situation of constant delivery—and ultimate dependence—emerges. "These are banana people, living on banana land," Swennen explains. "The only way to feed all of them, and to help them get out of the camps, was to give them something not just to eat—but to grow."

AS REAL, AND SIMPLE, as Swennen's solution sounds, making it happen seemed like a remote possibility. Since the arrival of Black Sigatoka in the African lakes region in the 1970s, it had been tearing through crops in Uganda, Tanzania, Rwanda, and Burundi. In the commercial world, Sigatoka can be battled with chemicals. Though treatment must become more aggressive as the leaf-destroying fungus becomes more resistant, our banana supply has remained constant. But most of Africa's bananas are grown in family plots, where spraying is impractical and too expensive. Instead, local villagers find themselves playing a high-stakes game: growing more bananas in an effort to get the yields needed to prevent starvation. The situation was especially bad in the region holding the Tanzanian refugee camps; that area was hard hit by banana maladies. "They were lucky to get 40 percent of plants to actually bear fruit," says Swennen. "Most never make it—they just fall over."

As discussed earlier, one of Swennen's first projects when he returned to the lab from Africa in 1993 was to create a banana that resisted Sigatoka. And he had remarkable results, coming up with multiple varieties that successfully avoided the disease. Swennen knew that even if only a small number of people adopted his fruit, it would have a major impact on hunger. Swennen also knew that with bananas so easy to grow, adoption by a few could lead to adoption by millions.

Yet Swennen faced the same problem that he does today: getting permission to test the fruit, even though the bananas he hoped to plant in Tanzania were developed using conventional modification methods (Phil Rowe's embryo rescue combined with the techniques Swennen developed to increase yield). The United States was also pushing for Africa to allow commercially modified products—corn and soy—to be imported to the continent. But the European Union was (as it is now) generally against the use of such foods and implied that African nations that allowed modified crops to be grown might be restricted from importing any agricultural goods across the Mediterranean for fear of cross-crop contamination.

"It wasn't just banana researchers like me caught in the middle," Swennen says. "It was millions of people."

Swennen thought his bananas could be an answer for the refugees; he thought they could be an answer for Africa. And he thinks they can be an answer for Panama disease. As the Rwandan crisis continued, Swennen traveled to the refugee camps and border areas. Fighting was still going on in some places; he recalls seeing houses burning and families fleeing in panic. The scientist knew he had to talk to local people, no matter how desperate the situation, to find out what the banana they needed would have to be like. As with the commercial Cavendish, an ideal African banana had requirements: It needed to be familiar enough to grow using existing techniques; It had to taste good and work as an ingredient in staple dishes like *matoke*; and it had to resist the maladies that had already spread, and continued to spread, across the region.

Back in Belgium, Swennen chose two dozen modified varieties, his own and from other labs (including FHIA), picking those he thought would yield fruit that was both resistant to Black Sigatoka and that would fit smoothly into traditional diets. The next step would be to take the chosen varieties back to Africa and test them in the field.

It took two years—two years of hunger, for those waiting in the camps—for officials to finally allow the trials. Finally, in 1997, fifty demonstration fields (the number needed to be high because twenty-one banana varieties were being tested) were set up in Tanzania's Kagera region. The miniature plantations were located on the grounds of churches, rural health facilities, and schools—anyplace where a community could work together to see the plants through the testing process.

The trial did get one unexpected boost: The bananas were good enough that local farmers began to secretly enter the plantations at night. They'd grab what fruit they could and plant it on their family farms—a process that greatly accelerated overall acceptance of Swennen's modified bananas.

Eventually, the farmers participating in the test chose fourteen acceptable fruits for wider distribution. "It was important," Swennen says, "that they picked what they wanted to grow." Swennen and his colleagues went back to the lab again and created seventy thousand plantlets in test tubes; these were moved to a series of Tanzanian demonstration fields, where they multiplied, and multiplied again. At each step, local farmers and families were brought in to test the fruit, to see if it would fit into traditional recipes and farming methods. The visitors weren't just impressed with how the fruit resisted Sigatoka. They were also astonished at the mammoth bunches the Belgian bananas produced. The bunches weighed 165 pounds, on average—five times more than was typical for equivalent village fruit. Finally, a well-intentioned outside organization was making food the way the people it was trying to help made food.

In 2000, the pool was reduced to just the few most desirable varieties. Swennen then offered to give the bananas to local farmers, under one condition: that they distribute the plants to their neighbors. Over the next three years, Swennen's bananas grew; they remained Sigatoka-free and helped restore agriculture across war-torn regions. The project was officially declared a success in 2003—it would no longer need to be monitored scientifically. "When we left," Swennen said, "2.5 million of our plants were growing."

In the end, Swennen estimates, 500,000 people benefited from the plants. That's about ten times more than a similar effort using nonresistant fruit might yield, but it still was just 2 percent of the region's banana crop. What Swennen hopes is that his bananas will spread, just as the first bananas did in Africa, more than a thousand years ago, and become an integral, and strong, part of the regional diet.

A success story? For the moment. But the future isn't as clear. Swennen's bananas remain susceptible to other banana maladies and pests. Though stronger bananas will likely be created, problems remain: So far none of today's lab-bred bananas are anywhere near perfect, even for the most desperate situations. Some of Swennen's bananas have proved to be highly susceptible to worm-like nematodes. Others yield less fruit than the typical healthy banana plant; still others lack the properties a commercial banana would require.

But the African project was more than a good start: It was the first step in a journey—one that will almost certainly include the use of the most modern techniques available, including full-scale genetic transformation—that is looking more and more essential.

AT HOME, WE HAVE THE CAVENDISH and only the Cavendish. But choices exist, even within the narrow sphere of our single banana. It isn't hard to see that America's fruit and vegetable aisles have undergone great changes in the past decade. Exotic fruit like kiwis, or even Thai rambutan, have begun to appear regularly. Even ordinary fruit, like apples, now comes from overseas. But the biggest addition is organics: Supermarkets are adding entire sections filled with pesticide-free apples, pears, carrots—and especially bananas.

Shoppers love organic bananas. Unlike similarly grown apples, the natural version of the world's favorite fruit is never scrawny or blemished: They're indistinguishable from their conventionally grown counterparts. They meet the standard bananas have had to meet for over a century.

Organic bananas are a feel-good product. They provide a substantial benefit to workers and the environment, and they're not that much more expensive than ordinary fruit. You've probably seen them in your local market, most likely grown in Ecuador, most likely under the Dole brand name. If you look carefully at the sticker on your banana, you'll see a numeric code printed right beneath the country of origin. On a conventionally grown fruit, the number is 4001. A supermarket cashier punches the digits in as she weighs your selection at the checkout counter, automatically matching price to weight to product. The numbers are part of the price look-up, or PLU, system administered by the International Federation for Produce Standards, and appear on nearly every item in your supermarket's greengrocer section. There are over five hundred codes for different kinds of apples. Cavendish bananas have just two basic identifiers: the 4001 mentioned above and 4186, for a miniature fruit. The codes can be further defined by adding a number at the beginning. Anything that starts with a nine is organic. The coding system is ready for genetically modified bananas: If they ever arrived at market, the identifier, as with other tranformed produce, would begin with an eight.

The problem with organic bananas is that they're hard to grow in quantity. In order to prevent them from succumbing to diseases— especially Black Sigatoka—the fruit needs to be grown in specially quarantined farms, usually located at higher elevations than traditional plantations. The cost is lower yields.

As beneficial as they are to the environment and especially to workers, who don't have to handle toxic chemicals, the truth is that organic bananas probably can't function as an answer to the banana world's most pressing problem: survival. Organic bananas are difficult to grow in the lowlands, where the huge plantations are. Even if organics could thrive in those areas, they'd have to be planted in clean soil, away from areas infected with Black Sigatoka or other banana diseases. That's hard to do without clearing additional forest, as banana companies have done for decades. Just as with fresh plantations during the Gros Michel area, they'd eventually get sick anyway. In a world of vulnerable fruit, an organic banana, by definition, is especially weak.

Organics also do little to increase wages or, beyond the very important issue of pesticide exposure, improve the day-to-day lives of workers. The banana that attempts to do that is called a "fair-trade" banana. If you buy coffee beans at Starbucks, you've likely seen the "fair-trade certified" label. Growers and importers of fair-trade goods agree to have those goods vetted by an independent organization. A fair-trade banana would be one that provides growers and laborers decent compensation, in safe working conditions, and that fosters movement toward independent farming communities. (A fair-trade banana would not necessarily be organic). In Ecuador, such bananas bring about eight dollars per box to the cooperatives that produce them, compared to a dollar or so for standard bananas. For fair trade to work, the movement needs to become much larger. Right now, far less than 1 percent of all Cavendish bananas are fair-trade certified; they work as proof of concept but little more. To make a difference, the big banana companies will need to embrace the idea. They'll need to forgo some profits. Ecuador is a good place to test this. A reform-minded president has, as his symbolic and literal adversary, a banana magnate. If fair trade can take hold there, it can work throughout the world's commercial banana operations.

Will it? That's hard to say. The reason Ecuador has become the largest grower of Cavendish bananas is because it is so cheap to operate there. Fair trade might prompt the big banana companies to move to even cheaper territory, though the spread of Panama disease in Asia may not give them much room to maneuver.

The only genuine way to make fair trade succeed is not to attempt to transform Chiquita or Dole or Ecuador or Honduras or even individual plantations themselves. The shift needs to begin not where bananas are produced, but where they're bought.

Consumers need to insist on fair trade, and governments need to mandate it. Only then will banana growers attempt the changes in infrastructure needed to make either fair trade or organics, or both, a possibility. Such a thing has happened in some parts of the world: Almost half the bananas bought in Switzerland are fair-trade products. Worldwide, the amount of organic and fair-trade fruit produced has more than doubled in the past five years. Though the target remains statistically distant, the process is the best hope for bringing a measure of justice to workers who, for over a century, have known very little.

WHAT IF AMERICA GIVES UP BANANAS? The beloved fruit, as we consume it, isn't practical. It never has been. There has always been a cost to the fruit's south-to-north trade, one that we, as shoppers, have never borne. The best solution for most of the social ills caused by the industrialization of food production is to give up the exotics—beef from Australia, mangoes from Malaysia, fish from China—that, like bananas, require huge infrastructures and rock-bottom operating costs to remain economical. We could grow and buy locally and only eat fruit in season, only eat meat raised and killed with humane practices. Our market baskets could be filled with items from small-scale concerns, purchased at local markets.

I don't wish to be cynical: This is an idea I believe in. But, again, to make it happen would require vast changes in public opinion, in the way business operates, and in the way government regulates companies. Bananas wouldn't make the cut in such a system, since they can't be grown locally for U.S. shoppers. It would be a sad day for anyone who relies on the fruit as an energy boost on the way to the gym or savors its fresh, creamy taste in breakfast cereal, smoothies, or ice cream. I'd miss the wonderful banana pancakes available at a diner just a five minute walk from my home in Los Angeles, which have started my day for nearly the entire length of this project (the sight of a slightly glazed-looking fellow, poring over a ream of banana-related papers, stories, and notes, is finally considered normal at that spot). Yet, as much as we love these things, the loss, I think, would be worth it.

If we intend to keep bananas, maybe the answer is a Cavendish replacement—a third generation in the history of our favorite fruit.

That has happened in Cuba and Brazil. The Caribbean island nation uses FHIA varieties; Brazil grows its more tart, more resistant banana. But neither of these bananas is easy to ship. Both of them taste, and look, strange to Americans: The Cuban fruit is greener and less sweet; the Brazilian banana is applelike in texture. The banana is a natural product, but conventional wisdom stills says that changing it would be as ill-advised as creating a new formula for Coca-Cola.

I say nonsense. The Cavendish naysayers were wrong in the 1950s, and similar arguments are wrong today. My nomination for a new banana is Lacatan. Of all the fruit types I tasted, the Philippine variety is, by far, my favorite. Lacatan has been grown successfully in the Caribbean. Lacatan was tried, in the 1920s, as a stand-in for Gros Michel. Nobody denied that it was delicious—tasty enough, perhaps, to overcome the fact that it is more red than yellow. But the variety is fragile. If you do find a bunch at your local natural foods market, you will notice immediately how bruised and, perhaps, mushy they are. Delicious as you now know the Lacatan to be, you might pass it by. Still, the banana industry managed to invent technologies to overcome the drawbacks of the Cavendish. I don't know if the same thing could be accomplished for the Lacatan, but I know that nobody has seriously tried.

DOES THE BANANA HAVE TIME ON ITS SIDE? Many would argue that the answer is yes. But that's thinking only about the Cavendish. There may be five or ten or thirty years left for our banana. Maybe Panama disease won't continue to spread so quickly. Maybe the Cavendish can be inoculated. Maybe we'll find a way to convert over to Lacatan.

That's not the issue.

As you now know, the Cavendish is not the only banana an ocean-jumping epidemic could affect. Here, an outbreak of banana disease affects our breakfast tables. In South and Central America, the spread of the malady threatens to make already-poor economic conditions worse. In India it means a loss of biodiversity; in the

Pacific it means the diminishment of an important locally grown foodstuff in favor of expensive imports.

But it is Africa where the cause is most urgent. And cultural shifts are making the outcome of a fast-moving banana epidemic potentially more tragic. Village life is changing. As in nineteenth-century Europe and America, as in Asia over the past three decades, Africans are moving closer to cities. In many cases, they may not be able to take their village fruit along. Instead, they'll need to buy bananas at market, just as we do. Urban bananas, whether in New York or Kinshasa, require upheavals in production. A disease that spreads from a few garden plots in one African village to another can be contained. But when Africans move to cities and want their *matoke*, they have to get their bananas from bigger and bigger farms: plantations, newly built, where diseases spread quickly, radiating outward from town to town, country to country, across a continent—and beyond.

An epidemic in the Cavendish—the global banana—could become an epidemic in the dozens of bananas human beings depend on locally and in the hundreds of bananas needed to maintain the diversity vital to fighting such an epidemic.

The circularity of it is depressing.

BUT REALLY, is all this doom and gloom likely? Isn't the Cavendish well isolated on its own plantations? For now, maybe. But the mechanism that could change that is now falling into place.

Disease is what forced banana companies to flee from country to country during the Gros Michel era. Today, that movement is stoked by economics and politics.

The world's trade wars centered around bananas are having an unintended effect. While Europe attempts to promote the interests of small growers by favoring their product over fruit produced farther away, the big banana companies are moving operations to the countries that Europeans can buy bananas from. In early 2007,

Chiquita announced that it was closing some plantations in Central America and moving them to the former French colony of Ivory Coast, in Africa. Bananas from there don't violate EU rules. Cavendish plantations are expanding across the rest of the continent.

The hunt for land has been renewed. And the banana moguls face the same issue they did a century ago. They need to make an impossible fruit cheap enough to buy but costly enough to be profitable. If Europe wants bananas, Chiquita must grow them in Africa. If Japan wants bananas, they'll be grown in the Philippines. Or Ecuador. Or India. Or Southeast Asia, as they were two decades ago, when a package of dirt arrived at a Florida scientist's door.

The banana race is on again: Dole, Chiquita, Del Monte, Great Britain's Fyffes, Ecuador's Bonita, and a half-dozen other companies based around the world are battling to become a favorite not just on the breakfast tables of Europe and America, but everywhere.

As bananas move to new soil, they—just as the Cavendish did in Malaysia and Sumatra—encounter new, virulent organisms. In 2001 a grower of beer bananas in the tiny Ugandan village of Bulyanti began to observe strange symptoms in freshly planted fruit. Buds were shriveling; fruit was ripening early and unevenly, with some bananas turning yellow, others staying green. When the bananas were cut open, they were purple instead of the usual yellowish white. The fruit quickly rotted and couldn't be eaten by humans or even livestock.

By the time agricultural inspectors arrived in Bulyanti, the malady had spread to the entire village. Then the region. The blight was at least as potent as Bunchy Top or Sigatoka. Within three years, the outbreak had grown into a full-blown epidemic, forming a circle whose diameter was constantly expanding, from ten, to twenty, to— today—thirty-two of Uganda's fifty-four districts.

The likely cause of the outbreaks has little to do with felling rain forest or mass contamination of huge plantations or the replanting of infected plants in clean soil. What has come to be known as "banana *Xanthomonas* wilt" (BXW) spreads, as Panama disease does in China, via people: through water, on vehicles, even in canoes bringing fruit from village to village.

The speed at which BXW traveled was especially disturbing. In 2004 the disease was reported outside Uganda: first in the neighboring Democratic Republic of Congo, and then in Rwanda. In 2006 it was seen in Tanzania. There is little doubt that it will keep moving, keep destroying.

BXW is a threat to the world's bananas all by itself. As with Panama disease, there is no cure available. Work on breeding resistant bananas has barely begun.

Scary enough. But the spread of BXW may also contain a prediction: When Panama disease arrives on our side of the world, it will likely move just as fast. The currency of Africa's latest crisis may be different, but the equation is the same as in our hemisphere: Save the banana—or watch it perish, and suffer the consequences.

THE SEARCH FOR ANSWERS has quickened in the past few years. Funds are beginning to flow to banana scientists, who have long since been at the far end of the receiving line compared to their counterparts working in wheat, rice, and corn.

In 2004 scientists in Taiwan reported success in developing a modified Cavendish that successfully resisted Panama disease (ultimately, that moment of promise ran aground when the fruit that grew well in Taiwanese soil failed to yield similar results at other plantations). An Israeli biotech company announced that it had made progress toward engineering a resistant version of the commercial fruit. And for the first time in decades, the world's biggest banana company has joined the search. Just three years ago, a Chiquita spokesperson scoffed when asked whether the company was trying to build a better banana. "That's not a productive avenue," he said. "We prefer to focus our research on traditional means of control." Pesticides over patrimony. But in 2005, the company returned to La Lima. It set up a private conventional breeding project at FHIA, in the labs and greenhouses it built five decades ago and abandoned in the 1980s. The Honduran researchers are operating under a strict gag order. So far, no miracle banana has been announced, but the world is waking up to the threats today's blights pose.

IF ONLY THE AVAILABLE SOLUTIONS WORKED. If only disease-free bananas stayed disease free. If only the breeding efforts undertaken over the past eighty years could somehow not reach dead ends. If only it was practical to sell and eat multiple varieties of fruit, grown in multiple places, the way we eat apples.

Maybe there will be some kind of breakthrough. Maybe it will happen.

But I don't think so.

But I also don't believe the outlook is bleak.

There is a way to build a better banana fast—fast enough that it may actually make a difference.

That way is Rony Swennen's way.

Like you, probably, and like many people, I began this project with a vague and uneasy suspicion of "genetic manipulation." Such foods, I believed, were created to increase corporate profits and not necessarily public health.

But I'm not talking about cloned beef or tomatoes that stay unnaturally "fresh" for weeks on end. This is about bananas. This is a crop in which every one is like every other. That means that once a healthy, safe banana comes out of the lab, it is not likely to change. We'd know how this banana will taste and grow and ship and survive. What we should also know is who it would help.

For a hundred years, we have allowed whatever risk there is in bananas to be borne elsewhere: in the town squares of Colombia, along railroad lines in Costa Rica, by the blue-skinned sprayers of Bordeaux mixture in Guatemala. We have thought only about a single banana, the only one we eat, and rarely about the ones people eat *only*. It seems to me that if we allow others to suffer the problems

that arise from growing and depending on bananas, and we refuse
to shoulder even a portion of that load, then we're doing nothing
but continuing a century of disregard and exploitation that began
with the first shipment of Gros Michel fruit aboard a sail-driven
schooner.

It would be hard to build a banana that resisted everything. But
even coming close could change the world. The lab-made banana
could be clean. It could be grown without pesticides. It could be
grown organically. It could be grown—because it is stronger, and
because stronger means cheaper—according to fair-trade principles.
It could be the banana that finally reverses history, that finally
makes each bunch a guilt-free choice, even a redeeming one, as we
load them into our shopping carts, as we argue over who first sliced
them into ice cream, as we sing ridiculous songs about them.

That banana—and only that banana—could, quite possibly, be
the world's most perfect fruit.

A BANANA TIME LINE

ABOUT THIS TIME LINE: There are several existing versions of banana time lines, both in print and online. The primary sources for the chronology published here are the ones compiled by the United Fruit Historical Society, available on that group's Web site (www.ufhs.com), and by Chiquita, available on that company's corporate Web site (www.chiquita.com). Many of the dates and items in this chronology are derived from Virginia Scott Jenkins's *Bananas: An American History*, published in 2001. Additional dates and historic information come from the sources cited in this book's bibliography.

GENESIS: Was the banana the forbidden fruit in the Garden of Eden? The Koran, in retelling the tale, implies as much, and over the centuries several Bible scholars have also reached that conclusion. And why not? The banana is lush, tropical, and sexually suggestive. It's far more tempting, in a purely allegorical sense, than an apple. (Eve, by the way, besides being chaste until that point, was a product of non-sexual reproduction: She was made from Adam's rib just as bananas are made, not from seed, but from parts cut from grown plants.)

PREHISTORY: Tiny, seed-bearing bananas—none much bigger than your index finger—grow wild in the tropical regions of Southeast Asia. These fruits are semi-edible but hardly substantial enough for humans to cultivate. But—and this is the first mystery of the banana—at some point seedless bananas emerge (possibly though a mutation or inadvertent crossbreeding via a windblown seed). Unlike the seeded bananas, these fruits are larger and easier to eat.

c. 5000 BC: Recently uncovered archaeological evidence suggests that bananas were cultivated in the western highlands of Papua New Guinea. A 2003 archaeological expedition found the oldest evidence of vestigial bananas there, providing further proof of early domestication in this and other parts of Southeast Asia.

500 BC: The first written accounts of human cultivation of bananas are created, in India. The fruits are grown in the same way they are today. Since they are seedless (and therefore sterile), they are propagated willfully: Humans harvest shoots from the large trees and replant them. This makes the banana a highly practical hedge against starvation, since the fruit can easily be cultivated and transported. The big mystery is how bananas got from the jungles of what is now Thailand, Malaysia, and Myanmar all the way to India. There's no doubt that bananas are important: Hindu legend calls them "the fruit of the wise men." But the actual path of the banana's dispersion is something today's genetic researchers are just beginning to uncover.

327 BC: Alexander the Great, returning from his conquests, brings bananas from India—the first time they appear in the Western world. Hindu mythology also places the banana, not the apple, in the Garden of Paradise.

50 BC: Pliny the Elder, writing in the first known compendium of natural history, discusses the origins of the banana. He suggests—probably based on records of Alexander's visit—that the banana, or *musa*, as he calls it (still the Latin term for the banana genus), comes from India, though other accounts over the coming century offer different origins, including Syria, Egypt, and China.

650: Middle Eastern armies and traders bring bananas to Africa. The fruit is given the name *banan*, which is a variation of the Arabic word for "finger." From the eastern side of the continent, it slowly migrates west, reaching Guinea. Cultivation centers around Lake Victoria, where it becomes the staple food. (Today, the "green circle" around the lake remains the place in the world where banana consumption is highest, and most essential, accounting for as much as 70 percent of regional caloric intake.) The banana also becomes part of a burgeoning slave trade between central and northern Africa, presaging a role it will take in the Caribbean and Central America a millennium later.

1402: Portuguese solders, part of early colonial expeditionary forces, bring the banana from Guinea to their Canary Islands colony. The island chain, today a possession of Spain, remains one of the world's key banana exporters, providing a large percentage of the fruit eaten by Europeans.

1516: Spanish missionary Father Tomás de Berlanga brings the banana to the Caribbean. The first cultivation is in Santo Domingo (now the Dominican Republic).

1600: Spanish settlers grow bananas in Florida, but—then as now—the southern tip of the United States is just a little wrong climatically: Winter frosts make efficient cultivation impossible. Bananas remain a local staple.

1750: Carolus Linnaeus, father of modern taxonomy, dubs the banana *Musa sapentium*, or "wise fruit."

1799: Captain James Cook finds bananas on Hawaii.

1826: While living in Mauritius, British naturalist Charles Telfair obtains the Cavendish banana from South China, providing yet another link in the journey of the yellow banana to the Americas.

1836: The Duke of Devonshire receives plants from Mauritius at his estate, Chatsworth, in England.

1837: The Chatsworth bananas are officially "described" to the British Linnaean society.

1848–55: Missionary John Williams brings Cavendish bananas to the South Pacific, leaving healthy plants on Tonga, Samoa, Tahiti, and Hawaii.

1870: Captain Lorenzo Dow Baker purchases 160 bunches of Gros Michel bananas in Jamaica, speeds back to the United States, and sells his stock in Jersey City for $2 a bunch. This is the first known commercial banana transaction in the United States.

1870: Baker's efforts lead to a minor banana craze, and for the first (and possibly only) time in the fruit's history, the banana is seen as a delicacy to be savored by the elite rather than as a handy and cheap staple. As related by Virginia Scott Jenkins, *The Domestic Cyclopaedia of Practical Information* offers advice on consuming the odd fruit: "Bananas are eaten raw, either alone or cut into slices with sugar and cream or wine and orange juice. They are also roasted, fried, or boiled and are made into fritters, preserves, and marmalades." Other household tomes offer advice on how to peel the suggestive fruit, a problem among Victorian diners first encountering it. Some merchants attempt to remedy the situation by selling sliced bananas in foil wrappers.

1871–80: Minor C. Keith, a twenty-three-year-old Brooklyn entrepreneur, secures a contract to build a national railroad in Costa Rica. The building of the railroad costs over five thousand lives, including those of Keith's two brothers. As a way to create business for the trains, Keith plants bananas in cleared rain forest along the trackside. This begins a long cycle of lopsided land deals and forest clearing operations benefiting banana entrepreneurs.

1876: The horticultural hall of the Philadelphia Centennial Exhibition features bananas—positioned, for the first time, as a cheap and healthy substitute for apples. It is the beginning of America's love affair with the fruit (the other major sensation at the exhibition: Alexander Graham Bell's telephone).

1885: As more and more American families find out what bananas are—and want them—Lorenzo Dow Baker starts the first banana importing company. Boston Fruit would later change its name to United Fruit and finally to Chiquita.

1894: The U.S. military intervenes in Nicaragua to quell possible land and labor reforms. The action is the first in a long series of North American exploits in Central America that happen mostly at the behest of the banana companies. Over thirty more instances of U.S. involvement, many of which still have bloody repercussions today, are recorded over the next century.

1899: *Scientific American* offers scholarly advice on the best techniques for peeling a banana.

1900: Boston Fruit changes its name to United Fruit; it won't officially become Chiquita until the 1970s. A rival company, Standard Fruit, is founded in New Orleans, the central arrival point for all U.S. banana imports. That company will also change its name, to Dole, in the 1970s.

1900: U.S. banana entrepreneurs begin to settle outposts throughout Central America, creating private, elite enclaves—some of them entirely raucous, with brothels and honky-tonks—that are far removed from the dismal conditions the workers they employ labor and live under. If there are protests, the U.S. military is quick to intervene.

1900: Panama disease, which would later decimate world banana crops, is identified in Java, though it has yet to be given a name. A variant of the disease is today attacking the banana variety that accounts for 99 percent of all U.S., Canadian, and European imports.

1901: Guatemala hires United Fruit to run its national post office; the company will soon assume governmental functions in most of its Central American client nations.

1902–35: United Fruit paints its shipping vessels white, dubbing them the Great White Fleet. It outfits the ships with fancy state-rooms and tourist amenities as a way of making sure that boats laden with bananas in one direction will carry some kind of cargo—in this case, wealthy Americans—in the other (the tourists return home by train). The enterprise is a huge success, and—though it is inter-rupted by World War I and finally terminated during the second global conflict—the company can claim credit as an innovator of the all-inclusive Caribbean cruise.

1903: Panama disease appears for the first time in Central America. How the blight got from the South Pacific to Panama remains a mys-tery, though it may be the first case of global commerce carrying a pathogen along with its economic benefits.

1904: United Fruit implements a radio technology that allows in-stantaneous communications between approaching cargo vessels and mainland plantations. The "tropical radio" system, in turn, allows precision harvesting of bananas. In the past, the picking began as soon as the boat appeared on the horizon, resulting in inefficient, all-night frenzies to harvest and load fruit before it spoiled. Now, with advance notice of a ship's arrival, picking can be perfectly timed—essential for the rapid delivery of a product with a shelf life of ten days or less.

1904: United Fruit is granted a ninety-nine-year, unlimited license to build railroads in Guatemala and cultivate all lands in a wide swath alongside the newly laid tracks.

1904: The banana split is invented in Pennsylvania.

1904: The banana split is invented in Columbus, Ohio.

1905: Honduras begins a nearly century-long reign as the world's largest banana exporter.

1906: The banana split is invented in Iowa.

1907: The banana split is invented in Wilmington, Ohio.

1910: An early banana laboratory is opened in Costa Rica. Scientists show some interest in breeding disease-resistant fruit, but then, as now, a key conflict emerges: Should efforts be focused on building better bananas, or finding more and more potent substances—pesticides, fungicides, and other chemicals—to stop pests before they damage crops? Nearly all the time, the banana companies choose the environmentally devastating latter alternative.

1910: Samuel Zemurray, future president of United Fruit, is challenged by the U.S.-backed government of Honduras. Zemurray organizes a private coup, led by a pair of gangsters named Guy "Machine Gun" Molony and Lee Christmas. It takes just four weeks for the Honduran regime to fall; a friendlier president is installed, and his first significant act is to grant a huge banana concession to Zemurray.

1911: A rebellion against the new Honduran government is quelled by U.S. troops, who are sent, ostensibly, to guard American banana workers.

1913: United Fruit strikes a land-for-railroads deal in Honduras.

1915: United Fruit's Great White Fleet now has ninety-five ships, each of which can carry up to a half million bananas.

1916: The Great White Fleet is temporarily dry-docked after legendary German naval commander Count Felix von Luckner targets—and sinks—several of the vessels.

1920: Guatemalan banana workers attempt to unionize. U.S. marines arrive to "police" the nation.

1920: The Fruit Dispatch Company is formed to distribute bananas in the United States. Over the years, the company—a subsidiary of Chiquita and its predecessor entities—introduces numerous technological innovations that transform, and actually help build, America's consumer culture. The driving force is that the banana importers are succeeding at the impossible: bringing highly perishable, tropical fruit to northern consumers year-round. Over the years, Fruit Dispatch develops refrigerated shipping, central warehouses for supermarkets, and product-tracking systems that will ultimately morph into today's sophisticated retail technologies, such as bar coding and freshness dating.

1922: Panama disease, in just under two decades, has spread to Australia, New Zealand, China, India, and the Canary Islands—basically following the same route that the earliest cultivated bananas did as they migrated west. Meanwhile, United Fruit's growing home economics department invents dried banana chips.

1923: Songwriters Frank Silver and Irving Cohn score a hit with their song, "Yes, We Have No Bananas." The lyric supposedly relates to the periodic shortages in banana supply that are beginning to crop up, the result of advancing difficulties in combating soil-based pathogens that destroy tropical crops. For the rest of the century, and through today, battling these pathogens becomes a more and more costly, intense, and difficult war for banana growers.

1924: United Fruit prints recipes for corn flakes with banana slices and encourages cereal companies to include discount vouchers inside their boxes; it is the first supermarket coupon to be packaged with another product.

1925: Panamanian banana workers go on strike; the rest of the nation soon follows. Bananas rot in the fields, the Panama Canal closes, and U.S. troops intervene.

1928: The entire Central American banana industry experiences labor unrest. Strikes, worker riots, and demands for better wages and conditions will grow through the next decade—as will the measures taken by banana companies to squelch them.

1928: The first human-bred banana is grown in Trinidad. This is one of the earliest attempts to find a replacement for the Gros Michel, the classic export banana that is rapidly succumbing to Panama disease.

1929: A banana-workers strike in Colombia is brutally suppressed. Vigilante squads, sponsored by United Fruit and trained by the U.S. military, act against the strikers and terrorize the nation. The action leads directly to the violent guerilla battles between the right-wing descendants of those squads and the left-wing gangs—both supported by drug money—that plague Colombia today.

1930: Banana companies build huge ripening rooms in the United States. Ethylene gas, a natural substance given off by ripening fruits, is used to control the level of ripeness. The rooms work by regulating temperature—cooler means the fruit matures slowly—while more ethylene hastens the process. The result is bananas that arrive at the market on their final green day, and which will last exactly seven days before turning brown. That such standardization could be introduced in a fruit is a symbol of how adept the banana companies are at manipulating and maximizing their profit potential.

1932: United Fruit fires striking Honduran banana workers. The strike's organizer is assassinated.

1935: Sigatoka disease is identified in Central America. This is the major blight facing today's global banana crops, but it is controllable (albeit with increasing and more expensive quantities of pesticides as the fungus develops resistance). The first attempt to control Sigatoka is with Bordeaux mixture, a toxic, thick, oily substance that causes illness in thousands of banana workers. At the same time, Panama disease devastates some Honduran fields so badly that an entire port-side town, Puerto Castillo, is abandoned. The strategy for dealing with the disease was to simply move operations to healthier areas; it was through this constant migration that banana companies cut down huge tracts of Central and South American tropical forest.

1935: Banana companies make some effort to improve labor conditions, but their fundamental control of Central American nations remains intact. Use of the term *banana republic* becomes common after it appears in an article in *Esquire* magazine. Another name, little known in the U.S. but seen as the complementary and explanatory counterpoint to the emerging English coinage, is El Pulpo. The Spanish word for "octopus" specifically describes United Fruit.

1939: In the United States, United Fruit begins to offer free textbooks to grade schools. The books are filled, of course, with information on bananas.

1941: Much of the Great White Fleet is commandeered into service by the U.S. Navy for World War II. Unable to get significant quantities of product to market, the banana industry suffers huge losses.

1944: As the war wanes, a new banana industry emerges: one that relies as much on marketing as it does on blunt tactics. The Chiquita brand name is introduced as part of this effort. The brand's famous jingle is inspired by the banana dances done by Brazilian bombshell Carmen Miranda, especially her over-the-top, suggestive number in Busby Berkeley's musical "The Gang's All Here." The Chiquita jingle advises "never" to refrigerate a banana. Doing so, it warns, will make the bananas brown (true enough, but that it will also extend the fruit's life by a week isn't mentioned). The original Miss Chiquita Banana is a cartoon character drawn by Dik Brown, who later created *Hagar the Horrible*.

1946: United Fruit owns nearly a million acres of land in Cuba, Jamaica, Honduras, Guatemala, Nicaragua, Costa Rica, Panama, and Colombia.

1947: Guatemala adopts a "worker protection code." United Fruit describes it as "communistic." The *New York Times Magazine* prints a recipe for bananas with ham, cheese, and mustard.

1950: Pablo Neruda's *Canto General*, a cycle of 350 poems, includes an entire chapter of poetry about the suffering created by the actions of United Fruit. At the same time, Standard Fruit develops a cardboard box with handles and holes, similar to the one now used to ship every banana (and many other fruit varieties). The ability to box bananas will become a major advantage when the Gros Michel, finally wiped out by disease, is replaced by the more fragile Cavendish. This event is less than a decade away, but, except for a few new technologies and some threadbare research, the problem is mostly denied by banana executives.

1951: Jacobo Arbenz becomes the first democratically elected leader of a Central American country. His ascendance to the presidency of Guatemala is not pleasing to the banana companies.

1952: Arbenz nationalizes a quarter million acres of unused United Fruit land, leaving only productive fields under company possession. The act enrages the United Fruit board, which begins to search for a way to "solve" the Arbenz problem.

1953: The first commercial Cavendish varieties are grown by Standard Fruit.

1953/1954: Samuel Zemurray, the ostensibly retired United Fruit chairman who engineered the first banana company coup in Central America, finances the publication of a book called "Report on Guatemala." The book, which seeks to prove that Arbenz is "under Moscow's control," is distributed to every member of the U.S. Congress. Armed with the Zemurray-commissioned report, Congress urges President Truman to act on the "crisis" that appears to be threatening U.S. interests in Guatemala (and, in an early version of the Vietnam-era domino theory, throughout the rest of the region). Truman authorizes CIA action, including the compilation of a list of fifty-four Guatemalans—among them, Arbenz and other members of his government—who are to be "eliminated." A coup is mounted, and the Arbenz government falls; Arbenz goes into exile. One of the witnesses to the coup is a young physician named Ernesto Guevara, who'll soon become one of the region's most prominent radicals, taking on the nickname "Che." Over the next thirty years, the dictatorship that took over from Arbenz will seek to stamp out any form of leftist or agricultural activism. Over 200,000 Guatemalans, including many ethnic Mayas, are killed.

1955: Fifteen million pieces of banana industry–produced literature are distributed to U.S. schoolchildren.

1957: *Green Prison*, a novel by Ramon Amaya Amador, is published in Honduras. It galvanizes workers with its accurate description of conditions on the banana plantations.

1958: The end of the Gros Michel era nears. Chiquita scientists, after decades of denial, begin experimenting with replacements.

1959: Chiquita begins sending scientists to Asia on collecting expeditions, hoping to find a suitable new banana for U.S. consumers.

1960: Chiquita opens a research program in banana genetics and breeding at La Lima, Honduras. The program is headed by Phil Rowe, who will go on to become the most successful breeder of new banana species in history.

1961: Cuban exiles, sponsored by the CIA, fail in an attempt to depose Fidel Castro. The Bay of Pigs operation is partially funded by United Fruit, which lends its shipping fleet to the invasion force.

The banana industry's alleged motivation? Revenge on Castro for nationalizing Cuban plantations following the 1959 revolution.

1961: Wide-scale adoption of the Cavendish banana begins, requiring huge changes in methods for handling the fruit. The variety, though tasty, is nowhere near as hardy as the Gros Michel, which could simply be cut down by the bunch and tossed into ships' cargo holds. The Cavendish needs to be handled delicately, so methods of boxing and bagging are adopted. This, in turn, leads to further developments, including the opportunity to brand bananas, via the sticker found on every other fruit in each supermarket bunch, and a technological system for tracking bananas from field to market (the use of numeric codes to identify price, origin, harvest, and destination information is the direct ancestor of today's bar codes).

1964: Standard Fruit changes its name to Dole.

1965: Ecuador becomes the largest exporter of bananas in the world, supplanting Honduras. (The lead will change hands over the ensuing decades.)

1967: Chiquita distributes ninety thousand recipe cards detailing an unheard-of creation: the peanut butter and banana sandwich.

1968: World banana consumption tops 4 billion pounds.

1969: A banana museum opens in Altadena, California.

1970: Replacement of the Gros Michel by the Cavendish is complete. The project is so successful, in fact, that it leads to an oversupply of bananas. Prices drop precipitously.

1972: Black Sigatoka, a disease that rots banana leaves, is first observed. Though it is controllable, treatment efforts require dangerous and costly chemical sprayings or constant moving of banana crops to virgin soil, resulting in the further destruction of rain forest.

1974: The Securities and Exchange Commission launches an investigation against Chiquita after it learns that the company gave a $1.25 million bribe to the president of Honduras. Chiquita chairman Eli Black leaps out the forty-third story window of New York's Pan Am Building, right above Grand Central Station. The Honduran government is overthrown and Costa Rica threatens to evict United Fruit from its territory.

1975: Honduras cancels Chiquita's lopsided concession to grow bananas in that country.

1978: United Fruit pleads guilty to bribery. The scandal that overthrew a government and drove Eli Black to take his own life is resolved for a fine of $14,000.

1980: Problems begin to emerge with the African banana harvest: Blights and pathogens that should be easily controllable with chemicals begin to show resistance. More and more spraying is needed, at greater and greater cost. Even with all this, production on the continent is cut by half as a result of these stronger diseases.

1981: Black Sigatoka, the leaf-rotting fungus, hits South America. Once again, the solution favored by banana growers is chemical spraying.

1983: Chiquita closes its research and development labs, ending an decades-long tradition of study and exploration.

1985: The Honduran government takes over La Lima and the "Zona Americana," the abandoned Chiquita compound that served as the company's Central American headquarters. The company swimming pool, movie theater, and horse-racing track are razed, and the facility is converted to the Honduran Agricultural Research Foundation. The primary constant? Phil Rowe, the world's most prolific banana breeder, stays on. In Southern California, another breeder, Doug Richardson, opens Seaside Banana Gardens. The short-lived botanical park and greenhouse facility introduces, for the first time, exotic banana varieties to the U.S. Most Americans still don't know that any banana other than the Cavendish exists.

1985–90: A new incarnation of Panama disease begins to appear in Asia. By 1990, it will destroy Cavendish crops in multiple countries. The question: How fast will it spread?

1993: Transcontinental banana wars begin as Europe and the United States battle over banana tariffs. Besides clothing, no single product has raised more contentious and nasty conflicts. U.S. banana companies pressure Congress to enact tariffs against Europe's closed markets.

1998: Hurricane Mitch destroys 80 percent of the Honduran banana crop, causing an economic and humanitarian disaster in that country. It will take nearly a decade to rebuild the industry, and Honduras will never again lead the world in banana production.

1998: The world's largest banana-processing plant, capable of handling fifty thousand bananas daily, is opened in Costa Rica.

1998: Reporters for the *Cincinnati Enquirer* publish the first of what was to be a series of articles detailing continued wrongdoing on the part of Chiquita. Chiquita's private investigators discover that reporters were given access to company voice-mail messages. The company complains to the paper's publishers about this possibly illegal invasion of privacy, and the rest of the series is abruptly pulled. The reporters are fired.

1998: The World Trade Organization rules that European banana growers competed unfairly against U.S. companies.

1999: U.S. banana consumption is one hundred fruits per person per year.

2000: A new series of tariff and free-trade fights begin over bananas. Activists, including the Rainforest Alliance, target the banana industry for pesticide use.

2001: The Catholic University of Leuven, Belgium, opens the first genetics research facility for bananas. Head researcher Rony Swennen leads an effort to gather over 1,200 samples of different banana varieties, by far the world's largest collection, and begins working to decode the banana genome.

2001: A new disease, called banana *Xanthomonas* wilt, begins to spread in Africa. It will turn out to be faster moving, just as virulent, and just as incurable as Panama disease.

2002: Master banana grower Phil Rowe commits suicide.

2003: Chiquita sells its Panamanian processing facility to a workers' cooperative. Dole begins working with activists to improve conditions for banana workers. The first organically grown bananas are exported from Ecuador.

2003: The governments of Rwanda and Burundi, facing possible starvation of millions of refugees, accept modified bananas, developed by Swennen, for cultivation. Over 2 million plants are subsequently grown.

2005: In Honduras, Chiquita subcontracts FHIA, the Honduran Agricultural Research Foundation that occupies the company's former lab facilities, for a secret project. Its goal is believed to be developing a Cavendish replacement in anticipation of what many now believe is inevitable: Panama disease will hit Central America.

2006: A national banana-research laboratory is opened in Uganda, the first on that continent. Its mission is to develop both conventional and bioengineered hybrids. Bioversity International, the umbrella organization for most of the world's banana research, launches a traveling exhibition designed to advocate increased research on the fruit. The name of the program is No End to the Banana.

2007: Chiquita is fined $25 million by the U.S. Department of Justice for payments made to an acknowledged "terrorist organization" in Colombia. Dole is sued in U.S. courts for using chemicals that render workers sterile.

THE FUTURE: Right now, little has changed. Biotech bananas still hold the greatest potential, and though progress has been made in the lab, extensive field testing has yet to begin. Panama disease continues to spread.

# BIBLIOGRAPHY

Books

Abella, Alex. *The Total Banana*. New York: Harcourt, Brace, Jovanovich, 1979.

Adams, Frederick Upham. *Conquest of the Tropics*. Garden City, NY: Doubleday, Page & Company, 1914.

Ancona, George. *Bananas: From Manolo to Margie*. New York: Clarion Books, 1982.

The Chiquita Banana Cookbook. New York: Avon Books, 1974.

Coates, Anthony G., ed. *Central America: A Natural and Cultural History*. New Haven: Yale University Press, 1997.

Cullather, Nick. *Secret History: The CIA's Classified Account of Its Operations in Guatemala, 1952–1954*. Afterword by Piero Gleijeses. Stanford, CA: Stanford University Press, 1999.

García Márquez, Gabriel. *One Hundred Years of Solitude*. New York: Alfred A. Knopf, 1995.

Gosden, Chris, and Jon Hather, eds. *The Prehistory of Food: Appetites for Change*. New York: Routledge, 1999.

Jenkins, Virginia Scott. *Bananas: An American History*. Washington, DC: Smithsonian Institution Press, 2000.

Langley, Lester D., and Thomas David Schoonover. *The Banana Men: American Mercenaries and Entrepreneurs in Central America, 1880–1930.* Lexington, KY: University Press of Kentucky, 1995.

Langley, Lester D. *The Banana Wars: United States Intervention in the Caribbean, 1898–1934.* Chicago: Dorsey Press, 1988.

May, Stacy, and Galo Plaza Lasso. *The United Fruit Company in Latin America.* New York: National Planning Association, 1958.

McCann, Thomas P. *An American Company: The Tragedy of United Fruit.* Edited by Henry Scammell. New York: Crown, 1976.

Merrill, Tim, ed. *Honduras: A Country Study.* 3rd ed. Washington, DC: GPO for the Library of Congress, 1995.

Pringle, Peter. *Food, Inc.* New York: Simon & Schuster, 2003.

Reynolds, Philip Keep. *The Banana.* Boston and New York: Houghton Mifflin Company, 1927.

Rosengarten, Frederic. *Wilson Popenoe: Agricultural Explorer, Educator, and Friend of Latin America.* Lawai, HI: National Tropical Botanical Garden, 1991.

Schlesinger, Stephen, and Stephen Kinzer. *Bitter Fruit: The Untold Story of the American Coup in Guatemala.* 1st ed. Garden City, NY: Doubleday, 1982.

Schneider, Ronald M. *Communism in Guatemala, 1944–1954.* New York: Frederick A. Praeger, 1958.

Simmonds, N. W. *Bananas.* 2nd ed. London: Longmans, Green & Co., 1966.

Stephens, Clyde S. *Bananeros in Central America: True Stories of the Tropics.* Alva, FL: Banana Books, 1989.

Stover, R. H., and N. W. Simmonds. *Bananas.* 3rd ed. New York: Wiley, 1987.

Striffler, Steve, and Mark Moberg, eds. *Banana Wars: Power, Production, and History in the Americas.* Durham, NC: Duke University Press, 2003.

Turback, Michael. *The Banana Split Book: Everything There Is to Know About America's Greatest Dessert.* Philadelphia: Camino Books, 2004.

Wardlaw, C. W. *Green Havoc in the Lands of the Caribbean.* London: W. Blackwood & Sons, 1935.

Wilson, Charles Morrow. *Dow Baker and the Great Banana Fleet.* Harrisburg, PA: Stackpole Books, 1972.

———. *Empire in Green and Gold.* New York: Greenwood Press, 1968. First published 1947 by Henry Holt.

Zemurray, Sarah. *One Hundred Unusual Dinners and How to Prepare Them.* Boston: Thomas Todd Company, 1938.

Articles

Bucheli, Marcelo, and Geoffrey Jones. "The Octopus and the Generals: United Fruit Company in Guatemala." Harvard Business School Case 9-805-146.

Bucheli, Marcelo. "Banana Wars Manoeuvres." *Harvard Business Review* (2005).

———. "The Role of Demand in the Historical Development of the Banana Market, 1880–1960." Presented at Stanford University, November 2001.

———. "United Fruit Company in Colombia: Impact of Labor Relations and Governmental Regulations on Its Operations, 1948–1968." *Essays in Economic and Business History* (1997).

———. "United Fruit Company in Latin America." In *Banana Wars: Power, Production and History in the Americas*, edited by Mark Moeberg and Steven Striffler. Durham, NC: Duke University Press, 2003.

Buddenhagen, Ivan. "Whence and Whither Banana Research and Development?" Presented at Costa Rica Banana Biodiversity Conference, January 1992.

De Langhe, Edmond. "Banana and Plantain: The Earliest Fruit Crop." In *INIBAP Annual Report* (1995).

———. "Diversity in the Genus Musa: Its Significance and Its Potential." *ISHS Acta Horticulturae 540* (2000).

Gallagher, Mike, and Cameron McWhirter. "Chiquita Secrets Revealed." *Cincinnati Enquirer*, May 3, 1998.

Langdon, Robert. "The Banana as a Key to Early American and Polynesian History." *The Journal of Pacific History* 28 (1993).

Marquardt, Steve. "Green Havoc: Panama Disease, Environmental Change, and Labor Process in the Central American Banana Industry." *American Historical Review* (2001).

———. "Pesticides, Parakeets, and Unions in the Costa Rican Banana Industry, 1938–1962." *Latin American Research Review* 37 (2002).

Pearce, Fred. "Going Bananas." *New Scientist* (2003).

Ploetz, Randy, and K. G. Pegg. "Fusarium Wilt of Banana and Wallace's Line: Was the Disease Originally Restricted to His Indo-Malayan Region?" *Australasian Plant Pathology* (1997).

Ploetz, Randy. "Panama Disease: Return of the First Banana Menace." *International Journal of Pest Management* 40 (1994).

———. "Panama Disease, an Old Nemesis Rears Its Ugly Head, Parts 1 and 2." *Plant Health Progress* (2005).

Robinson, Raoul A. "Crop Histories." sharebooks.ca. ISBN 0-9731816-4-8.

Sheller, Mimi. "The Ethical Banana: Markets, Migrants, and the Globalisation of a Fruit." Presented at Lancaster University, Center for Mobilities Research, February 2005.

Smith, Jeremy. "An Unapeeling Industry." *The Ecologist* (2002).

Soluri, John. "Accounting for Taste: Export Bananas, Mass Markets, and Panama Disease." *Environmental History* (2002).

————. "People, Plants, and Pathogens: the Eco-Social Dynamics of Export Banana Production in Honduras, 1875–1950." *Hispanic American Historical Review* (2000).

"Tainted Harvest: Child Labor and Obstacles to Organizing in Ecuador's Banana Plantations." Human Rights Watch (2002): hrw.org.

ACKNOWLEDGMENTS

I N THE THREE YEARS SINCE THIS PROJECT BEGAN, I've met and spoken to many people in the banana world, and every one of them has been generous with their time, frank with their opinions, and patient with my learning curve. I'd especially like to thank Rony Swennen and the researchers and staff—especially the endlessly helpful Marleen Stockmans—at the Laboratory of Tropical Crop Improvement, Division of Crop Biotechnics, at the Catholic University of Leuven in Belgium. I was shown equal courtesy and beyond-the-call-of-duty assistance by Adolfo Martinez, Juan Fernando Aguilar, and the entire staff at the Honduran Agricultural Research Foundation, in San Pedro Sula, Honduras. Houbin Chen, at the South China Agricultural University in Guangzhou also welcomed me.

I also was privileged to conduct extensive phone interviews with Randy Ploetz of the University of Florida's Institute of Food and Agricultural Sciences and Gus Molina of the International Network for the Improvement of Banana and Plantain.

Ann Lovell and Ken Bannister, both directors of their own banana museums, spent considerable time helping me to understand the American passion for the fruit. Ann was particularly generous in sharing postcards and archival images from her collection, many of which are reproduced in this book.

This project would have been impossible to complete without referring to the detailed and illuminating research conducted by the following scholars: John Soluri, Steve Marquardt, Ivan Buddenhagen, Mimi Sheller, Edmond de Langhe, Stephen Schlesinger, Stephen Kinzer, and Marcelo Bucheli. Specific references to their work can be found both in the text and in the bibliography.

Marina Carter, who is studying the life of Charles Telfair—a historical figure who was instrumental in developing the type of banana we eat today—helped provide vital clues in the effort to chart the path that particular fruit took as it spread throughout the world.

The United Fruit Historical Society (UFHS) is a valuable public resource, making freely available historic information on the company we now know as Chiquita. I took particular advantage of the UFHS biographies of the early banana pioneers, as told in Part III of this book.

The magazine article that launched this project was printed in the August 2005 issue of *Popular Science*, and I'm indebted to the editors of that publication—especially Mark Jannot and Kalee Thompson—for giving me my first opportunity to write about bananas. Several of the images that originally accompanied that article appear in this book. They were generously provided by Jeffrey Weiss, the photographer who accompanied me on that assignment.

Laureen Rowland, my original editor at Hudson Street Press, and Laurie Liss, my agent at Sterling Lord Literistic, both believed in the project and were endlessly patient as I worked my way through it. My friends Jocelyn Heaney and Michel Martinez encouraged me and refused to allow me to be a lazy writer. Sia Antunes was the best and most efficient research assistant imaginable. Danielle

Friedman at Hudson Street provided much-needed continuity through the project's twists and turns as well as a sharp final edit. Special thanks to Luke Dempsey, editor in chief at Hudson Street, who stepped in at a late stage and nurtured the book to completion.

Despite this formidable roster of assistance and inspiration, I'm sure I haven't learned nearly enough about bananas. Any mistakes in this book are mine and mine alone.

Finally, a note on the frontspiece: This gorgeous image has appeared in two previous banana books—*The Banana*, by Philip Keep Reynolds, published in 1927, and 2000's *Bananas: An American History*, by Virginia Scott Jenkins. I hope that this book proves as worthy a companion to that illustration as those were.

INDEX

ABOUT THE AUTHOR

Dan Koeppel is a nature, outdoors, and science writer whose work has appeared in national magazines including *Wired*, *Popular Science*, *Elle*, *Audubon*, *Backpacker*, *Bicycling*, and the *New York Times Magazine*. He is a contributing editor at *National Geographic Adventure* and the author of *To See Every Bird on Earth*, a memoir published by Hudson Street Press in 2005. He has written for television and movies, including *Star Trek: The Next Generation*, and is a member of the Mountain Bike Hall of Fame. He grew up in Queens, New York, and lives in Los Angeles, a place in the vicinity of which nearly every kind of fruit—except bananas—was once grown.

4 (EDEN & APPLE), 52 (BANANAS & SENSIBILITIES)
91 (COLOMBIA), 113 (DOM. REP. + NEWS?)
117 (DIMINUITIVE), 128 (GUATAMELA), 143, 146 (HOW TO RIPE)
152-156 ($ *) 165 (BLACK - *)

∴ BAN. REPUBLIC COINED BY O'HENRY IN 1935?